The Seventy Wonders of the Ancient World

THE GREAT MONUMENTS AND HOW THEY WERE BUILT

The Seventy Wonders

THE GREAT MONUMENT

With 333 illustrations, 140 in color

EDITED BY CHRIS SCARRE

of the Ancient World

ND HOW THEY WERE BUILT

Thames & Hudson

Contents

(Half-title) The Statue of Zeus at Olympia.
(Frontispiece) Angkor Wat.

Pages 4–5 (l–r) The pyramids of Giza; the sarcophagus of Pakal, Palenque; the minaret of the Sankore mosque, Timbuktu.
Pages 6–7 (l–r) The Canopus, Hadrian's Villa, Tivoli; Sacsawaman; the Pont du Gard; Easter Island statues.

Designed by Norman Reynolds

© 1999 Thames & Hudson Ltd, London

First published in the United States of America in 1999 by Thames & Hudson Inc., 500 Fifth Avenue, New York, New York 10110

thamesandhudsonusa.com

Reprinted 2002

Library of Congress Catalog Card Number 98-61827
ISBN 0-500-05096-1

Printed and bound in Hong Kong

The Seven Wonders

Tombs & Cemeteries

Temples & Shrines

Palaces, Baths & Arenas

Fortifications

Harbours, Hydraulics & Roads

Colossal Statues & Monoliths

List of Contributors

Dr Chris Scarre is Deputy Director of the McDonald Institute for Archaeological Research in the University of Cambridge. He has directed several archaeological excavations in France and is a specialist in the later prehistory of western Europe. **(8, 18, 19, 48, 61, 70)**

Dr Robin Coningham is Lecturer in South Asian Archaeology in the Department of Archaeological Sciences at the University of Bradford. He has conducted excavations at early city sites on Sri Lanka and more recently in the Northwest Frontier Province of Pakistan. He is also a UNESCO consultant. **(17, 26, 27, 30, 31, 41, 53, 69)**

Dr Janet DeLaine is Lecturer in Roman Archaeology in the Department of Archaeology at the University of Reading. An expert on Roman architecture, she is the author of a major monograph on the Baths of Caracalla at Rome. **(28, 38, 39, 40, 56, 57, 58, 67)**

Dr Susan Toby Evans is Adjunct Professor of Anthropology in the Department of Anthropology at the Pennsylvania State University. She has conducted archaeological surveys and excavations in the United States, Mexico and Honduras, and specializes in the archaeology of Mexico, particularly during the Aztec period. **(25, 34)**

Professor Brian Fagan of the Department of Anthropology in the University of California at Santa Barbara is a leading archaeological writer. He has written major studies of climate change, Egypt and the history of archaeological discovery, as well as the standard textbook *Ancient North America* (Thames & Hudson, 3rd ed., 2000). **(29, 32, 59)**

Adriana von Hagen writes on the archaeology of Peru and currently co-directs an archaeological project in the cloud forest of northeastern Peru. She is co-author (with Craig Morris) of *The Cities of the Ancient Andes* (Thames & Hudson, 1998), a survey of the major archaeological sites in Peru and Bolivia. **(14, 23, 43, 52, 60, 66)**

Dr Timothy Insoll is Lecturer in Archaeology in the Department of Art History and Archaeology at the University of Manchester. He has conducted excavations into the origins of the West African cities of Gao and Timbuktu, and has written widely on the archaeology of Islam and religions in general. **(33)**

Simon Kaner is a specialist on the prehistory of Japan and lectures and writes on the archaeology of East Asia. **(15)**

Dr N. Claire Loader has conducted research at the University of Durham into Mycenaean architecture and building techniques. Among her recent publications is a major study of cyclopean masonry, including Mycenae and Tiryns. **(3, 4, 5, 6, 9, 24, 35, 45)**

Ann Paludan is an authority on Chinese sculpture and has written about the Ming emperors and the classical tradition of Chinese statuary. She is also the author of *Chronicle of the Chinese Emperors* (Thames & Hudson, 1998). **(12, 50, 55)**

Dr David Phillipson is Director and Curator of the University Museum of Archaeology and Anthropology at Cambridge, and formerly was Director of the National Monument Commission of Zambia. He has undertaken major fieldwork at the Ethiopian city of Aksum and is the author of the standard textbook *African Archaeology* (Cambridge University Press, 2nd ed., 1993). **(44, 68)**

Dr Julian Reade is Assistant Keeper in the Department of Western Asiatic Antiquities at the British Museum, and is a specialist in the archaeology and history of the ancient Middle East. His publications include *Assyrian Sculpture* (British Museum Press, 1983). **(2, 13, 20, 36, 37, 42, 46, 47, 51, 54)**

Dr Kate Spence is a British Academy Postdoctoral Fellow in the Faculty of Oriental Studies, Cambridge, and specializes in the architecture and archaeology of ancient Egypt. She is currently engaged in an analysis of the orientation of ancient Egyptian architecture. **(1, 7, 10, 21, 22, 62, 63, 64)**

Dr Nigel Spivey lectures in Classical Archaeology at the University of Cambridge. He has excavated at the Etruscan city of Cerveteri, and is the author of several books, including *Etruscan Art* (Thames & Hudson, 1997). **(11)**

Professor David Webster of the Department of Anthropology at the Pennsylvania State University specializes in the archaeology of the Maya of Mexico and Central America. He has excavated at numerous Maya sites, including Becán, Copán and Piedras Negras. **(16, 65)**

Professor Roger Wilson is an expert on Classical archaeology in the Department of Archaeology, University of Nottingham, where he is also Head of Department. He specializes in the Greek and Roman archaeology of Sicily and the central Mediterranean. He is the author of *Sicily under the Roman Empire* (Aris & Phillips, 1990). **(49)**

Preface

EVERYONE HAS HEARD of the Seven Wonders of the Ancient World. Pyramids, temples and statues, they embodied the greatest technological achievements known to the Greek-speaking world a couple of centuries before the birth of Christ. That world, of course, was essentially small in scale, centred on the lands around the East Mediterranean. But it provides the idea behind the present book, where an international team of scholars takes not seven but seventy monuments of the past, from every region of the globe. The aim is to describe what up-to-date archaeological research reveals of the way the individual monuments were brought into being, representing as they do the culmination of technological achievement in their different societies.

The monuments we cover in this book are built and (on the whole) extant structures, whether statues, canals, temples or palaces. We have deliberately chosen not to include the many other types of human accomplishment which might be considered 'wonders' in popular parlance. These, such as rock art or cave art, or portable objects and devices, certainly represent great and enduring achievements. Their exclusion here is in no way to deny the creativity or inventiveness of their creators. Many societies unrepresented here were the authors of artworks, or were consummate in other areas of cultural activity such as music, ritual and dance which have left no material expression. Their achievements must properly be the subject of another book, with a different emphasis from the one we have taken.

We must also clarify what we mean by 'the ancient world'. Strictly speaking, 'ancient' simply means old, with the added flavouring of a slightly archaic quality. Let us at once agree that there is no natural entity which we can call the 'ancient world'; it does not automatically and of itself include or exclude particular periods or regions. What we cover in the present book, then, are the first major monuments in their respective regions. Had we chosen a strict time bracket, with an arbitrary cut-off date, we would have found ourselves excluding some regions altogether. Were we to decide, for example, that the end of the ancient world from a Eurasian perspective falls at the dissolution of the Roman empire in the 5th century AD or the spread of Islam in the 7th century, we could not have included major monuments of the native Americas and sub-Saharan Africa.

There is a degree of arbitrary choice in these decisions, and not everyone will agree with the selection of monuments presented here. We hope, however, that they are spread widely enough in space and time to illustrate both the diversities and similarities of technologies and achievements in different parts of the world.

A word of explanation as to how the book has been structured. The seventy entries are divided into seven thematic sections, each one devoted to similar kinds of monument from different regions or societies. Naturally enough, we begin with the traditional Seven Wonders themselves. The sections which follow cover the separate categories of monument: tombs and cemeteries; temples and shrines; palaces and other structures for luxury and leisure; fortifications; roads and hydraulics; and finally the outsized statues or monoliths, conceived and executed on a colossal scale, which are among the most striking examples of ancient 'wonders'; many of them are still as impressive in the modern technological age as they were in the past.

CHRIS SCARRE

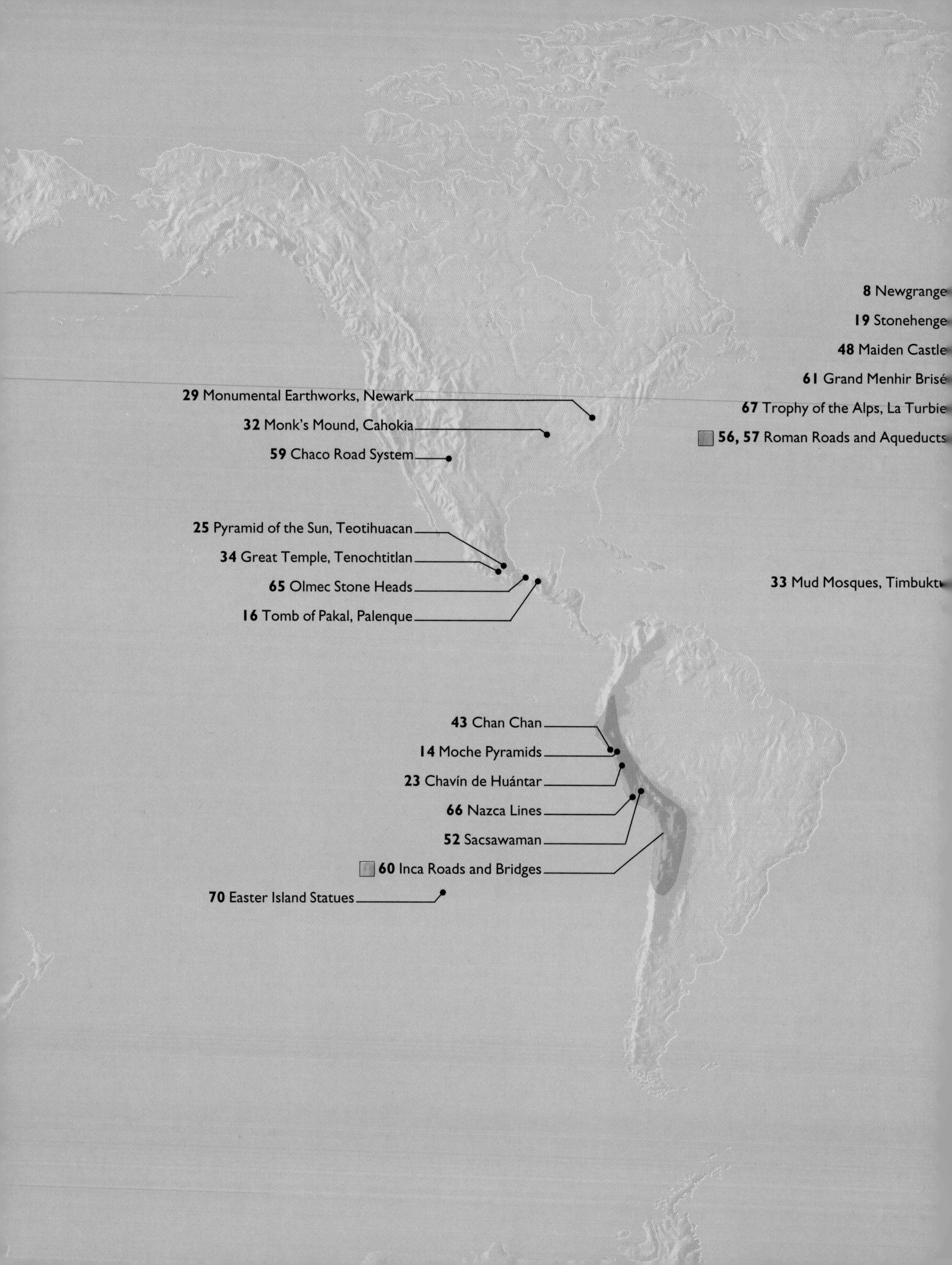

8 Newgrange

19 Stonehenge

48 Maiden Castle

61 Grand Menhir Brisé

67 Trophy of the Alps, La Turbie

56, 57 Roman Roads and Aqueducts

29 Monumental Earthworks, Newark

32 Monk's Mound, Cahokia

59 Chaco Road System

25 Pyramid of the Sun, Teotihuacan

34 Great Temple, Tenochtitlan

65 Olmec Stone Heads

16 Tomb of Pakal, Palenque

33 Mud Mosques, Timbuktu

43 Chan Chan

14 Moche Pyramids

23 Chavín de Huántar

66 Nazca Lines

52 Sacsawaman

60 Inca Roads and Bridges

70 Easter Island Statues

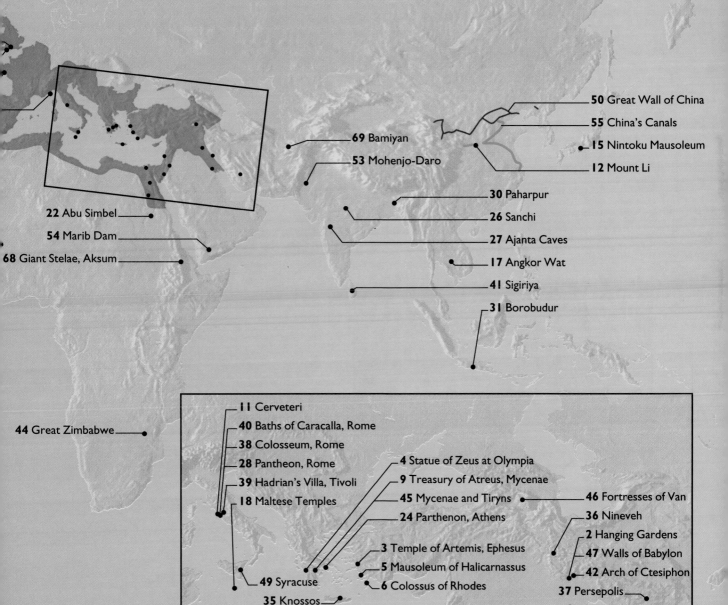

50 Great Wall of China

55 China's Canals

15 Nintoku Mausoleum

12 Mount Li

69 Bamiyan

53 Mohenjo-Daro

30 Paharpur

26 Sanchi

27 Ajanta Caves

17 Angkor Wat

41 Sigiriya

31 Borobudur

22 Abu Simbel

54 Marib Dam

68 Giant Stelae, Aksum

44 Great Zimbabwe

11 Cerveteri

40 Baths of Caracalla, Rome

38 Colosseum, Rome

28 Pantheon, Rome

39 Hadrian's Villa, Tivoli

18 Maltese Temples

4 Statue of Zeus at Olympia

9 Treasury of Atreus, Mycenae

45 Mycenae and Tiryns

24 Parthenon, Athens

46 Fortresses of Van

36 Nineveh

2 Hanging Gardens

47 Walls of Babylon

42 Arch of Ctesiphon

37 Persepolis

20 Ziggurrat of Ur

3 Temple of Artemis, Ephesus

5 Mausoleum of Halicarnassus

6 Colossus of Rhodes

49 Syracuse

35 Knossos

58 Caesarea

51 Masada

13 Petra

7 Pharos of Alexandria

62 Great Sphinx

1 Pyramids of Giza

21 Karnak

10 Valley of the Kings

63 Egyptian Obelisks

64 Colossi of Western Thebes

Introduction

Memorials of Power

'My name is Ozymandias, King of kings:
Look on my works, ye Mighty, and despair!'
Nothing beside remains...

PERCY BYSSHE SHELLEY, 'OZYMANDIAS', 1817

SHELLEY'S FAMOUS sonnet 'Ozymandias' was written after a visit to the British Museum in 1817, where he saw the massive granite torso of Ramesses II recently taken by Belzoni from the Ramesseum at Thebes in Egypt. Belzoni had been prevented from removing the foot of a second, larger statue which he saw nearby; it was the account of this foot which inspired Shelley's poem.

The statue to which the foot belonged may originally have weighed 1000 tonnes. Colossal statuary on such an enormous scale was designed to inspire feelings of awe and wonder. Such feelings outlive even the collapse and ruin of the monument itself, for the massive remains – the foot of Ramesses II, or the hollow bronze limbs of the fallen Colossus of Rhodes seen by Roman travellers – continue to fire the imagination.

Above **The Inca 'fortress' of Sacsawaman above Cuzco, with its zigzag terrace walls incorporating huge stone blocks jointed together with amazing accuracy.**
Left **The uprights and lintels of Stonehenge involved the shaping and manipulation of massive blocks weighing up to 40 tonnes apiece.**
Right **The Great Sphinx of Giza was carved from the natural rock into the features of an Egyptian pharaoh (probably Khafre, c. 2500 BC), with the elongated body and outstretched forepaws of a lion.**

Ancient wonders in the modern world

The Colossus of Rhodes is one of the Seven Wonders of the Ancient World. These have been a staple part of the Classical heritage since at least the Renaissance. Here, however, we have expanded the concept to include not seven but seventy monuments, spanning the whole world, from monolithic standing stones of Brittany of the 5th millennium BC to the Great Temple of the Aztecs in Tenochtitlan, which so astonished the Spanish conquistadores when they arrived in Mexico in the 16th century AD.

'Wonders of the world' may seem an outmoded concept in the modern age, yet there can be few better ways to express the visual and emotional impact of these creations. That impact was always a vital element of their meaning and remains so today. When we stand before the rock-cut temples at Abu Simbel, or walk a surviving section of the Great Wall of China, we cannot fail to be impressed. In so doing, we are responding as their builders intended. The Abu Simbel temples were powerful propaganda of the might of pharaoh Ramesses II, and of the Egyptian state. The Great Wall of China was much more than a military work; it too was a symbol of power, which conveyed its message through visual impact, through the line of the wall continuing mile upon mile across the landscape. Monuments such as these were designed to grab the attention – too enormous to be overlooked, they led the viewer on to imagine the labour needed to create them and the control of resources which lay behind such a mighty work. But that was not all. They were also symbols of technological skill.

Rediscovering ancient technologies

Each of the monuments presented here provides us with crucial insights into the ancient technologies used in different parts of the world. In some cases, the ancient skill has been lost. Yet even though it is hard to understand how the pyramids were built or the stones of Stonehenge raised into position, recent experiments have gone a considerable way to show how such feats might be achieved without the benefit of modern cranes. It is a constant surprise to the modern world how much could be achieved by apparently simple means – by large teams of men hauling on ropes, or paddling rafts (for the Stonehenge bluestones and colossal Olmec heads), or by stone-cutters persistently chipping away, year after year, in the quarries. These monuments reveal to us societies capable of co-ordinated effort; who possessed technological skills painstakingly acquired and carefully passed down across the generations; and who were determined to modify the world around them and leave their mark upon it. We must nevertheless recognize the evidence of occasional

Below **The Via Appia south of Rome; dating from 312 BC, this road connected the city with areas under Roman control.**

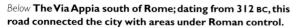

ancient failure – the Aksum stela that fell as it was being raised, the Aswan obelisk left unfinished in its quarry, or the Colossus of Rhodes toppled by an earthquake less than 50 years after it was completed.

Much of our information comes from archaeology: the careful study of material remains, drawing additional support from texts and representations. Sometimes, only archaeology can now tell us how the structure or monument originally appeared; the Great Temple of the Aztecs, described by the Spanish conquistadores, was levelled by the conquerors and the site itself rediscovered only in 1978. Archaeology also throws new light on famous and ever-visible monuments, such as the pyramids or the Sphinx, or on those more recently 'discovered', such as the Maya cities of Central America or the temples of Angkor in Cambodia.

The monuments featured here are all consummate examples of human achievement in hewing stone, moulding mud-brick, carving ivory or casting metal. They show technology pushed to the limit by past societies seeking to commemorate, immortalize or simply to impress through the deployment of skill and labour power on a massive scale. They include, in the Bamiyan Buddha and Abu Simbel temples, some of the largest shapes ever cut from the living rock. They reveal astonishing success in

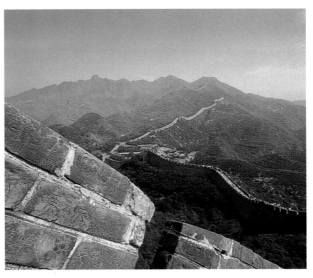

Left **The Flavian Amphitheatre, or 'Colosseum', at Rome was capable of seating at least 50,000 spectators.** Above **The Great Wall of China crossing the mountainous terrain to the north of Beijing.** Below **The so-called 'Pyramid of the Sun' at Teotihuacan rises to a height of 60 m and incorporates over a million cubic metres of material.**

The Hypostyle Hall of the temple of Amun-Re at Karnak: the massive columns once supported a now-vanished roof.

The message of the monuments

In many respects the instinctive response to these monuments is the right one; it is the response which most of them were explicitly created to elicit – whether in subject peoples, rival powers, or simply posterity. For the size and construction of these monuments was one way of securing remembrance – their solidity ensured, as far as any human undertaking could, that they would survive down the ages, and with them the memory of the ruler or society who created them. Even where designed ostensibly for the dead rather than the living – as the resting place of Khmer rulers, Chinese emperors or Maya lords – most were highly visible monuments.

The quest for prestige and remembrance naturally applies unequally to the different monuments considered here. Indeed, one might consider Roman roads and Chinese canals to be purely practical constructions; yet it is interesting to note how milestones along Roman roads lauded the emperors who

the transport and erection of huge monolithic statues or stelae weighing hundreds of tonnes. They demonstrate, in richly carved temples and palaces, not only architectural genius and artistic skill, but also the ability to manipulate massive quantities of materials, sometimes dragged from a distance. They include spectacular engineering feats in bridges, aqueducts and enormous canals.

Archaeology is uniquely qualified to reveal just how these successes were achieved. By studying details of the structures themselves, by careful excavation of their sites, by precise survey of their dimensions and orientation, and by a more general understanding of ancient technologies, we can begin to understand how even the most perplexing of these monuments was created. Yet in stripping away some of the mystery, we must not lose sight of the message.

built them; and the Sui rulers of China engaged in canal-building as a dynastic goal, which contributed largely to their overthrow because of the massive drain on resources it involved. No human work on such a scale can possibly fail to carry a message of rulership, authority and legitimacy. The mighty obelisks of female pharaoh Hatshepsut challenge anyone to doubt the legitimacy of her rule, albeit that she was a woman. Such great works sometimes mark the transfer of power and the rise of a new dynasty: the largest of the Egyptian pyramids come at the beginning of the Old Kingdom; the Colosseum at Rome marked the accession of the Flavian emperors; the Great Wall of China was established by the first emperor Shihuangdi.

Technological difficulty adds to the aura of power, and the enigma of how they could have been achieved must have been as much a puzzle for ancient societies as it is for the modern visitor. The huge size and weight of the largest monoliths at Stonehenge have led to more theories than there are stones in the structure; how were they dragged to the site, how set upright, how were the lintels raised? In the 12th century, Geoffrey of Monmouth was equally impressed but expressed this through recourse to a magical explanation: Stonehenge had been built by Merlin, who brought the stones by magic power from Ireland. We can be confident that this sense of wonder, giving rise to numerous and varied legends about the building of Stonehenge, goes back deep into the past, well beyond the beginning of written records.

We may never know exactly how these monuments were viewed by the societies who created them, though contemporary texts, where they survive, can provide a measure of insight. Where writings are absent, archaeologists must rely on the surviving remains, seeking to understand these structures as products of pre-modern societies which in many respects were very unlike our own.

Above **A colossal Olmec head, 2.85 m tall, from San Lorenzo in the Gulf Coast Lowlands of Mexico. Such heads are thought to be portraits of powerful chiefs or rulers.**
Left **The aqueduct of San Lazaro, one of two bringing water to the Roman city of Mérida in southern Spain.**

The Seven Wonders

THE SEVEN WONDERS of the Ancient World were a collection of monuments, of diverse types and times, united by the quality of 'wonder': their capacity to inspire awe and admiration in those who beheld them. This distinction was achieved through sheer size (the largest stone building), magnificence (the richest sculptures), impressive engineering (the tallest bronze casting), or through some combination of these.

In the Western world, the idea of drawing up a definitive list of humanly made wonders goes back at least as far the Greeks. Herodotus, writing in the 5th century BC, tells us of 'the three greatest works to be seen in any Greek land', all of them the work of the Samians: the tunnel aqueduct, the harbour mole and the great temple of Hera, on the island of Samos. The concept of the Seven Wonders is an extension of this idea.

Their origin lies in the Hellenistic period, in the wake of the conquests of the Macedonian king Alexander the Great. Older civilizations – Egypt, Babylonia and Persia – were absorbed into the new polyglot world where Greek culture was the dominant influence and Greek was the lingua franca. The number seven itself came probably from the Near East, as (a little later) did the seven-day week. All seven of the wonders fell within the realms conquered by Alexander, but not all were in the Greek tradition. The pyramids were already vastly old; the Hanging Gardens of Babylon (or indeed the Walls of Babylon in the alternative versions) owed nothing to

The pyramids of Giza in Egypt, built c. 2551–2470 BC, were the oldest monuments to be included among the traditional Seven Wonders of the Ancient World.

the Greeks. But in placing their own works alongside these, they were able to compare their achievements with those of the realms that Alexander's successors now controlled. Not surprisingly, perhaps, it is Greek cultural achievements which win through in the analysis, five of the seven traditional wonders being carved, cast or constructed by Greek or Hellenistic artists and architects.

In its earliest form, the list of Seven Wonders can be traced back to the 3rd or 2nd century BC, though even so it is not quite the same as the list we are familiar with today. One early source is a short poem, attributed variously to Antipater of Sidon (d. *c.* 125 BC) or Antipater of Thessalonica (fl. *c.* 20 BC to AD 20). The poet praises in turn the statue of Zeus at Olympia, the Colossus of Rhodes, the Hanging Gardens of Babylon, the Pyramids of Egypt, the Mausoleum of Halicarnassus and the Temple of Artemis at Ephesus. Instead of the Pharos or lighthouse of Alexandria, however, he names the Walls of Babylon, broad enough for a chariot to be driven along them. So while the general nature of the list, and the number seven, were clearly established by this time, the particular contents were not yet fixed. Indeed, the list goes on changing throughout the Roman period, as various writers sought to include new monuments which fitted their own particular

agendas. The Roman poet Martial, in the late 1st century AD, added the newly completed Flavian Amphitheatre (the Colosseum) at Rome. The Christian writer Gregory of Tours (6th century AD) included Noah's Ark and the Temple of Solomon. Surprisingly, the Pharos does not appear in any surviving list until after the Roman period. The Alexandrian lighthouse was, however, a key element in that particular list of the Seven Wonders which was revived during the Renaissance.

Each of the Seven Wonders represented the epitome of human achievement in a different aspect of technical skill. So the Pyramids of Egypt were the supreme example of building in stone, the Hanging Gardens of Babylon of skill in harnessing running water, the Colossus of Rhodes of casting in bronze. Yet in a very real way the whole concept was a fiction, a literary conceit. Despite Antipater's claim, he can never have seen the Hanging Gardens, since they had perished many centuries before. Nor was the Colossus of Rhodes still standing at the time he wrote, though it was visible as a ruin. But this hardly matters. Archaeology shows that all seven of the wonders were indeed amazing achievements, and the methods used to create them provide striking evidence of the capabilities of ancient technologies.

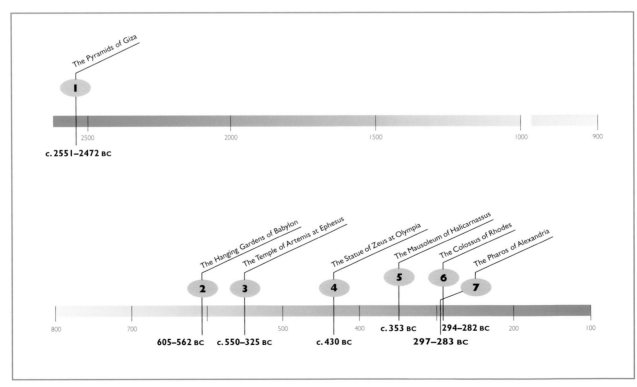

20

The Pyramids of Giza

Time: c. 2551–2472 BC
Location: Giza, Egypt

On approaching these colossal monuments, their angular and inclined form diminishes the appearance of their height and deceives the eye ... but as soon as he begins to measure by a known scale these gigantic productions of art, they recover all their immensity.

VIVANT DENON, 1803

OF THE SEVEN WONDERS of the Ancient World, only the pyramids of Giza are still standing. Although they have lost much of their white limestone casing and the temples around them have fallen into ruin, the sheer size of these enormous structures still amazes visitors. Their construction stands out as one of the most astonishing achievements in history, but even today the methods used by the ancient builders are a matter of some controversy.

There are actually more than 80 pyramids in Egypt, built over a period of around 1000 years, but those at Giza are the largest and among the best preserved thanks to the solidity of their construction. The Giza pyramids were built by three kings of the 4th Dynasty, Khufu (also known as Cheops), Khafre (Chephren) and Menkaure (Mycerinus). The pyramid of Khufu (c. 2551–2528 BC)

The Giza pyramids: that of Khufu is in the foreground and behind it are those of Khafre and Menkaure. In front of Khufu's pyramid is the pit that originally contained a wooden boat in which the dead king would travel to the afterlife.

FACTFILE

Pyramid of Khufu

Period of construction	c. 23 years
Length of base	230.33 m
Height	146.59 m
Inclination of sides	51° 50' 40"
Average deviation from true north	0° 3' 6"
Volume	2,600,000 cu. m
Number of blocks used	c. 2,300,000
Average block weight	c. 2.5 tonnes
Weight of granite roofing blocks	50–80 tonnes
Size of workforce	20,000–30,000

is the largest and is known as the Great Pyramid: for over 4000 years it was the tallest built structure in the world.

Meaning

Egyptian pyramids of the Old and Middle Kingdoms were the superstructures of royal tombs. Their solidity and bulk were designed to protect the king's body, but the choice of the pyramidal shape must also have been governed by symbolic considerations. The pyramid was intended to assist the king in his ascension to heaven, and the shape is often interpreted as a ramp up to the sky. It is also associated with the primeval mound which emerged from the waters of chaos at the time of creation. In addition, the pyramidal shape may be a solar symbol, representing in solid form the oblique rays of sunlight which are sometimes seen breaking through the clouds. Whatever the interpretation of the shape, it is also clear that the Egyptians were trying to build the tallest structure possible: a pyramidal stack of solid masonry would have been the most successful method of achieving this.

The pyramid itself was only one part of the royal burial complex. Each pyramid stood in an enclosure with a mortuary temple on its east side and there was also a valley temple near the river which was linked to the upper temple by a long causeway decorated with reliefs. Khufu's causeway was still largely intact when Herodotus visited Giza in the 5th century BC. In his view, the carved decoration on the walls was almost as impressive as the pyramids themselves.

Layout and preparation of the pyramid site

Great care was taken in choosing an appropriate site. The Giza plateau was probably selected because it holds a commanding position above the Nile Valley and was on the west bank – west was

Left **The Giza pyramids from the southwest: in the foreground is Khafre's pyramid, with the pyramid of Khufu behind. Around Khufu's pyramid are the tombs of the nobles and to the southeast are the pyramids of Khufu's queens. The white limestone casing of Khafre's pyramid is still intact at the summit.**
Above **A view of the corbelled Grand Gallery of the Great Pyramid, leading to the king's burial chamber.**

The Giza plateau showing the pyramids (Menkaure, Khafre and Khufu), the ancillary structures and the stone quarries from which core blocks for the pyramids were extracted.

In recent years there have been several attempts to attribute a significance to the diagonal layout of the three major pyramids at Giza. It is extremely unlikely that there is any underlying master-plan. The pyramids were built at different times and as separate projects. Furthermore, the pyramid enclosures are not linked together as one would expect had the overall plan been important. The diagonal layout is a direct result of the construction process: the pyramids are aligned to true north, and each was therefore built obliquely to the edge of the plateau and set back from the preceding monument both to keep to the ridge and also to provide a clear view of the northern stars for accurate alignment.

Quarrying and transport of stone

The blocks used for the core of the Great Pyramid were quarried just to the south of the pyramid by the same methods used to excavate the trench around the Sphinx (p. 258). However, the builders considered the quality of the local limestone too poor for the casing blocks, so fine white limestone was brought from quarries across the river at Tura to a harbour at the edge of the plateau. On average the limestone blocks used in the pyramid weigh 2.5 tonnes, although they decrease in size slightly towards the top. In addition, granite blocks were brought from Aswan, 935 km (580 miles) to the south, to line the burial chamber and to provide impenetrable plugs for the inner corridors in the vain hope of discouraging tomb robbers. Granite was also used for the lowest course of the casing of Khafre's pyramid and at least the bottom sixteen courses of Menkaure's.

associated with the setting sun and with death. In addition, the limestone ridge provided a solid foundation for the massive weight of the structures and also ample material for building their solid cores.

The site was then prepared for construction. Work began with the rough laying-out and levelling of the area to provide a good footing. The Egyptians seem to have used simple tools, such as square-levels and plumb-lines, but were able to achieve an astonishing degree of accuracy: the level of the pavement around the Khufu pyramid varies by only some 2 cm (*c.* 0.78 in). Although the area around the pyramid base was cut down to provide a level foundation, the natural rock inside the perimeter was left intact to form a solid core for the lower courses of masonry.

When the site had been prepared, the surveyors could begin to lay out an accurate square for the base of the pyramid. Each pyramid was carefully aligned so that the sides faced the four cardinal directions. First, either the east or the west side was aligned to north using the circumpolar stars. Again Egyptian masons achieved great accuracy: the sides of the Great Pyramid deviate from true north by an average of around 3 minutes of a degree. Once one side had been aligned the other sides were constructed from it geometrically and were marked out on the pavement.

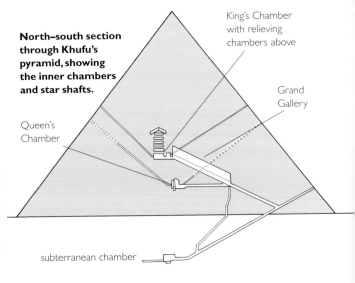

North–south section through Khufu's pyramid, showing the inner chambers and star shafts.

King's Chamber with relieving chambers above

Grand Gallery

Queen's Chamber

subterranean chamber

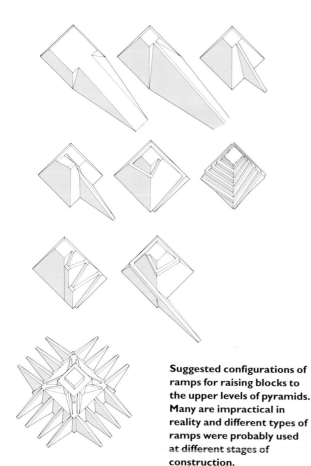

Suggested configurations of ramps for raising blocks to the upper levels of pyramids. Many are impractical in reality and different types of ramps were probably used at different stages of construction.

sidered and most scholars now agree that ramps of some sort were used. These would have been dismantled on completion of the pyramid. At Giza, although no firm evidence of ramps is preserved, the rubble and chippings which fill the Khufu quarries could be their remains. Evidence from other sites suggests that a number of different types of ramp were used. Some theories can be ruled out for practical reasons: there is insufficient space for a straight ramp leading to the top of the Great Pyramid while a spiral ramp would have obscured the corners of the pyramid, leading to distortion of the structure.

It seems likely that different solutions for raising blocks were used as the project progressed. Approximately 96 per cent of the volume of a pyramid is in its bottom two-thirds and during construction of the lower courses many small ramps may have ensured a high flow rate of blocks to the working levels. Towards the summit of the pyramid the flow rate would have been slower to allow for the difficulty of raising the blocks, and at the very top a considerable amount of improvization would have been necessary to lift and position the blocks.

Each block was cut to shape when it had been moved to its final position so that it fitted exactly to its neighbour: the casing blocks of the Great Pyramid are so closely set that it is often impossible to slide a knife-blade between them. Gypsum mortar was used to fill any gaps and may also have served as

The so-called King's Chamber in the Great Pyramid is lined with red granite and still contains Khufu's sarcophagus, also carved from granite.

On arrival at the harbour, blocks were loaded on to wooden sledges and dragged with ropes up to the base of the pyramid. The size of the team dragging a block would be determined by its weight. One of the supply routes to a Middle Kingdom pyramid at Lisht has been excavated and was found to consist of a series of smooth timbers set into a solid mud runway: such a track would considerably reduce friction and aid the passage of the sledges.

Contrary to popular opinion, the pyramids were not built by slaves but by conscripted labour. At least some of the workforce was permanent but much of it may have been seasonal: summer probably saw the largest workforce as the annual Nile flood prevented work in the fields. In addition to those actually building the pyramids, there was a huge support network dedicated to feeding the workers. Recent estimates suggest that the Khufu pyramid employed a workforce of 20,000–30,000 who were housed nearby.

Ramps and construction

One of the most controversial aspects of pyramid construction is the method of raising blocks on to the pyramid structure. Many different schemes of lifting, levering and dragging blocks have been con-

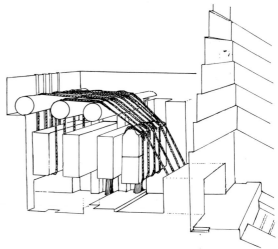

Left **Unfinished granite casing at the base of Menkaure's pyramid. Only the blocks in the centre have been dressed. Bosses to ease manoeuvring can still be seen on some of the undressed blocks.** *Above* **Portcullis system for lowering three granite slabs to block the entrance to the burial chamber of Khufu's pyramid.**

a lubricant to ease positioning of the blocks. It seems likely that the corner blocks were laid and dressed at the beginning of each course to make sure that each layer of stone was correctly aligned. Diagonals were measured to check that the structure was square, while sighting down the corners prevented torque.

Internal layout of the pyramids

Khufu's pyramid is unique in the complexity of its internal arrangements. There are three inner chambers: the lowest is carved from bedrock beneath the pyramid while the two upper chambers are built within the body of the pyramid. The King's Chamber is entirely lined with red granite from Aswan and contains a sarcophagus of the same material. Above it are five relieving chambers, roofed with huge granite beams, designed to deflect the weight of the pyramid away from the ceiling of the burial chamber; in the Grand Gallery which leads to the King's Chamber the same end is achieved by corbelling. Narrow shafts approximately 20 cm (8 in) square lead from the two upper chambers and are aligned towards Orion and the circumpolar stars to allow the dead king's 'soul' to travel to these stars. The architects also invented elaborate portcullis and plugging mechanisms to seal the entrance corridors, but later robbers tunnelled around them.

The inner chambers of the pyramids of Khafre and Menkaure lie below ground level and were excavated from bedrock. Khafre's pyramid contains only two simple chambers with pented ceilings, while Menkaure's pyramid has a small but more complex sequence of rooms and passages, one of which is decorated.

Finishing the pyramid

While the edges of casing stones were probably cut to shape when they were laid, the outer surface of the stone was not dressed until the pyramid was finished: the surplus stone protected the casing during construction of the higher levels. The final dressing took place from the top downwards. As the workmen moved down the sides of the pyramid the construction ramps would have been gradually dismantled. Much of the granite casing of the lower courses of Menkaure's pyramid had not been dressed when construction was abandoned, and handling bosses can still be seen on many of the blocks.

Apart from robbers' tunnels, the Giza pyramids remained essentially intact until the Middle Ages when they were systematically quarried for their stone. Fine limestone was required for building work in Cairo and it proved far easier to strip the casing blocks from the pyramids than to quarry new material. Thankfully a small portion of the casing survives at the top of Khafre's pyramid, providing a tantalizing glimpse of its original appearance.

Exploration and mapping of the Giza plateau has been underway since the 17th century and is still in progress. Careful observation and excavation continue to provide information about building methods and about the people who constructed these extraordinary monuments.

The Hanging Gardens of Babylon

Time: 605–562 BC
Location: Babylon, Iraq

He built the so-called hanging paradise because his wife, who had been brought up in the area around Media, wanted mountain scenery.

JOSEPHUS, 1ST CENTURY AD

MAJESTIC GROVES and baroque fountains suspended on interlacing arches, miracles of mountainous Iranian scenery transported to the dreary Mesopotamian plain – the Hanging Gardens of Babylon combine technical virtuosity with romantic dream. Unlike the other original Seven Wonders, they are a monument not to glory but to love – a gorgeous Valentine built by a king to gratify his homesick wife. It is a charming tale, but is it an illusion? Did Nebuchadnezzar and Amyitis ever stroll together along those shadowy paths? Was this where Alexander the Great, dying, desperately tried to cool his fever?

Artist's reconstruction of the Hanging Gardens, with the trees on the uppermost level which amazed visitors, the terraces resembling a theatre, and waterfalls tumbling from hidden sources.

Area	120 sq. m
Height	25 m
Vertical piers	6.6 m wide and 3.3 m apart
Irrigation techniques	pipes, screws, water channels

The ancient descriptions

The first reputable historian to mention the gardens is Berossus, a Babylonian writing about 270 BC. He states that Nebuchadnezzar (605–562 BC) built a new palace in 15 days, with stone foundations or terraces resembling mountain scenery. Trees were planted there, and this, says Berossus, was the 'so-called' hanging park, made to please the queen.

There is nothing implausible in this. Ancient alliances were often sealed by a royal wedding, and it is very likely that Nebuchadnezzar married an Iranian princess. One of Nebuchadnezzar's own records, obviously known to Berossus, describes his New Palace: it was as high as a mountain, partly made of stone, and allegedly completed in 15 days. There is no specific mention of a park, yet palaces did tend to have one.

Later Greek accounts add far more detail. One says that the gardens were 120 m (394 ft) square and about 25 m (82 ft) high, the height of the city wall. They were terraced like a theatre, with small buildings among them. The base consisted of many walls, each about 7 m (23 ft) wide and 3 m (9.8 ft) apart, which supported beams of stone. Above the

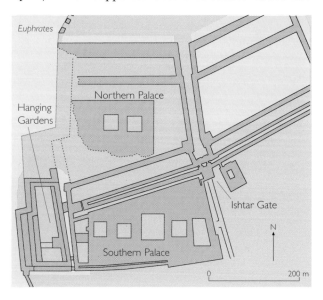

beams were three separate layers – reeds laid in bitumen, two courses of brick-work, and an uppermost casing of lead. The soil of the garden rested on top, and water for the trees was provided by hidden machines fed from the river below.

A second account speaks of 20 supporting walls. A third says that the garden rested on vaults of brick and bitumen; Archimedean screws alongside a stair-way provided the water. Another describes a sub-structure of stone columns supporting wooden beams: the beams were the trunks of the date-palm which, instead of rotting, provided sustenance for the roots of trees in the garden above, and the whole area was irrigated by an ingenious network of fountains and channels.

But where were they?

Because of the contradictory descriptions, some people have doubted whether the gardens ever existed. Yet none of the architectural features mentioned, except the indestructible tree-trunks, would be surprising. Greek visitors must have seen a wooded elevation rising above the palace, and we

Left **An Assyrian king sitting in his garden, about 645 BC.** *Below* **Drawing of a fragment of a sculpture showing a palace with trees at Nineveh – a city with magnificent gardens destroyed, but also imitated, by the Babylonians.**

may legitimately look for its remains among the modern ruins. Unfortunately the palaces of Babylon have been devastated over thousands of years by people keen to reuse the magnificent baked bricks. Normally foundations alone survive.

Early explorers looked for the gardens in the high Summer Palace; this is roughly 180 m (590 ft) square,

screw enclosed in cylinder; optimum angle 37°

Above **The Archimedean Screw: water is lifted as the screw is turned. Ancient texts from Iraq seem to contain descriptions of this screw device long before the birth of Archimedes, the Greek scientist after whom it is named.** *Opposite* **Plan of Babylon showing one supposed location for the Hanging Gardens.**

and incorporated elaborate wells, but there is inadequate space for terraces and trees. One archaeologist located the gardens above some brick vaults he had found in the Southern Palace; again there are wells, but the vaults are the basement of an administrative area, and may have been a prison.

Anyone looking at a groundplan of the palace quarter, however, will notice that the Southern and Northern Palaces are flanked on the north and west, close to the Euphrates, by structures of remarkable thickness. Any of them could have incorporated terraced gardens, and maybe several did, but much the most impressive is the Western Outwork. This enclosure, about 190 × 80 m (623 × 262 ft) in size, has outer walls some 20 m (65 ft) wide, made of bricks laid in bitumen. There were rooms at the northern end, and at the southern end a square with some kind of stairway in one corner. On this unique structure it would have been possible to create a square garden, close to the required dimensions, with summer-houses and an artificial terraced mountain.

And so the question rests. It may yet be resolved by new excavations or by some undiscovered document from Nebuchadnezzar's reign. Until then we can imagine the Hanging Gardens, with or without vaults and fountains, in whatever way we choose.

The Temple of Artemis at Ephesus

Time: c. 550–325 BC
Location: Ephesus, Turkey

The arts of Greece and the wealth of Asia had conspired to erect a sacred and magnificent structure.

EDWARD GIBBON, C. 1776

THE TEMPLE OF Artemis won its place among the Seven Wonders through the magnificence of its architecture and its sheer size. Significantly larger than the Parthenon (p. 111), it was one of the largest temples ever built by the ancient Greeks. Standing near Ephesus on the Ionian coast of modern-day Turkey, both temple and city derived great wealth from the pilgrims attracted to this splendid shrine, home to the cult of a mysterious goddess ('Diana of the Ephesians'), who though assimilated with the Greek goddess Artemis was in fact an ancient Anatolian deity.

The Temple of Artemis was not only one of the largest Greek temples; it was among the earliest to be built entirely in marble. It was constructed on the site of earlier shrines in around 550 BC with financial support from Croesus, the fabulously wealthy king of the neighbouring kingdom of Lydia. In 356 BC, however, this magnificent structure was burned down by a pyromaniac seeking to immortalize his name. Within decades a new temple rose on the spot, modelled closely on the earlier building.

FACTFILE

Croesus Temple	(Temple D)	c. 550 BC
	55 × 110 m (on upper step)	
Classical Temple	(Temple E)	c. 325 BC
	78.5 × 131 m	
Unsupported span	6.5 m	
Architrave blocks		
Length	8.75 m	
Weight	40 tonnes	
Columns		
Height	20 m	
Diameter	c. 6.5 m	

The restored temple survived into the Roman period, when the Roman writer Pliny marvelled at its size and construction. Three large windows pierced the roof pediment, the central one provided a window of appearance through which worshippers at the altar could see their goddess, Artemis. The altar itself was a splendid colonnaded building in its own right, standing in front of the temple.

The original temple measured 55 × 110 m (180 × 360 ft) on its upper step and was surrounded by a double row of columns on three sides, and a deep columned porch fronting the entrance. When it was rebuilt in the 4th century BC, the foundation and some of the superstructure of the earlier temple were reused, but it was now raised some 2 m (7 ft) and the platform surrounded by a flight of stairs. Thirty-six column bases on the entrance front were decorated with relief carvings, an unusual feature for Greek temples; the columns themselves were carved with 40–48 shallow flutes. Around the temple above the columns ran a frieze, and there were lion-headed waterspouts. With unsupported spans often exceeding 6.5 m (21 ft), involving blocks of stone up to 8.75 m (29 ft) long, the structure pushed the builders to their limits.

Artist's reconstruction of the Classical Temple of Artemis at Ephesus, with the large altar building in front.

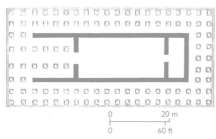

Plan of the Classical Temple and altar.

Building the temple

The scale of the undertaking is conveyed by the story that the architect of the first temple, Chersiphron, contemplated suicide when faced with the problem of raising the great entrance lintel. Greek builders were certainly using cranes by 515 BC, but many of the blocks in the Temple of Artemis were simply too heavy. And raising the large blocks was not the only problem – Chersiphron also had to ensure that the architrave blocks were set exactly in place. To achieve this he built a ramp of sandbags which rose slightly higher than the position in which the block was to be set. Once the block had been hauled up the ramp, the sandbags were emptied at the bottom so that the surface of the ramp slowly sank until the stone settled into its correct position.

The marble for the building came from quarries located 11 km (7 miles) away, far enough to make the transport of massive blocks weighing 40 tonnes another challenge. Wagons could simply not have supported weights of this scale, but Chersiphron devised an ingenious alternative: column drums were fixed with central pivots within a wooden frame so that they could rotate like huge rollers and be hauled by a team of oxen. This concept was adapted by Chersiphron's son, Metagenes, so that the rectangular architrave blocks could be moved in a similar way, each end of the block being encased within a massive wooden wheel.

Thus did necessity become the mother of invention, the sheer size of the temple and the blocks used in its construction requiring new techniques for transporting and raising the stones. While Chersiphron's methods never became popular elsewhere, the colossal temple was truly a testament to his ingenuity. Alas, little survives to this day, save for the excavated temple podium and a solitary reconstructed column.

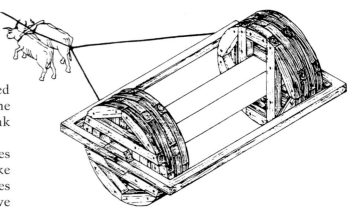

Above **Metagenes' method for transporting the huge architrave blocks.** *Left* **A view of the scattered remains and single reconstructed column of the Temple of Artemis today.**

The Statue of Zeus at Olympia

Time: c. 430 BC
Location: Olympia, Greece

[Pheidias] has shown Zeus seated, but with his head almost to the ceiling, so that we have the impression that if Zeus stood up, he would unroof the temple.

STRABO, 1ST CENTURY AD

AROUND 437 BC Pheidias, exiled from Athens on political grounds, travelled to Olympia at the request of the council of the sanctuary of Zeus to begin work on a figure that was to become another of the Seven Wonders of the Ancient World: the statue of Olympian Zeus. He had already created the famous chryselephantine statue of Athena for the Parthenon (p. 111) and an equally spectacular statue of the same goddess that stood close to 10 m (33 ft) high on the Acropolis. By the time he arrived in Olympia, he was beyond question the leading Greek sculptor of his time.

Pheidias' task in Olympia was to design and erect a cult image of Zeus to be housed in the Doric temple built in 466–456 BC and dedicated to Zeus. The result was outstanding: he crafted a 13-m (43-ft)

View of the Sanctuary of Olympia where many Greeks came to worship and take part in the Olympic games. Buildings from several periods reflect the continuous growth of the sanctuary over time.

high statue of ivory and gold set on a 1-m (3.3-ft) marble base. The whole work completely filled the western end of the temple – a difficult feat considering the materials and size of the space – and could only be viewed at a distance since painted screens around its base prevented closer inspection.

Pheidias portrayed Zeus seated on a throne, maximizing his size in the space available: if he were standing he would have been over 18 m (59 ft) tall. In his right hand Zeus held a winged Victory figure symbolizing triumph in the Olympic games, and in his left a sceptre decorated with metal inlay denoting his sovereignty as king of the gods. Perched on the sceptre was an eagle, the very emblem of Zeus. Zeus himself was completely fashioned in ivory, but gold was used for his robe and sandals. Fine details of lilies and animals were carved into his clothing and his head was adorned with an olive wreath. His whole massive body rested on an elaborate throne of ebony and ivory – a magnificent work in its own right, being carved with mythological figures and scenes and decorated with gold and precious stones. His feet rested on a large footstool, in front of which was a black marble basin used to collect the olive oil that was poured over the statue, probably to help prevent the ivory from cracking.

Although no certain work by Pheidias has come down to us, it is clear that he could execute fine, larger-than-life sculpture and was accomplished in working ivory. Yet never had he – or anyone else for that matter – worked ivory on such a massive scale, until he created his Athena for the Parthenon. The technique was not straightforward and required skill in working metal and wood as well as ivory.

FACTFILE

The core of Olympian Zeus

Roughly 780 cu. m (27,545 cu. ft) of wood, from local sources, made up the core of the statue, to which the ivory was fixed. The core would have been nearly the height of the statue and was made in sections which were assembled in the temple – it would have been impossible to move the core to, and into, the temple as a single unit. The timber was shaped only slightly, as musculature would have been carefully moulded in ivory and metal.

Pheidias' workshop was outside the sanctuary, to the west of the temple, and it is here that he planned and executed parts of the statue. He himself would have directed the work and been responsible for the finer details of moulding and carving, but others would have overseen the supply and movement of materials. Equally, other sculptors would have participated in the preparation of the materials and wooden core, fixing the sheets of ivory and gold and providing general assistance to Pheidias.

Shaping the materials

It has often been assumed that ivory tusks were sectioned and attached to wooden cores, yet the detail that Pheidias was able to achieve in the statue of Zeus, notably the carefully rendered musculature of

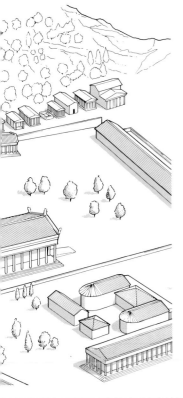

Left **Reconstruction of the Sanctuary of Olympia. The temple housing the statue of Zeus is in the centre.** *Right* **The workshop of Pheidias was converted into a Byzantine church in AD 391.**

Below **Simplified plan of the Sanctuary of Olympia in the 5th century BC.**

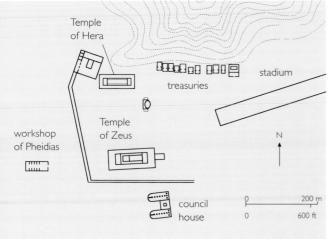

ials for softening and shaping ivory, including fire, beer, vinegar and boiling with mandrake, all of which would have been available to Pheidias. Once softened, smooth sheets formed the throne while others were pressed into terracotta moulds to fashion flesh. Each completed piece of ivory was then moved into the temple where it was secured to the core by means of rivets and the natural adhesion that occurs between wet sheets of ivory.

Gold was used for Zeus' sandals and robe, for the Victory figure in Zeus' right hand and parts of the throne. A number of techniques were used to work the gold. To decorate parts of the throne large sheets were probably beaten over a shape. Moulds may have been used for other parts, however, such as the solid gold lions at the sides of the footstool, and the drapery of Zeus' robe. Gold was melted at extremely high temperatures and then poured in liquid form into the moulds. Terracotta examples used for drapery details have been found.

The whole structure was thus built up piece by piece until finally the ivory was polished and the gold shined. The result was a magnificent wonder that sufficiently amazed the ancients to be recorded in the writings of Strabo, Cicero, Callimachus and Pausanias, to name only a few.

his chest, would suggest that some other finer technique of working ivory was known. Production of furniture in ancient times, with which Pheidias was likely familiar, provides a clue. Furniture makers knew that larger, thinner sheets of ivory could be obtained by unrolling ivory tusks rather than by sectioning them. Not only was it easier to cover a larger area with these sheets, but their thinness would have made the ivory easier to mould once softened. Ancient sources record various methods and mater-

Towards the end of the 4th century AD, Christians banned all pagan cults. The sanctuary at Olympia was no longer used and the Olympic games ceased to be celebrated. Yet the statue of Olympian Zeus continued to attract wonder, so much so that it was moved to Constantinople (Istanbul). In AD 462, however, a massive fire seriously damaged the city and the statue was destroyed. No copies of the Olympian Zeus were ever made – all that we know of the statue today comes from descriptions in ancient writings and rough depictions found on ancient coins.

Artist's reconstruction of Pheidias' great masterpiece, the Statue of Zeus. The sheer size of the seated god and his reflection in the pool of oil before him were awe-inspiring.

The Mausoleum of Halicarnassus

Time: c. 353 BC
Location: Bodrum, Turkey

that sepulchrall monster that Queen Artimise made to her husband Mousolos the Carian King.

WILLIAM BIRNIE, 1606

T HE MAUSOLEUM of Halicarnassus on the southwest coast of Turkey was built to house the remains of Mausolus, ruler of Caria. His grandiose tomb was completed after his death in 353 BC, probably by Artemisia, his sister-wife. It was a truly monumental structure, eclipsing any other contemporary tomb both in size and grandeur: standing almost 45 m (148 ft) high, it covered an area of more than 1216 sq. m (13,089 sq. ft). Although little remains of the Mausoleum today, many details of its construction are known from historical accounts and archaeological excavations.

The remains of the Mausoleum today. Scattered column drums, building blocks and foundations provide some clues as to the form the tomb once took.

FACTFILE

Podium		Colonnade	
Height	20.2 m	Height	12 m
Length	38 m		
Width	32 m	**Chariot group**	
Volume of stone	24,563 cu. m	Height	6 m
Pyramid			
Height	6.8 m		
Volume of stone	2853 cu. m		

Various reconstructions of the Mausoleum have been proposed, with differing views as to the form of the podium and, particularly, the arrangement of the statues, as seen in the two illustrated here by G.B. Waywell (below), **with surviving fragments shown, and** (opposite) **K. Jeppesen.**

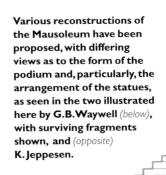

The Mausoleum was almost square in plan, with the east and west sides slightly longer than those on the north and south. It rested on a large podium measuring 38 × 32 m (125 × 105 ft), above which was an Ionic colonnade running around all four faces; the whole edifice was topped by a 24-stepped pyramid. Blue limestone and white marble blocks were used to face the structure, while the core was of green volcanic stone. A network of drains and subterranean galleries kept the structure dry and well supported. A suitably grand setting for this magnificent monument was provided by the large walled precinct, covering some 2.5 ha (6 acres) and entered from the east through a monumental gateway.

Five of the best sculptors of the Greek world were reputedly employed in decorating the Mausoleum: Scopas, Bryaxis, Leochares, Timotheos and Praxiteles. Four were each responsible for one side of the tomb, while the fifth fashioned the huge four-horse chariot on the very top of the stepped pyramid. Two friezes ran continuously around all faces of the tomb, one depicting the battle of the Lapiths and Centaurs and the other the battle between the Greeks and Amazons, while freestanding figures and lions, life-size or larger, stood on blue limestone bases.

Quite when the tomb collapsed (perhaps toppled by an earthquake) we do not know; some have even suggested that it was never completed. All knowledge of the site had been lost by the 15th century when the Knights of St John quarried into it, burning the marble to make lime mortar and using the building stone to fortify their castle at Bodrum. It was they who came

upon the tomb chamber of Mausolus at the base of the monument in 1522; unfortunately its contents were quickly looted and few details are recorded.

Building the Mausoleum

Pliny the Elder tells us that the tomb rose to a total height of 45 m (140 Greek ft or 148 ft), close to one-third of which was occupied by the colonnade. The height of the pyramid can be calculated as 6.8 m (22.3 ft), while remains of the chariot group suggest that it stood an impressive 6 m (19.7 ft) high – around twice life-size. This would then leave 20.2 m (66 ft) for the podium.

The podium alone would have required around 24,563 cu. m (867,442 cu. ft) of stone to be sourced, cut, transported and put in place. Only the green lava used in the interior was available locally, while analyses have shown other stones came from different sources further away. The marble of the Amazon frieze came from the island of Kos, while the chariot frieze is probably of Phrygian marble from the Afyon region inland. This marshalling of materials from widespread locations may have owed much to Mausolus' standing as a major player in regional power-politics.

Excavations carried out in the 19th century and again in the 1960s and 1970s have recovered the ground plan of the Mausoleum and show something of how it was built. A necropolis already occupied the site, making it necessary to level the ground and to cut and fill corridors and chambers to provide a solid support. Blocks of the local lava almost a metre in length formed both the foundation and the core of the podium. Clamping adjacent blocks with metal rods helped to bind and support walls and it is likely that further strength was provided by metal dowels joining blocks in different courses. The colonnade and pyramid were equally well planned, with each column of the colonnade separated from the next by 3 m (9.8 ft) so that there were 36 Ionic columns in total. Above the columns metal clamps were again used to bind blocks of the architrave.

These statues, found north of the Mausoleum during excavations in 1857 and now in the British Museum, have been identified as portraying Artemisia and Mausolus, though this is not certain. In the reconstruction, left, they are shown in the centre of the colonnade.

The scant archaeological evidence and the ambiguities in ancient accounts of the Mausoleum make it difficult to determine how the blocks were raised. Cranes must have been used to position column drums above the podium on account of their sheer size and the height to which they were raised. Once in place the drums were fitted with wooden dowels that joined and secured them. Podium blocks may have been lifted in the same fashion, perhaps with ropes lashed around lug ends that were cut off once the stones had been put in place. Raising blocks for the pyramid would have been even more difficult as any device would need to have been proportionately strengthened to counter not only the size of the stones, but also the height to which they had to be raised – approximately 32–39 m (105–128 ft).

Raising and fixing the sculptural decoration would have been equally problematic, if not more so. Hoisting a building stone carries with it the risk of fracture and this is increased when raising finely carved sculptures with fragile limbs. Yet works equal to and larger than life size were raised as part of a carefully planned sculptural programme.

It was the wealth of ornament, notably the free-standing sculpture, which qualified the Mausoleum for a place among the Seven Wonders of the World. Numerous fragments survive, some with traces of paint: red-brown on hair and beards, and red, blue and purple on cloaks and clothing. The lion figures around the edge of the roof were painted yellow-ochre. Yet how all this freestanding sculpture was arranged remains a subject of great controversy. Some argue that to accommodate it all, the podium must have been stepped, creating ledges upon which the statues rested. Others have tried to stick closer to the historical accounts that do not mention a stepped podium, but as a result they have been unsuccessful in accommodating all the sculpture. Even those that advocate a stepped podium cannot agree on the number of steps.

We are on firmer ground with the tomb chamber itself: a rectangular room built into the base of the edifice, approached down a flight of steps and closed by massive marble doors. Just within the entrance is

One of three reliefs now in the British Museum depicting the battle of Greeks and Amazons. Found in the foundation area of the Mausoleum, the reliefs form one part of a continuous frieze that ran around all sides of the tomb.

a massive squared block of stone, with holes and slots for the dowels which originally fixed it in position. Within this chamber, in 1522, the Knights of St John came across a marble urn or coffin. When they returned the next day, however, the coffin had been broken into and only a scatter of gold roundels and fragments of cloth of gold remained. A few such roundels were found in recent excavations. This is all that we know about the original burial.

Why was such an elaborate monument built for this particular ruler of Caria? Politics may provide the answer. Mausolus was keen to found a Carian empire, uniting Greek and non-Greek people, and his tomb symbolized his desire for unity by combining Greek, Lycian and Egyptian architectural features. One of the Mausoleum's innovations was to bring together architecture and sculpture in a new relationship, creating a balance between the two that was echoed in many subsequent ensembles. Mausolus also found a kind of immortality through his tomb, which was much copied (on a smaller scale) in Hellenistic and Roman monuments, and has given us the word 'mausoleum' which we still apply today to any grand funerary monument.

Artist's reconstruction of the Mausoleum of Halicarnassus.

41

The Colossus
of Rhodes

Time: 294–282 BC
Location: Rhodes

Few people can get their arms round one of its thumbs, and its fingers are bigger than most statues.

PLINY, 1ST CENTURY AD

OF ALL THE Seven Wonders of the Ancient World, we perhaps know least about the Colossus of Rhodes. There are no eyewitness accounts to tell us what it looked like when it still stood, and unlike many other Classical statues no copies seem to have been made of it. Even its exact location is disputed. Did it stand by the harbour entrance? It was certainly common practice to erect large statues on podiums at harbour mouths to impress visiting seafarers, but others have argued that the Colossus was further away from the water's edge, at the top of the Street of Knights where an old Turkish schoolhouse now stands. Yet we do know how the Colossus was made, thanks to the ancient writer Philo of Byzantium. And indeed it was the technical achievement of casting a gigantic bronze figure over 33 m (110ft) high – even its fingers were bigger than most statues of the time – that qualified it for inclusion among the Seven Wonders.

Essentially the Colossus was a thank-offering to the sun god Helios – the patron deity of Rhodes – for the city's deliverance from a siege by Demetrius 'Poliorcetes', ruler of Syria, in 305 BC. His name means 'the besieger', but in Rhodes he met his match. When he withdrew from the island he abandoned his siege engines, which the Rhodians promptly sold, thus financing the Colossus.

The project was entrusted to Chares, who probably designed a figure with its head crowned by an aureole of pointed flames and loose, curled locks of hair as if blown by the wind. These were features characteristic of the sun god, and the Colossus may have had the realistic, almost cherubic, face, with lips slightly parted, which is found on coins of the period depicting Helios. Glistening in the sun and towering over the buildings of the city, it cannot have failed to impress both native Rhodians and foreign visitors alike.

FACTFILE

Height	33 m
Chest	18.5 m
Armpits (length)	6.2 m
Thigh	3.5 m
Ankles	1.5 m

Above **The entrance to the Mandraki Harbour, with the Fort of St Nicolas on the far side.** *Left* **An 18th-century reconstruction reflecting the erroneous belief that the Colossus straddled the harbour entrance.**

The head of Helios depicted on a Rhodian coin.

Building the Colossus

The sheer size of the Colossus made it impossible to cast limbs and body in separate parts and then fix them together. Philo tells us that Chares instead cast the figure *in situ*, but in sections. Work began in 294 BC with the feet, which were first cast and then set in position on a white marble base. The next stage – the lower legs – was then cast on to the feet, again using carefully prepared and sculpted moulds. And so the Colossus rose, section upon section. It was a hollow structure, secured internally by an iron framework with horizontal crossbars and weighted by blocks of stone.

As work on the Colossus progressed upwards, a mound of earth was continuously raised, providing the artisans with a platform from which they were able to mould and cast the next part. The skill of the whole process lay in the fact that Chares never saw what the statue looked like until the very last part was cast and set in place, since only when the mound of earth was removed was the Colossus revealed in all its glory.

The quantity of bronze required for the statue would have consumed the island's stocks of copper

A possible reconstruction of the Colossus of Rhodes. Stability was achieved in the simplicity of the pose, but its sheer size, materials and prominence could not fail to have attracted attention.

and tin, but Rhodes was a major trading centre and further supplies would have been imported by sea. Obtaining the necessary quantities of bronze may be one reason why the Colossus rose only 2–2.5 m (6–8 ft) per year. Another reason was the sheer time it would have taken to melt and cast the bronze, to construct and raise the earthen mound, and to build the Colossus itself.

For such a tall statue to withstand the forces of wind and weather it had to be columnar in shape. Arms must have been held close by the sides or raised directly above, as their weight and size would have rendered any other pose unstable. We can also rule out the idea that the Colossus straddled the harbour mouth; this would have required a span of over 120 m (400 ft) and is simply the imagining of a 15th-century pilgrim. Paradoxically, given its fame, the Colossus in fact stood for little more than 50 years; completed in 282 BC, it was toppled by an earthquake in 226 BC. The ruins themselves became a tourist attraction, until they were carted away by a Syrian merchant in the 7th century AD.

The Pharos of Alexandria

Time: 297–283 BC
Location: Alexandria, Egypt

Pharos is an oblong island ... and has upon it a tower that is admirably constructed of white stone with many storeys and bears the same name as the island.

STRABO, C. 64 BC–AD 21

THE PHAROS OF Alexandria was traditionally the seventh wonder of the ancient world. A lighthouse designed to guide ships safely to the harbour of Alexandria, its construction is said to have taken fifteen years and to have cost the vast sum of 800 talents. It was built under Ptolemy I and dedicated around 283 BC in the reign of Ptolemy II. With the exception of the pyramids at Giza, it was the tallest building in the ancient world.

The Pharos stood on an island at the entrance to the harbour of Alexandria on the site now occupied by the medieval Arab fortress of Qait Bey. The central tower of the fort was probably built on the foundations of the Pharos and may therefore reproduce its ground-plan and dimensions. Much of the material used to build the fort comes from the Pharos. It is, however, remarkably difficult to reconstruct its exact appearance, despite schematic representations on ancient coins and mosaics and written descriptions by Classical and Arab authors. A ruined tower at Abusir is also thought to have been modelled on the Pharos. This was all that was known until the 1960s, when an Egyptian diver discovered huge blocks and statues on the seabed around the fort of Qait Bey. These are thought to come from the ruined lighthouse and are currently being studied by

A diver from the French underwater team examines a huge block which may once have been part of the Pharos.

FACTFILE

Height	c. 135 m
Cost	800 talents
Range of beacon	c. 35 km

a French team consisting of divers and archaeologists.

Built in three tiers, the Pharos is thought to have been about 135 m (443 ft) high. The lowest tier was square in plan and contained rooms for the permanent garrison of the lighthouse, their animals and supplies. The entrance was raised and was reached by a ramp from a platform around the tower. Within this square lower tier was an inner wall supporting the upper sections of the lighthouse; these were reached by an internal spiral ramp. The middle tier was octagonal and above this was a circular section surmounted by a statue of Zeus.

Construction of the Pharos

We can speculate a little about the construction of the Pharos. It was built of a white stone, most probably local limestone rather than marble as is often thought. Granite was probably also used in appropriate places as it is much stronger than limestone and could withstand the greater loads at the bottom of the tower and above doorways. Many of the blocks now lying on the seabed are of granite and some weigh up to 75 tonnes.

Alexandria was part of the Hellenistic world and in terms of style the Pharos seems to have been a Hellenistic rather than an Egyptian monument,

although the French underwater team has located a substantial number of Egyptian statues in the vicinity. Colossal statues of Ptolemy and his queen stood outside the lighthouse.

Raising blocks into position on such a tall building must have required considerable ingenuity, and Hellenistic building techniques, including sophisticated cranes and lifting devices, would have been available to the builders. It is also possible, however, that much of the stone for the upper storeys was dragged up the spiral ramp inside the building.

Even the location of the fire which lit the lighthouse is uncertain: it was probably at the top, either beneath or alongside the statue of Zeus. Fuel could have been carried up the spiral ramp by pack animals and then hauled to the top with lifting devices. Some sort of reflector may have been used to magnify and direct the light of the fire but there is no actual evidence for this.

Despite some damage and repairs, the Pharos remained largely intact until the 14th century AD. At some point before the 12th century it was badly damaged in an earthquake, following which the square base was buttressed and a mosque was built on top. The entire structure finally collapsed in 1303 in another serious earthquake and was eventually replaced by the fortress of Qait Bey in 1479.

Opposite **An artist's reconstruction of the Pharos of Alexandria, cut away to show the interior.** *Above* **Schematic representation of the Pharos on a coin of the Roman emperor Commodus (AD 180–192).** *Right* **Drawing of a detail of a mosaic from St Mark's basilica, Venice (13th century), showing a boat arriving in the harbour at Alexandria; when this mosaic was made the Pharos was still standing.**

Tombs & Cemeteries

MANY OF THE most famous buildings of the ancient world were not palaces or temples for the living, but tombs for the dead. Whether it be the pyramids of Egypt, the tomb of Chinese emperor Shihuangdi, or the prehistoric burial mounds of Europe, funerary monuments were frequently built with both a view to impress and an eye to eternity. In dynastic Egypt, for example, the structures of everyday life – even the royal palaces – were usually built in mud-brick, and have therefore left only denuded remains; whereas it is the temples and burial places, stone-built or rock-cut, which have left enduring traces.

Thus it is that some of the greatest constructional efforts of the ancient world went into the creation of imposing tombs. The result was often a massive monument which dominated its surroundings. Of the Seven Wonders of the Ancient World, the Pyramids of Giza and the Mausoleum of Halicarnassus may be placed in this category, as may the tombs of the Nabataean rulers at Petra with their ornate façades fronting comparatively simple rock-cut chambers. At Angkor Wat in Cambodia, the entire tomb takes the form of an elaborate temple heavily embellished with sculptures and rich in cosmic symbolism. These were designed to place the semi-divine ruler on his correct footing within the cosmic order. The pyramids at Moche or the keyhole-shaped mound of the Japanese emperor Nintoku were likewise intended to dominate by their sheer external size.

The megalithic chambered tomb of Newgrange in Ireland, dating back to 3100 BC, is one of the largest prehistoric burial monuments in western Europe.

Yet behind the dynastic message of a massive tomb was the need to provide for the dead ruler in the afterlife, according to the beliefs of the time and the society concerned, and impressive external structures often hide equally elaborate burial chambers. The tomb of Chinese emperor Shihuangdi beneath Mount Li was sealed up after his death. Nobody knows exactly what it contains, but ancient accounts refer to an underground palace with rivers of mercury.

Indeed, in cases where the burial chamber has been revealed, it frequently shows much greater constructional skill than the external structure in which it is concealed. The resting place of the Maya ruler Pakal at Palenque, for example, at the heart of a pyramid, is more remarkable than the pyramid itself. Likewise the Treasury of Atreus at Mycenae: from within, the beehive-shaped chamber is strikingly impressive, both in scale and construction, but externally the tomb was largely buried within the hillside. The same was true of Egyptian royal tombs in the Valley of the Kings. Other than the entrance, there was little on the surface to indicate the presence of elaborately decorated complexes, such as Seti I's cut deep into the valley sides.

Over hidden tombs such as these, burial monuments above ground have one significant advantage: being visible, they can carry enduring messages, whether these messages be overt or implicit. The Etruscan cemetery of Cerveteri in Italy is an entire burial ground, with tombs of different sizes and styles extending over a period of several centuries. Here the observant viewer can begin to grasp changes in tradition – for few practices remain constant for many years – and variations within society. The large circular tombs of the earlier phase are later succeeded by streets of more modest, more regimented tombs, reflecting perhaps the townscape of the city of Cerveteri itself.

For the truly enigmatic, however, we must turn to prehistoric tombs such as Newgrange in Ireland. Impressive both in overall scale and in the decoration carved on its kerbstones, passage and chamber, this monument took enormous effort to build. Yet the human remains found within – scattered and trampled by centuries of visitors – provide little insight into the exact practices carried out here. Towards the close of every year, however, the sun's rays at sunrise shine through the roofbox and down the passage to flood the floor of the central chamber with light. It is hard to imagine a more evocative symbol, as the dying sun illumines the place of burial, offering hope of rebirth. In the absence of written evidence, the exact meaning of the beliefs may now escape us, but the imagery can still be grasped through the structure of the tomb.

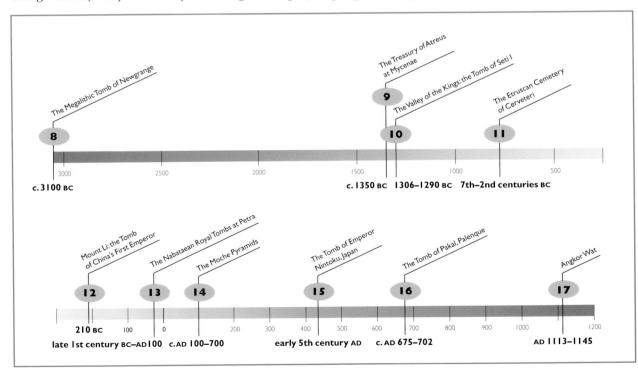

The Megalithic Tomb of Newgrange

Time: c. 3100 BC
Location: Boyne Valley, Ireland

I also met with one monument in this kingdom very singular. It stands at a place called New Grange and is a Mount or Barrow of very considerable height encompass'd with vast stones pitch'd on end round the bottom of it.

EDWARD LHWYD, 1700

ONE OF the largest burial monuments in western Europe, Newgrange is situated on a low ridge facing south across the Boyne Valley, some 50 km (30 miles) north of Dublin. Built around 3100 BC, it stands in a passage-grave cemetery of two other large mounds (Knowth and Dowth) and several smaller ones. The defining feature of a passage grave is the stone-built passage which gave access to the burial chamber, allowing successive burials to be placed there. What makes Newgrange unusual, however, is its size, its 'roof-box' and the richness of its megalithic art.

The Newgrange roof-box is a narrow stone-lined slot built directly above the entrance to the passage. For a few days either side of the winter solstice (21 December), the rising sun shines through the roof-box, along the passage and lights up the burial chamber. Several years of careful observation would have been required to achieve this effect, perhaps marking out the correct position of the mound and its structures with wooden poles. It was an astonishing feat of accurate planning.

Above **Newgrange, and its neighbour Knowth, have the greatest concentration of megalithic art in western Europe, with designs including spirals and lozenges.** *Left* **Cross-section of the tomb, showing the ray of light that illuminates the chamber at midwinter.**

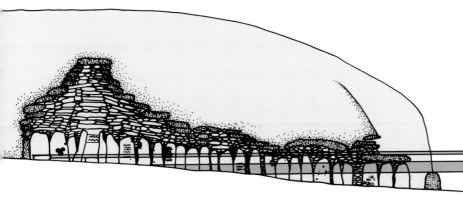

Traces of this original planning survive in the most richly decorated stones at Newgrange – the two kerbstones, one in front of the entrance (K1) and the other at the back of the tomb (K52). Unlike other kerbstones, these were decorated after being put in position and incorporate in their design a vertical line marking the exact axis of the mound. This may have been used as a sighting line, though it most likely also had a symbolic significance. The axis passes through the back stone of the burial chamber (C8) close to one edge, at a point marked on the stone itself by two opposed triangles. Measurements show that a unit of around 13.1 m (43 ft) was used in planning the tomb; K1 is 26 m (85.3 ft) from C8, which in turn is 52 m (170.6 ft) from K52. Key points on the perimeter of the mound are related to each other using the same unit, and were presum-

ably measured into position before the rest of the kerb was laid out.

Some 550 slabs were required for the kerb, passage and chamber. With few exceptions they are of a coarse grey-green slate, known as greywacke, from outcrops to the north of Newgrange. These were probably collected as boulders rather than quarried. Even so, the transport of these stones to the Newgrange ridge was a formidable undertaking for what was probably only a small team of builders.

Constructing the tomb

Laying out the kerb and building the passage and chamber may have proceeded in parallel. The most difficult operation was roofing the chamber. In some tombs of this kind, the chamber was capped by a single huge block of stone, but the builders of

FACTFILE

Quantity of mound material	200,000 tonnes
Number of kerbstones	97
Number of decorated kerbstones	31
Stones of passage and chamber	c. 450
Decorated stones in passage and chamber	44
Maximum diameter of kerb	85.3 m
Length of passage	18.95 m
Height of corbelled vault	6 m

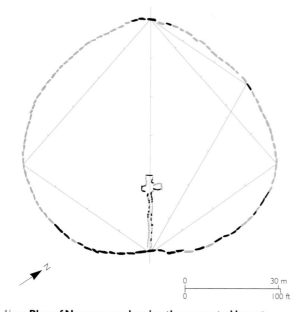

0   30 m
0   100 ft

Above **Plan of Newgrange showing the suggested layout in units of 13.1 metres. The stones shown in black are decorated.** *Right* **Newgrange today, as reconstructed following the excavations of 1962–75.**

Newgrange chose an alternative solution. They constructed a corbelled vault, with successive courses of stone slabs oversailing the one below, narrowing the gap until it could be closed by a single slab.

The structure owed its solidity to the way the stones were closely packed; any tendency for the stones to tilt or settle would have wedged them more tightly together. A further advantage of this method was that it did not require massive communal effort, as would moving a megalithic capstone, but could have been handled by a small team, perhaps a few dozen people. It did require considerable skill, however, as did the positioning of the 'roof-box' above the passage entrance .

Once passage and chamber were complete the mound itself could be constructed. Huge quantities of water-worn stones were dug from the gravel ter-races of the River Boyne. Alongside this local material was black granite and grandiorite from the north, and white quartz from the Wicklow Mountains to the south. Pieces of quartz, granite and grandiorite were found around the entrance, and Newgrange has today been reconstructed as a drum-shaped mound with a steep outer face, fronted by a near-vertical wall of quartz with granite and grandiorite inclusions forming an impressive façade. Whether this is correct, or whether the quartz and the granite and grandiorite formed a paved forecourt, is still unclear. What is beyond question is that Newgrange was a magnificent structure, edged by kerbstones that were not only richly carved but most likely also brightly coloured, concealing within its depths a burial chamber covered by a soaring corbelled vault and lit every midwinter by the rays of the rising sun.

Above **Looking out along the passage at Newgrange, with the tall corbelled vault of the burial chamber rising above.**

The Treasury of Atreus at Mycenae

Time: *c.* 1350 BC
Location: **Mycenae, Greece**

The plan of the tomb reveals clear thinking and a definite intention as well as bold imagination. …
This unknown master of the Bronze Age who designed and built the Treasury of Atreus deserves to rank with
the great architects of the world.

A.J.B. WACE, 1949

THE TREASURY of Atreus is in fact a tomb, but due to its magnificence it was long believed that it once held the treasures of King Atreus, the father of Agamemnon. It was built around 1350 BC, and although the identity of its original occupant is unknown, it is truly befitting a king, with a chamber soaring to over 13 m (43 ft) in height and an entrance passage 37 m (121 ft) long. It stands to the southwest of the citadel of Mycenae in the Greek Peloponnese, and the prestige and wealth of the dead within and of the community as a whole could be measured by its monumentality: it exceeded all practical purpose. A spectacular achievement of ancient architecture, the Treasury of Atreus is the finest example of its type, both by virtue of its size and the fineness of its finish.

The Mycenaean tholos tomb was reserved for burials of important officials or members of the ruling class. Cut back into a hillside, the tholos tomb is circular in plan – hence its name – and rises to a pointed dome. From their shape, these tombs are also referred to as bee-hive tombs. Believed by many to have its origins in Crete, the tholos tomb succeeded simple shaft graves in the mid- to late Bronze Age. Earlier examples are known, but the form dominates the early part of the late Bronze Age when it is widespread across the Greek mainland. Regional variations occur, but generally the form and certainly the function remain the same.

Building the tomb

The entire tomb was constructed of well-dressed stone. Its façade was ornamented in green and red marble, with half-columns flanking the door, each supporting another smaller half-column. These

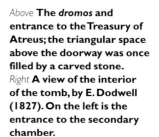

Above **The *dromos* and entrance to the Treasury of Atreus; the triangular space above the doorway was once filled by a carved stone.**
Right **A view of the interior of the tomb, by E. Dodwell (1827). On the left is the entrance to the secondary chamber.**

FACTFILE

Dromos (entrance passage)		***Stomion*** (entrance gate)	
Length	37 m	Width	2.6 m
Width	6 m	Height	5.4 m

Chamber	
Diameter	14.5 m
Height	13.2 m

were carved with zigzag and spiral patterns, and spirals decorated the stone that once filled the triangular space above the lintel, now empty.

To construct the tomb, the entrance passage was first cut back into the hillside and the earth and stone removed. The time taken for this would have been dependent on the number of labourers available, but may easily have been two months or more. Then the soil and stone filling the area needed for the tomb was excavated.

The first stones to be laid were those of the entrance passage, to prevent the sides of the passage from slipping inwards. The building stone was local and quarried no further than 1 km (0.6 miles) from the tomb. Blocks were extracted from the quarry by channelling around the desired stone, which was then freed using wedges and levers. The lowermost course would have been the easiest to lay as the blocks could be simply shifted into place, but to lift the blocks of the upper courses required more effort and ingenuity. Ropes would have been lashed about the blocks and teams of labourers situated on the hill above the entrance passage would have hoisted them into position. This same method would have

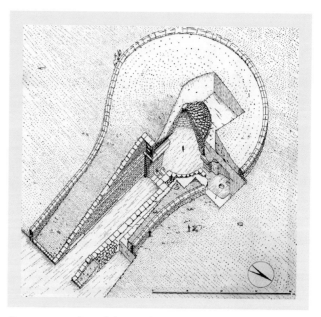

A reconstruction of the tomb, showing the interior of the main chamber, the side chamber and the corbelled vault.

been used to raise the blocks in the chamber itself. Here, however, blocks were not placed directly on top of each other, but positioned slightly to project beyond the course below. This method of corbelling enabled builders to fashion the curving walls that spanned the diameter of the tomb.

The gateway would have been started once the chamber was two-thirds complete and before the uppermost courses were laid. As with the entrance passage and chamber, the doorway was finished with dressed and tightly fitted blocks. Two massive lintel stones, one of which exceeds 100 tonnes, would have been shifted into place along the top of the entrance. Above the lintel stones, the walls were corbelled so that a triangular empty space was left, helping to direct the huge weight of the dome to the side walls of the entrance rather than on to the lintel itself. The space above the lintel was filled with a carved stone. The doors, now vanished, may have been made of wood.

The whole effort would have taken more than half a year to build, and probably closer to one year. Men were needed to quarry and transport stones and to hoist blocks into position. Sculptors were also required to shape columns for the entrance and to apply decoration to the tomb's façade. It is a wonder that so much effort went into building the tomb since, when finished, it was covered over and hidden from view.

The Valley of the Kings: The Tomb of Seti I

Time: c. 1306–1290 BC
Location: Luxor, Egypt

In beauty of execution it [the tomb of Seti I] far surpasses all the other tombs of the Bîbân el-Mulûk [Valley of the Kings].

GEORG STEINDORFF, 1902

THE VALLEY of the Kings is without question one of the greatest archaeological sites in the world. Lying beneath the pyramidal mountain peak of el-Qurn on the West Bank of the Nile at Luxor and hidden by a ridge of rock, the valley contains 62 tombs belonging to kings, queens and high officials of the New Kingdom. Today, the most famous tomb is undoubtedly that of King Tutankhamun, discovered by Howard Carter in 1922. Although its contents were indeed extraordinary, the tomb itself is actually one of the smallest and least imposing in the Valley. The most remarkable sepulchre belongs to the great king Seti I (c. 1306–1290 BC): it is the most complete in the entire Valley and has the finest architecture and decoration. It is also one of the most spectacular structures of its kind to have survived from antiquity.

A tomb in the Valley of the Kings was only part of royal mortuary provision. The tomb, designed to protect the body and burial goods, was also associated with a temple close to the Nile where the mortuary cult was conducted. Seti I constructed his

1 Excavating and plastering a chamber.
2 Burial chamber: the decoration is sketched out.
3 Correcting sketches and carving the relief.
4 Side chamber: painting the relief.
5 The sarcophagus is carefully manoeuvred into the tomb.

FACTFILE

Length of construction period	c. 16 years
Length of tomb	c. 110 m
Size of workforce	c. 30–50 men
Volume of stone excavated	c. 3000 cu. m

mortuary temple at Qurna, over 2 km (over 1 mile) east of his tomb in the Royal Valley, and he also built a cenotaph and temple at Abydos.

Planning a tomb

Work usually commenced on a new royal tomb almost as soon as the previous king had been buried. Sites in the valley were chosen carefully: the first burials had been high in the cliffs but later kings, Seti I among them, were buried closer to the valley floor. Plans of existing tombs and their locations were probably kept to ensure that new excavations did not hit earlier burials, but collisions did occasionally occur. Initially great care was taken to disguise tomb entrances – security was presumably one of the main reasons for the choice of this remote

valley as a royal necropolis – but after the reign of Seti I the entrances became increasingly ornate.

Seti I's tomb is a complex series of descending passages, pillared halls and a protective well, and is closely modelled on the earlier tomb of Horemheb. Contemporary plans of royal tombs have survived, although some could have been made as a record after completion of the tomb rather than as part of the design process. The decorative programme of Seti I's tomb must have been carefully planned and recorded, as the scheme established here became the model on which the tombs of subsequent kings were based. Most of the decoration is taken from religious texts dealing with the night journey of the sun and related underworld themes. There are also representations of Seti I with different gods and astronomical paintings.

Excavating the tomb

Before excavation began a foundation ritual took place: deposits consisting of offerings and model tools have been found in pits outside a number of tombs in the Valley of the Kings. Rubble was then cleared from the surface of the site and stonemasons

The Valley of the Kings: the top of the entrance to the tomb of Seti I can be seen in the bottom left corner.

Above **A stone mason with a chisel and wooden mallet. Sketch on a flake of limestone from the workers' village at Deir el-Medina.**

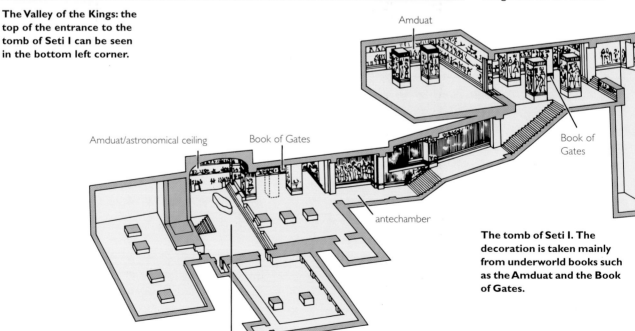

Amduat

Amduat/astronomical ceiling

Book of Gates

Book of Gates

antechamber

burial chamber

The tomb of Seti I. The decoration is taken mainly from underworld books such as the Amduat and the Book of Gates.

started work. The tombs were cut into the soft lime-stone of the valley, which varies considerably in quality. Fissures in the rock occasionally forced an alteration to the plan, and hard flint nodules could not always be removed from the walls. The masons worked with copper or bronze adzes and chisels and wooden mallets. Careful records of the issue and return of tools were kept to discourage pilfering: the metal chisels blunted particularly easily and were frequently returned for sharpening. As the masons hacked away at the rock, the limestone chips were loaded into baskets and carried out of the tomb.

Once excavation had progressed beyond the first passage, plasterers arrived to prepare the wall sur-faces for decoration. Where the quality of the rock was good, only a thin skim of the gypsum-based plaster was needed to smooth the surface, but on poorer quality rock plaster was extensively used to fill cracks and disguise uneven surfaces.

Decoration

After the preparation of the wall surfaces, draftsmen were then brought in to sketch out the decoration

Litany of Re

Amduat

of the tomb. When the appropriate texts and vignettes for each wall had been chosen, they were sketched on to the pre-pared surface in red ink. Often the decoration formed several registers and the scale of the text and figures had to be adjusted accordingly. Once a wall

had been fully drafted in red, the chief draftsman checked the content and layout of the hieroglyphs and figures and made his final corrections in black ink. Inevitably royal tombs were unfinished at the time of the king's burial and examples of drafted but uncarved decoration exist in many tombs.

Skilled masons were then brought in to carve the drafted designs into raised relief. First, a less skilled workman cut around the hieroglyphs and other designs and removed the background to an even depth. Then a senior mason carved the detail into the raised figures on the wall. Finally, painters were brought in to add colour. The Egyptians used solid blocks of bright colour applied with brushes from small pots. Outlines were added in black, red or white. Some parts of tombs, such as ceilings, were not usually carved: the decoration was painted directly on to the smoothed surface.

For much of the construction period the tomb must have been very crowded. Excavating, plaster-ing, drafting, carving and painting were all going on at the same time in different parts of the tomb and basket-carriers with chippings must have been con-tinually jostling past the skilled workers. As work progressed deeper into the tomb light levels became increasingly low and wicks of twisted linen soaked in fat or oil were burned in shallow pottery bowls – but these cannot have provided much light, making the precision of the decoration even more astonish-ing. Careful records of the number of these 'candles' issued have been found, and one scholar has used them to suggest that an eight-hour working day was the norm in the Valley of the Kings.

Right **Painted decoration on the ceiling of the burial chamber of Seti I, showing the northern constellations.**

The workmen

One of the most fascinating aspects of the tombs in the Valley of the Kings is that we know so much about the people who built them. The workmen lived in the village of Deir el-Medina beneath the mountain on the river side. They walked to work over the mountain ridge; entrance to the Valley was restricted to ensure maximum security for the king's burial. There was an exceptionally high level of literacy in the village and records of the workers' daily lives have survived in the form of letters, notes, accounts, legal documents and other texts.

The workmen were organized under a foreman into two groups called the 'right' and 'left' sides, although it is not clear whether this is a literal reference to each team being responsible for one side of the tomb. The workforce varied in size according to the stage of work in the king's tomb: if a king was particularly old or infirm on accession a large workforce was probably considered sensible. Under Seti I's successor, Ramesses II, the workforce numbered about 52 but later fell to around 35 as the tomb neared completion. Attendance registers show that absenteeism was common: excuses included mum-

The goddess Nephthys, protecting deity of the dead, with outstretched wings: one of the fine painted reliefs from the burial chamber of Seti I.

mifying relatives, family rows, brewing and drunkenness. The workers also put considerable time and effort into constructing their own tombs on the slopes of the mountain above the village.

Recent history

When Belzoni discovered the tomb of Seti I in 1817 it was beautifully preserved: the reliefs were intact and the colours almost as pristine as the moment when the tomb was sealed. Since then the tomb has been badly damaged: many reliefs were destroyed in attempts to remove blocks to sell to tourists, ceilings were blackened by smoke from the torches of early travellers and streams of visitors have accidentally rubbed the colour from the walls. The increased humidity caused by visitors has also badly damaged the paintings. The tomb has now been closed to the public for a number of years and will remain so while conservators battle to preserve this extraordinary and beautiful tomb for posterity.

The Etruscan Cemetery of Cerveteri

Time: 7th–2nd centuries BC
Location: central Italy

The tombs feel so easy and friendly, cut out of rock underground. One does not feel oppressed, descending into them. It must be partly owing to the peculiar charm of natural proportion which is in all Etruscan things of the unspoilt, unRomanized centuries.

D.H. LAWRENCE, 1932

'NECROPOLIS' translates simply as 'dead city'; or more sympathetically as 'city of the dead'. And that is just how the Etruscan necropolis of Cerveteri seems – like a community or settlement for the afterlife. Whether ramshackle or ordered, the structures of this cemetery atmospherically retain the cosiness of any long-term human habitation. And yet the necropolis was never properly 'inhabited'; hence its familiar name, *la Banditaccia*, from *terra bandita*, 'forbidden (and foreboding) land'.

In the Banditaccia (as it is still usually signposted) the inhabitants of the Etruscan city of Cerveteri – situated on an opposite plateau – effectively set up a mirror-image of their own urban and domestic space. The necropolis presents to us now a simulacrum of the lost city of the living; carved and con-structed in volcanic stone for the durable benefit of posterity. These tombs were meant to last. Though mostly despoiled (long ago) of the remains and accoutrements of those laid to rest there, the necropolis preserves an essential Etruscan identity. To modern visitors it is a marvel; to those who created it, the Banditaccia was reassuringly familiar in all its detail and layout.

A main street, rutted with cart-tracks, runs through the Banditaccia as a longitudinal axis of the cemetery. This route (called the Via degli Inferi, or 'ghost-road') once also connected the Cerveteri of the dead to the Cerveteri of the living, via the city's north gate. Tomb-lined but now shaggily over-grown, this is the course that would have been fol-lowed by every funeral cortège, complete with mourners and musicians: deposition was then

Aerial view of the Banditaccia necropolis. Circular tombs of the 7th–6th centuries line the side of the Via degli Inferi.

Interior of the Tomb of
the Shields and Thrones
(mid-6th century BC).
Lintels, rafters and couches
replicate in stone wooden
originals; the throne may
be a copy of a bronze model.

marked by festivities conducted directly outside the entrance of the destined tomb.

Wandering along the extent of the Via degli Inferi within the necropolis today can be misleading, for archaeological restoration has made evident many tomb structures and entrances that were once discreetly concealed. But the two principal phases of general layout in the Banditaccia can readily be distinguished. In the first phase – between the 7th and 6th centuries BC – we see a number of imposingly large circular tumuli, which may contain several separate burials. These large mounds seem randomly disposed, yet ringed by smaller satellite tombs of similar shape. The tomb-chambers within are excavated into tufa bedrock, each one accessed by a door from the perimeter, additional grandeur is provided vertically by piling up earth above. It seems reasonable to suppose the aristocratic structure of archaic Cerveteri is reflected in this pattern.

In the second phase, beginning around 500 BC, a distinct 'levelling' occurs. Orthogonal sequences of regular cuboid tombs appear to be imposed as the result of central planning: the uniformity may come from a more 'egalitarian' urban model. Later, as space within the necropolis became tighter, families created deep subterranean hypogea, and some measure of competitive extravagance returned, albeit underground. The most notable is the late 4th-century BC 'Tomb of the Reliefs', whose walls were tricked out with polychrome stucco sculptures.

Throughout its period of use – up till the 1st century BC, when Cerveteri fully ceded to Roman administration – the Banditaccia was home to tombs that looked like homes. This explains why the ceilings of many rock-carved tombs have been given mock roof-beams, when there is no roof to support; or cross-hatched with a chisel, to suggest thatching. Likewise chairs and couches are fashioned out of rock in obvious replication of wooden furniture. Originally there were many further indications of domesticity: the archaic 'Tomb of the Dolia', for instance, takes its name from eleven enormous food-storage jars found within its chambers. But there were also elements of folly or aspiration too. The rounded or squared base-profiles of the larger circular tombs seem drawn from no obvious features of wooden hut construction. And the internal display of carved stone columns, complete with various capitals (including the Oriental-derived 'Aeolic' shape, as in the mid-6th century BC 'Tomb of the Capitals'), was surely meant to evoke not so much a house as a temple. But then the occupants of these tombs may have been priests in their time. And in any case, to their family descendants, the Etruscan dead were demi-gods.

FACTFILE

Extent of visitable site	10 ha
Number of tombs	over 1000

Mount Li: The Tomb of China's First Emperor

Time: 210 BC
Location: China

The whole universe
Is Qin Shihuangdi's realm...

INSCRIPTION, 219 BC

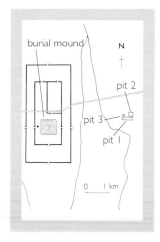

T HE TOMB of the First Emperor of China, Qin Shihuangdi, who died in 210 BC, lies halfway between Mount Li and modern Xi'an. According to a 1st-century BC description by China's first historian, Sima Qian, the tomb was designed to reproduce the universe below ground. Over 700,000 men (more than twice the number needed for the Great Wall) were conscripted to build it; the underground chamber containing the coffin was filled with models of palaces, towers and buildings and furnished with officials and precious rarities. The great waterways of China, the Yangzi and Yellow rivers, and the ocean were represented in mercury and made to flow mechanically. On the ceiling the heavenly constellations were depicted, while below lay a representation of the earth. Lamps were filled with whale oil to provide permanent lighting and the underground complex was protected by automatic crossbows to slay grave robbers. Such were the wonders of the tomb that the First Emperor's underground terracotta army which so impresses us today was not even mentioned by the historian.

In its heyday the tomb must have been an awe-inspiring sight. The tumulus, originally 115 m (377 ft) high and planted with trees and grass, was enclosed by double walls, 10–12 m (33–39 ft) tall, with corner- and gate-towers. Within these enclosures were large temples, halls for imperial use and administrative buildings. The entire burial complex extended over 2.5 sq. km (1 sq. mile), well beyond the tomb walls, and over 400 deposits with grave goods have been excavated. In addition to the terracotta army, these include a pair of exquisite bronze chariots, each with four horses and a charioteer, a large stable pit and several hundred small pits with kneeling figures beside live horse burials or animal

Left **Plan of the tomb area. The army pits face outwards on the eastern approach.**
Below **The tumulus over the burial chamber: even after two millennia, the mound is still around 50 m (165 ft) high, with a circumference of 1.5 km (nearly 1 mile).**

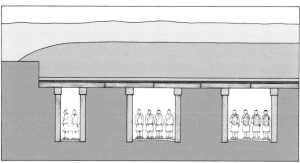

The pits containing the terracotta army had a roof of planks supported by wooden crossbeams carried by massive beams set in the trench walls. The roof planks were covered with woven mats plastered with clay.

FACTFILE

Total grave area	2.5 sq. km

Tumulus

North–south	350 m
East–west	345 m
Height (original)	115 m
(present)	43–76 m

Outer wall

North–south	2165 m
East–west	940 m
Base	8 m wide
Height (original)	10–12 m
(present)	small stretch 2–3 m

Inner wall

North–south	1355 m
East–west	580 m

Underground wall

North–south	460 m
East–west	392 m
Depth	2.7–4 m below ground

Distance from outer wall to Pit I with terracotta warriors 1225 m

skeletons, representing the imperial stables and menageries.

Apart from the tumulus and some rammed earth foundations, little remains above ground today, but archaeological finds such as tiles, drainage pipes and bronze fittings reveal much about the original architecture. Buildings were constructed in the traditional way on a rammed earth terrace with wooden beams on stone socles supporting an overhanging tiled roof; the non-weight-bearing walls of brick and rubble were covered with painted plaster. Floors were paved with large, hollow-patterned tiles. Beneath these, in the rammed earth terrace, was an elaborate drainage system with water cisterns and pipes. Bronze casings for strengthening beam corner joints and covering ceiling beams have been found, as well as thousands of bronze pendants, confirming contemporary descriptions of shining rafters hung with pearls, jade ornaments and green feathers.

The tomb itself has not yet been opened, but an examination of earlier and later tombs throws some light on its construction. During the Warring States period (475–221 BC) tomb mounds were introduced

Pit I contained 6000 warriors placed in perfect battle formation in 11 parallel trenches 200 m (656 ft) long. The floors were paved with bricks laid with a slightly convex surface to facilitate drainage.

and traditional pit tombs – in which the coffin was placed at the bottom of a wood-lined shaft with side ledges for grave goods – were enlarged. Chambers were carved into the side of the shaft creating separate rooms for grave goods. These catacomb tombs were made to resemble palaces. The rammed earth walls were baked, plastered and painted with curtains, windows and parapets; some rooms had lacquer wall paintings and inlays of jade or stone plaques. The base of the shaft was protected from moisture by layers of sand, charcoal and sticky clay.

The most elaborate catacomb tomb yet excavated, at Pingshan, Hebei, has a stepped tumulus with a tile-roofed gallery running round the mound on its second level. Stone walls with buttresses, on a thick stone foundation, flanked the grave chamber lined with courses of cypress logs sealed with metal alloy. The tomb had two storeys: above the grave chamber was a square wooden structure supported by a post and beam construction measuring nearly 25 sq. m (269 sq. ft) and 4.6 m (15 ft) tall.

After Qin Shihuangdi's death, the use of horizontal tombs, tunnelled into rocky cliffs or hillsides, brought even greater realism. The tomb of Liu Sheng, king of Zhongshan (d. 113 BC) at Mancheng, Hebei, was designed and furnished like an underground palace with stables for horses and chariots, wine and food store-rooms, a large audience hall and a rear chamber where the body, in a jade suit, lay in a lacquered coffin lined with jade. The front hall and side chambers were built like houses with timber framework and tiled roofs; the burial chamber was faced with stone slabs and had stone doors. The entrance to the tomb was blocked by iron barriers poured into place on the spot.

Qin Shihuangdi's tomb is thus almost certainly composed of many separate halls or buildings reproducing a palace-complex. Sima Qian refers to bronze casings and his description of mercury rivers has been confirmed by soil tests showing a high concentration of mercury forming regular patterns over an area of 1200 sq. m. (12,900 sq. ft) beneath the tomb mound. Archaeologists have found ramps leading to a wall enclosing the grave chamber, around 3 m (10ft)

This bronze chariot, with charioteer and horses, was reconstructed from nearly 3500 pieces and weighs 1200 kg.

below the tumulus. Made of large sun-dried bricks, the wall has corner towers like a palace wall and five openings on the main, eastern approach and one on each of the other sides.

Materials and logistics

The logistical requirements for such a project are staggering. To the basic manpower requirements for digging pits, building the walls and the tumulus, and the tens of thousands supplying food for three-quarters of a million men and providing and transporting the materials and fuel for brass foundries and kilns, must be added skilled workers in wood, bronze, clay and jewels, and the thousands more refining mercury from cinnabar (sulphide of mercury) brought from mines in distant Sichuan for the underground waterways.

The entire construction programme depended on ruthless discipline, an extraordinary degree of organization and a

Left **The varied origins of the emperor's soldiers, who were drawn from all over the empire, are reflected in the different features and hairstyles of the terracotta army.** *Opposite* **A lightly armoured soldier (left) and an infantry general with epaulettes.**

uniquely Chinese system of mass-production. The method developed for producing tens of thousands of large ritual bronzes from clay moulds in the Bronze Age a thousand years earlier was adapted to other lines of production. Based on a conveyor-belt division of labour, with specialist workteams under supervisors enforcing strict quality control, and the use of prefabricated interchangeable parts, it was possible to produce technically perfect pieces of uniformly high quality in virtually unlimited numbers. This system became the basis for all future mass-production in China, and analysis of the terracotta warriors shows how the method worked.

The figures were made from hollow moulds of rough clay split front and back for humans, and left and right for horses. The choice of moulds was limited, ranging from two for feet to eight for heads, but by varying the angles at which the head and limbs were attached, it was possible to produce a wide range of figures. Once assembled and dry, the figure was covered with several layers of very fine clay in which features, such as mouths and eyes, were individually carved and moulded noses, ears, uniform straps and toggles were added before firing at 950–1000°C (1742–1832°F). The figures were then painted in the distinctive colours of different army sections. This combination of mass-produced, standard moulds with individual modelling and carving made it possible to produce over 7000 figures so life-like that at first it was believed that they were individual portraits.

The same production methods were used for pipes, tiles and bricks, and for bronze architectural fittings. In each case, interchangeable parts made from moulds were used to create complicated end-products. The vital prerequisite was that the finished product had to be clearly envisaged and specified before work started. The degree of detail is impressive: drainage pipes, for example, had string patterns on the outside to prevent slipping and their ends were grooved for tight connections. Pipes leading from water cisterns were bent, creating a sucking effect to draw the water away more quickly.

Metal weapons and the bronze chariots show the same meticulous attention to detail and quality control. The double-edged swords, treated with chromium preservative to prevent corrosion, can still cut through a thick shield; and the alloy used for each part of the gold, silver and bronze harnesses on the chariot horses varies according to the strain it would bear.

The Nabataean Royal Tombs at Petra

Time: late 1st century BC–AD 100
Location: Petra, Jordan

It is astonishing that a people should, with infinite labour, have carved the living rock into temples, theatres, public and private buildings, and tombs, and have thus constructed a city on the borders of the desert, in a waterless, inhospitable region, destitute of all that is necessary for the sustenance of man.

A.H. LAYARD, 1887

THE CELEBRATED line from Burgon's poem on Petra, 'a rose-red city – "half as old as Time"', suggests a more seductive image than that of the quote above, but the truth lies somewhere in between. This harsh environment is an extraordinary setting for one of the most elaborate and elegant achievements of the ancient world.

It was the incense trade that transformed this remote corner of the southern Jordanian desert. Camel caravans from Yemen, over 1600 km (1000 miles) to the south, carried incense to be burned on the altars of Persia and the Greco-Roman world, and the Nabataeans controlled the northern section of

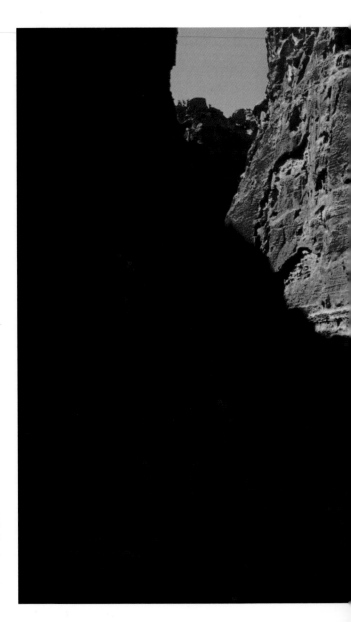

FACTFILE

Treasury of Pharaoh (Khasna Far'un)
Height   39.1 m
Width   25.3 m
? Abud or Obodas II (30–9 BC)

Urn Tomb (al-Mahkama)
Height   26 m
Width   16.49 m
? Harith (Aretas) IV (9 BC– c. AD 40)

Corinthian Tomb
Height   28 m
Width   27.55 m
? Malik II (c. AD 40–70)

Deir
Height   48.3 m
Width   46.77 m
? A royal prince (c. AD 70–90)

Palace Tomb
Height   over 46 m
Width   49 m
? Rabbel II (c. AD 70–106)

the route. It was at their capital city, Petra, that many caravans turned west to Gaza, Egypt and the Mediterranean; some continued north to Syria, others turned east. Incense was indispensable, and the merchants could ask almost any price. So could the tax-collectors through whose territory they passed. Between about 400 BC and AD 100 the rulers of Petra became phenomenally rich. The creation of magnificent buildings and monuments was one way of spending their money.

The so-called Treasury of Pharaoh dominates the narrow gorge which is the main entrance to the city of Petra.

Houses for the dead
Traditionally the Nabataeans of Petra had buried their dead in the sandstone cliffs that surround the city. There are hundreds of these tombs: many of them are simple rock-cut chambers, but others are more ambitious. The rock was soft and easily carved. It was no great effort to provide a tomb with a modest architectural framework, and there came a time, in the later 1st century BC, when ostentatious opulence began to outface modesty. The Royal Tombs of Petra, royal by tradition though no ancient names are attached to them, were no longer mere chambers for the dead. In their construction, the traditional skills of the Nabataean mason were

The principal group of 'royal' tombs at Petra. Most of them are entirely carved out of the cliff, but the Palace Tomb on the left was so large that part of the superstructure had to be built up with blocks of stone.

employed to imitate, adapt and enhance the latest and most ambitious architectural fantasies of cosmopolitan cities like Alexandria. The style, with its prominent urns and broken pediments, is an eclectic mix of local and imported features, an ancient equivalent of 17th-century baroque.

This is architecture in reverse, where effort was expended not in building walls and columns, since these already existed as solid rock, but in excavating and clearing the spaces between them. First a suitable cliff was dressed smooth, then the façade was carved from top to bottom. Regularity was probably ensured by the use of plumb-lines hanging free, and by narrow water channels that were subsequently removed; holes in the rock alongside some tombs may have supported scaffolding for the masons. Accurate calculations were essential for the interiors, as a rock-fall could be disastrous, but if all went well, and the many tons of superfluous rock had been safely removed, the result was much more durable than a freestanding structure.

The rooms behind the tomb façades are relatively small: there is an outer chamber, occasionally with benches also carved from the rock, while the burial chamber is usually cut into the wall behind. Virtually immune from demolition, the façades of the tombs of Petra, despite centuries of neglect, earthquake, erosion and casual vandalism, still dominate the landscape and provide a more authentic impression of 1st-century architecture, complete to the

highest elevations, than anything that survives in Alexandria itself.

The fine detail on the façades would probably have been the work of local stone-cutters; signatures on tombs at Madain Salih, another Nabataean site, suggest that a stone-cutter usually had a working life of about 25 years. The rougher work of quarrying was probably done by slaves.

The 'rose-red' city

Once these tombs were covered with plaster, made of crushed limestone and sand, and gaudily painted. Wind and sand have stripped the plaster away, exposing bare rock, but the brilliant range of colours displayed by the rock itself, constantly changing with the sun, brings these tombs to life in a way never intended by their creators. 'Fresh blackcurrant,' writes J. Taylor, 'blackcurrant ice-cream, peach, apricot, mulberry, saffron, raw steak, buttermilk and caramel.'

Petra lost its independence in AD 106, and became part of the imperial province of Arabia. One of the latest grand tombs at Petra was built for a Roman governor, and in AD 446 the Urn Tomb was converted into a church. The incense route through the desert was dying, replaced by maritime routes down the Red Sea, and urban life in the desert was increasingly precarious. Eventually the tombs decayed, the statues were defaced, and the rock-chambers for the dead became rock-shelters for shepherds.

The Moche Pyramids

Time: c. AD 100–700
Location: north coast of Peru

In the time of the paganism of the Indians [it] was one of the most important sanctuaries that existed in that kingdom. People came in pilgrimage from many parts and to carry out their vows and promises and to pay homage and make offerings.

ANTONIO VÁSQUEZ DE ESPINOZA, 1628

FROM *c.* AD 100 to 700 the Moche held sway over a series of valleys along the northern desert coast of Peru. They built massive, terraced adobe pyramids such as the Huaca del Sol and Huaca de la Luna which were the largest of their time in the Americas. Once embellished with murals and friezes depicting gods and rituals, some pyramids contained the burials of Moche nobles. Skilled Moche craftspeople created stunning works of art in pottery, cloth and metal, much of it destined to accompany Moche lords in the afterlife. Most Moche tombs have long since been looted, but intact elite tombs have been excavated at Sipán and their breathtaking range of burial goods and precious objects gives us some idea of what other Moche tombs might once have contained.

Sited at the political and ceremonial centre of the Moche valley, construction of both the Huaca del Sol (Pyramid of the Sun) and the Huaca de la Luna (Pyramid of the Moon) began around AD 100.

Aerial view of the Huaca del Sol, or Pyramid of the Sun; much of its original cross-shaped plan was washed away in the 17th century by Spaniards in search of buried treasure.

FACTFILE

Area of temples and surrounding community 300 ha
Estimated population   10,000

Huaca de la Luna
Six construction episodes, built over 600 years
Base   290 m N–S
          210 m E–W
Height   32 m
Estimated number of adobe bricks   50 million

Huaca del Sol
Eight building stages, completed by AD 450
Length   345 m
Width   160 m
Height   40 m
Estimated number of adobe bricks   143 million

Destruction wrought by centuries of looting, flooding, invading sand dunes and intense but sporadic rainfall makes it hard today to envisage the thriving community that resided there. At its height, some 10,000 people may have lived and produced a wide array of crafts in the plain between the two huacas.

The Huaca del Sol

Originally, the Huaca del Sol measured some 345 m (1130 ft) in length, 160 m (525 ft) in width, and rose some 40 m (130 ft) above the valley floor. Little remains of its original grandeur, however, because in 1602 Spanish treasure hunters diverted the waters of the Moche river, washing away most of the huaca. The approach to the summit of the roughly cross-

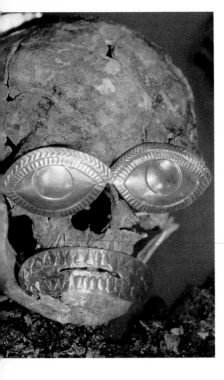

Above **The skull of the Lord of Sipán (Tomb 1) was covered with two eyes of sheet gold and a band of teeth.**
Right **A reconstruction of the Lord of Sipán's tomb; platforms adjacent to temple mounds contained rich tombs.**

shaped and terraced huaca may have been via a ramp on its largely destroyed north side. Much of the monument was once painted red, and perhaps other colours. The Huaca del Sol may have served as the residence of Moche leadership, or had an administrative function, while the Huaca de la Luna, which it faced, may have had a religious role.

Archaeologists have identified eight stages in the construction of the Huaca del Sol, with most of it completed before AD 450. Its builders used some 143 million mould-made adobes (sun-dried mud-bricks), arranged in tall, column-like segments. Adobes in some segments share so-called makers' marks –

curious markings ranging from hand- and footprints to circles and squiggles – impressed on each brick. More than a hundred of these marks have been identified and they may have served to distinguish bricks made by different groups as their labour obligation to the Moche leadership.

The Huaca de la Luna

Built at the foot of Cerro Blanco, a low hill of granite banded with diorite, the Huaca de la Luna is an adobe structure measuring 290 m (950 ft) from north to south and 210 m (690 ft) from east to west, and rising some 32 m (105 ft) above the plain. Excavations have

painted in white and red and yellow ochre. Many of the murals and friezes feature the Decapitator, a fanged, half-human deity often shown holding a ceremonial crescent-shaped knife in one hand and a severed human head in the other, connected to ceremonies of human sacrifice.

Human sacrifice

The Huaca de la Luna served as a setting for ceremonies of human sacrifice and also for burial rites that commemorated the sealing of earlier structures and heralded new building episodes. Evidence for human sacrifice comes from an enclosure at the back of the Huaca de la Luna, where excavators found the remains of more than 40 men ranging in age from 15 to 30. Their scattered bones lie buried in thick layers of sediment, suggesting that they had been sacrificed during the heavy rains that accompanied a Niño event (the periodic reversal of Pacific Ocean currents associated with adverse weather). The men were apparently beaten with maces and pushed from a stone outcrop in the enclosure. Some skeletons are splayed as if they had been tied to stakes; a few had their femurs forcibly torn from pelvis joints, and many of the bones have cut marks. Several victims were decapitated and had their lower jaws removed. This was not an ordinary Niño event, but a mega-Niño that only occurs about once every century. Some victims may have been sacrificed to the gods in a bid to stop the rains, while others were sacrificed after the rains had ended.

Sipán

In 1910 looters discovered a rich tomb at the foot of the Huaca de la Luna that yielded several gold masks, suggesting that members of the Moche elite or even its leaders were buried there. Unfortunately, looting at the Huaca de la Luna has been so intense that it is impossible to determine what its adjacent tombs originally contained. But at Sipán, a Moche site some 100 km (60 miles) north of the Huaca de la Luna, excavations have uncovered a wonderful and complete record of the contents of the tombs of Moche lords. In a platform at the foot of Sipán's larger adobe mound several royal tombs have yielded a wealth of gold and silver ornaments. Many of the objects and their imagery link those buried at Sipán with Moche sacrifice ceremonies. The chilling evidence from both the Huaca de la Luna and Sipán shows that human sacrifice was a key ritual in Moche religion and the ceremony or rituals connected to it.

recorded at least six construction phases, spanning almost 600 years. Corridors and ramps connected the structure's three platforms and four plazas, some of which were roofed. A huge looters' pit made in colonial times destroyed more than two-thirds of the uppermost platform.

Builders employed an estimated 50 million adobes in its construction, filling earlier plazas to create platforms for new constructions. This careful sealing of earlier structures was accompanied by the burials of priests who officiated over the rituals that took place at the Huaca de la Luna. Murals and friezes decorated many courtyards, while some exterior walls were

The Tomb of Emperor Nintoku, Japan

Time: early 5th century AD
Location: Osaka, Japan

67th Year [of Nintoku's reign], Winter, 10th month, 5th day. The Emperor made a progress to the plain of Ishitsu in Kahachi, where he fixed upon a site for a misasagi [tomb]. 18th day. The building of the misasagi was commenced.

NIHONGI, AD 697

SOME 1600 years ago, on a low river terrace in the modern Osaka prefecture of southern Japan, one of the largest monuments of the ancient world was raised to house the remains of a great ruler. Documents from later centuries tell us that this huge 486-m (1595-ft) long structure, the Daisen Mounded Tomb, held the burial of the Emperor Nintoku. Japanese tradition holds that the shadowy Nintoku was the 16th emperor of Japan and ruled in the early 5th century AD. His tomb dominates a cemetery of 15 burial mounds known as the Mozu Tomb Cluster. Though none is as large as the Nintoku mausoleum, they too were the final resting places of early Japanese emperors and their supporting elites.

Viewed from the air, the Nintoku mound takes the distinctive keyhole-shape characteristic of many of the great burials of early Japanese rulers. The central mound is isolated from its surroundings by three concentric moats separated from each other by two green strips. The whole mausoleum occupies an area of 32.3 ha (80 acres). The mound was constructed in three steps or terraces, with a protrusion on each side of the front platform. The same structure can be seen in many Chinese tombs, and these are the ultimate source of the Japanese keyhole design. The stepped construction method

would have helped in the actual building of the huge tombs, but it is also employed in smaller mounds where problems would have been less, and it is probable therefore that it had some deeper symbolic significance to the builders, long since lost.

The Nintoku tomb was a massive engineering undertaking. Some 1,387,533 cu. m (49 million cu. ft) of earth make up the mound and it would have taken over 1000 people more than four years of continuous hard labour to complete. When finished, the surface of the mound was covered by cobbles and on its slopes were at least 20,000 terracotta cylinders or 'haniwa' arranged in seven rows. These pottery haniwa were produced in huge numbers in nearby kilns, and were intended to provide symbolic

FACTFILE

Length of mound	486 m
Ground area	32.3 ha
Diameter of circular rear mound	249 m
Width of triangular front mound	305 m
Volume of mound	1,387,533 cu. m
Estimated number of haniwa cylinders	20,000

The construction of the enormous mounded tombs of the early Japanese rulers, such as this one belonging to Ojin, second only in size to Nintoku's, required the harnessing of labour on a scale unprecedented in the archipelago.

Above **The great Daisen tomb dominates the Mozu tomb cluster, final resting place of the early Japanese emperors and their elites.** *Left* **Only from the air is it possible to appreciate fully the monumental scale of the Nintoku tomb.**

The great Nintoku monument has never been excavated. Identified as the tomb of an imperial ancestor, the huge mound and its contents are now protected by the Imperial Household Agency. Some idea of the contents has none the less been gleaned from limited investigations and from the excavation of similar tombs.

In 1872 a minor landslide brought down part of the front platform, exposing a small pit-style stone burial chamber. The stone chamber was megalithic in construction, measured almost 4 m (13 ft) long and 1.5 m (5 ft) wide and contained a massive stone coffin lid that was 2.5 m (8 ft) long and nearly as wide as the chamber. Iron armour and weapons, gilt-bronze ornaments and a Persian glass bowl were reburied after being recorded. This was not the burial of Nintoku, however, but merely a secondary interment, though judging from the contents it must have been a person of high status. From evidence of smaller excavated keyhole tombs, we may deduce that the primary burial in the Nintoku mausoleum is located beneath the circular mound at the rear.

The Nintoku mausoleum is one of a series of massive keyhole-shaped tombs constructed during the 5th century AD on the Osaka Plain and across the mountains in the Nara Basin. They are the largest Japanese keyhole tombs ever built, and mark out the Kinai region which was the centre of the Yamato state. The rulers of this kingdom were the first to bring most of Japan under their hegemony, and played a role in the international sphere which included Korea and China. The monumental scale of the Nintoku mausoleum was therefore both a marvel of engineering and an ostentatious display of new-found power.

protection for the tomb and its occupant. In addition to cylinders there were specially shaped haniwa, one taking the form of a human head (perhaps a female shaman), another in the shape of a horse. The female haniwa is very similar to ones excavated from the Mozu Umeo-cho kiln site a little to the east, lending support to the idea that they were locally produced. The examples from the Nintoku mausoleum stand at the beginning of a long and varied tradition of Japanese figural haniwa. Later tombs were to see the development of a multitude of different forms, including warriors, musicians, acrobats, buildings and boats, dogs, wild boar and deer, illuminating many aspects of elite life in 5th-century Japan.

The Tomb of Pakal, Palenque

Time: c. AD 675–702
Location: Palenque, southern Mexico

*America, say historians, was peopled by savages;
but savages never reared these structures, savages
never carved these stones.*

JOHN LLOYD STEPHENS, 1842

MONUMENTAL architecture in the form of huge temples, palaces, ballcourts and roadways is a dominant feature of Late Classic Maya civilization, which thrived in the tropical forests of southern and eastern Mesoamerica between AD 600 and 900. The largest Maya buildings are pyramid-temples that reach heights in excess of 60 m (200 ft). Despite their impressive scale, however, Maya buildings are not really megalithic in character; these structures were made of earth and rubble fill contained by thin skins of external retaining walls. Most of the individual stones used in construction were small enough to be carried by a single worker, and the Maya penchant for covering raw masonry with thick coats of plaster and paint means that the stones would generally have been invisible, no matter what their size. Occasionally the Maya used

Pakal's tomb, a vaulted chamber of huge limestone blocks deep inside the Pyramid of the Inscriptions, contains his elaborately carved sarcophagus.

FACTFILE

Pyramid

Maximum length	60 m
Maximum width	42.5 m
Height	27.2 m

Summit temple

Length	25.5 m
Width	10.5 m
Height (including roof comb)	11.4 m
Largest stones	12–15 tonnes

Sarcophagus (limestone block)

Length	3 m
Width	2.1 m
Depth	1.10 m
Weight	c. 8 tonnes

Total volume of pyramid and temple c. 32,500 cu. m	
Labour	125,000 person days

The Temple of the Inscriptions, built in the late 7th century AD, was especially designed to accommodate the tomb of Pakal, Palenque's greatest ruler. The tomb, located on ground level at the base of the pyramid, was linked to the summit temple by a monumental stairway that descended through the solid rubble core of the building's substructure.

The image of King Pakal is carved on the monumental limestone lid covering the sarcophagus in which his body lay.

lapse during construction, so that its builders had to depart from their original plan to shore up the sides. Much of the rough construction was done by unskilled labour, exploiting limestone and fill from the immediate vicinity, and locally made plaster.

It is not the Temple of the Inscriptions itself, however, but the huge tomb built beneath it that makes this monument so important. This tomb is one of the most sophisticated and impressive of Classic Maya constructions. Large blocks of especially fine limestone had to be transported from several kilometres away, and required skilled workers to fashion them into their final forms.

The tomb within the pyramid

During excavations between 1949 and 1952, the Mexican archaeologist Alberto Ruz found a stone slab with holes in it set into the floor of the temple on the top of this pyramid. The slab covered the entrance to a descending passageway with a monumental stairway. At the very base of the pyramidal substructure, the stairway ended at the entrance to a huge masonry tomb oriented to the cardinal directions. This was the first incontestably royal tomb ever found in the Maya Lowlands, and it provided powerful evidence that Classic Maya polities were ruled not by priests, as most Mayanists then believed, but by dynasties of kings. It also showed that some pyramid-temples of the Maya, like those in Egypt, were used as mortuary monuments for rulers. Clearly the Temple of the Inscriptions had been planned as a mortuary monument from the beginning, because the tomb and stairway were integral parts of its construction.

Finely finished stones weighing some 12–15 tonnes were used in various parts of the tomb. Huge slabs of limestone laid down on the old ground surface formed the floor of the mausoleum, which was roofed with a steeply sloping corbelled vault 6 m (19.7 ft) high. The single largest block of stone was the 3-m (9.8-ft) long sarcophagus. When Ruz and his workmen lifted the rectangular lid they found a curious lambda-shaped cavity containing a male skeleton. A mask of jade mosaic covered the face and other richly worked artifacts of jade, mother-of-pearl and pyrite were found in the coffin.

Inscriptions and iconography

The walls of the chamber and the sarcophagus, along with its lid and supports, were covered with carvings and stucco images. Depictions of elabo-

particularly large stones for impressive façade elements such as stairways and balustrades, but they reserved their principal megalithic efforts for carved stelae, altars and (occasionally) tombs.

The Temple of the Inscriptions

Probably the most famous Classic Maya building is the Temple of the Inscriptions, erected in the 7th century AD at Palenque, a great royal centre in the tropical forests of southern Mexico. The temple is partly built into a steep hill and threatened to col-

Above **King Pakal is depicted on his sarcophagus lid at the moment of his death. Dressed as the Maize God, he descends into the underworld realm of the ancestors, where he will be reborn as an ancestral deity.** *Below* **A mask made of pieces of jade found in the tomb of Pakal.**

we now know to be the occupant of the tomb and the royal patron of the Temple of the Inscriptions. His name was Hanab Pakal (usually written simply as Pakal), the 10th ruler in the Palenque dynastic sequence, who became king in AD 615 at the age of 12. After a long career of rituals, diplomacy and war, he began the construction of his mortuary temple around AD 675. Pakal died eight years later at the great age of 80, so the building was completed by his son, Kan Balam, who took great pains in his own sculptural programme on the summit temple to link himself to his illustrious father and their royal ancestors.

Such linkage was more than simply iconic. Ruz discovered a hollow stone tube along one edge of the stairway leading down from the temple floor to the tomb chamber. This 'psychoduct' was apparently intended to allow communication between the dead king and living participants in rituals taking place in the temple far above.

The most important insights come from the images and inscriptions in the tomb chamber itself, and particularly the lid. On it Pakal's artists showed the king at the moment of his death, sinking into the jaws of a supernatural snake forming the portals to the Otherworld, the place of the ancestors. He is garbed as the Maize God, a deity associated with the creation of the world and with the principle of resurrection. Behind Pakal is a great world tree with a celestial serpent entwined in its branches, and at the top perches a supernatural bird associated with shamanism and sorcery. The overall message is that Pakal at the moment of death is being reborn as a deity and sacred ancestor.

Whoever designed the compositional themes of the temple and the tomb took great pains to place this profound event – the death and transformation of Palenque's most powerful king – in a larger historical, mythological and dynastic context. Calendrical inscriptions link Pakal's accession date to a god-ancestor 1,246,826 years in the past, and a second date associates his birth with a day thousands of years in the future. Other texts celebrate important events in the life of the king, such as his marriage and the visit of a ruler from the great kingdom of Tikal, far away to the southeast.

rately dressed humans or gods were accompanied by hieroglyphic inscriptions and calendrical dates. Although the dates were comprehensible, no one at this time could read the hieroglyphs. Since then, epigraphers have largely decoded Classic Maya writing, and we now understand much better the complex meanings of the associated images, allowing us to place tomb and temple in their wider historical context.

The central focus is the sarcophagus lid, one of the finest products of Classic Maya art. On it is a human figure whom

The Temple of the Inscriptions at Palenque. Pakal's tomb is at ground level within it, with access from the shrine at the top.

Ancestors were extremely important to the ancient Maya, and the sides of the sarcophagus depict six generations of male and female ancestors who were members of the royal lineage. Nine other personages modelled in stucco on the walls of the tomb probably represent the rulers who preceded Pakal. Small figures on the ends of the tomb lid and on the supports of the sarcophagus are identified by name and title glyphs as *sahals*, or important court officials – perhaps the architects and administrators (themselves great lords) who oversaw the construction of the temple and tomb.

We know that the tomb was begun about AD 675, and was finished before the death of Pakal's son and successor about AD 702. Assuming 90 days of dry season labour each year over this whole interval, only 50 workers or so would have been required. If, as seems more likely, temple and tomb were built over a shorter time (say a decade), then this figure would be up to three times higher, though still not unduly large. Transportation of materials and the production and application of plaster were the most time-consuming parts of the operation, though we must not forget the skilled craftsmen who carved and coloured the reliefs, and fitted the huge stones.

At Palenque the Maya effectively blended monumental construction and complex symbolism. Because we can now understand Maya art and writing, this great mortuary complex is not an anonymous place, like Stonehenge, but one richly personified by references to real men and women whose names and titles we know. Just as importantly, we can appreciate not only the engineering skills of the Maya, but also what the Temple of the Inscriptions meant to its patron and its builders. Pakal's extraordinary tomb was both a spectacular archaeological find and a source of revolutionary insights into the nature of Classic Maya society and its world view.

The Temple-Mausoleum of Angkor Wat

Time: AD 1113–1145
Location: Angkor, Cambodia

One of these temples – a rival to that of Solomon – might take an honourable place beside our most beautiful buildings. It is grander than anything left to us by Greece or Rome.

HENRI MOUHOT, 1861

A MASTERPIECE of engineering and the largest medieval step-pyramid in mainland southeast Asia, the 12th-century AD temple-mausoleum of Angkor Wat is located in central Cambodia among the ruins of Angkor. This city was the capital of the Khmer empire which encompassed Cambodia and parts of Vietnam, Laos and Thailand.

Nominated by some as the world's most extreme expenditure of energy on the disposal of a corpse (that of the Khmer ruler Suryavarman II), the whole complex consists of an ornate 65-m (213-ft) high step-pyramid covering 1 sq. km (0.38 sq. mile), with five cardinally oriented concentric courtyards. The outermost is enclosed by a moat and wall, with its principal entrance on the west approached by a 200-m (655-ft) long stone causeway. The main monument stands at the centre of this courtyard, reached by a further causeway terminating at an inner wall pierced by 12 thresholds, three in each cardinal direction.

Bas-relief from the first courtyard depicting Suryavarman II in his audience hall, surrounded by his court.

FACTFILE

Overall			First terrace	
Height	65 m		Height	3.2 m
Area	1 sq. km		Area	187 × 215 m
Volume	272,336 cu. m			
			Second terrace	
Outer courtyard			Height	6.4 m
Moat	180 m wide		Area	100 × 115 m
Outer wall	1000 × 815 m			
			Third terrace	
Corner towers			Height	12.8 m
Height	32 m		Area	75 × 73 m
Central tower				
Height	42 m			

Within this second courtyard are three more superimposed terrace-courtyards. The first, defined by a gallery formed by an inner wall and two rows of pillars, has cardinal gates and corner structures. The gallery wall is decorated with almost 1000 sq. m (10,764 sq. ft) of reliefs depicting scenes from Hindu epics – the Ramayana and Mahabharata – as well as representations of courtly Khmer life, warfare and hell. Its main entrance is connected by a galleried courtyard to the second terrace, again defined by a gallery with cardinal gates and corner towers. From its western entrance the main path arrives at the foot of a central staircase rising steeply up to the third terrace. This final terrace is square in shape

The elaborately decorated western façade of the central monument, seen from the cruciform platform.

with 12 staircases, three in each cardinal direction, and is defined by linked arcades. Its corner staircases are surmounted by four towers with lotus-shaped pinnacles. Further arcades lead from central gateways to the central tower, 42 m (138 ft) high and crowned by a pinnacle in the shape of a lotus, which rises 65 m (213 ft) above the landscape.

The historical context

Angkor Wat was built during the reign of Suryavarman II (AD 1113–1145). A regional warlord with princely connections, he had to defeat two rivals before he could declare himself ruler of Angkor. He then campaigned against the Khmer's traditional enemies, the Chams and the Annamites. Despite 19 years of war he largely completed Angkor Wat, which is one of 15 major royal monuments within the city of Angkor. Founded by Yasovarman I in AD 889 to the north of the great lake or the Tonle Sap, Angkor, originally known as Yasodhapura, was the capital for almost 500 years. It consisted of a moated enclosure, measuring 4 × 4 km (2.5 × 2.5 miles), centred on a step-pyramid, the Phnom Bakheng, built on a natural hill. It is clear that Yasovarman's

constructions were to act as a model for later rulers, who added their own step-pyramids within the city; Angkor Wat represents the architectural zenith of this development.

Materials and construction techniques

Angkor Wat was built without the use of mortar or the arch. Two types of sandstone were employed in the construction: medium-grained for the walls and finer-grained for the elaborately carved gallery walls. Both were quarried at Mount Kulen, 45 km (28 miles) to the northeast, and the blocks were probably rafted down the Siem Reap river and brought to the site by networks of canals. In 1861 Henri Mouhot, one of the first European visitors, noted that most blocks had holes 2.5 cm (1 in) in diameter and 3 cm (1.2 in) deep drilled into one side, and that the number of holes increased with the size of the block. While some scholars have suggested that these were for joining slabs with iron dowels, it has now been proposed that they secured temporary pegs for manoeuvring the blocks into place, presumably using a combination of elephants, coir ropes, pulleys and bamboo scaffolding.

In the absence of the true arch, the monument's vaulting is constructed on the corbel principle – thus superimposed courses of overlapping ashlar are held together by weight and gravity. A number of towers on the first and second terraces still contain the remains of their timber construction frames. Techniques derived from woodworking are used for stone elements, for example the pillars of the three galleries are joined by ashlar beams to the walls using mortise-and-tenon joints, while in other areas of the complex there are occasional examples of blocks dovetailed together for added strength. These techniques both characterized and limited architectural styles since a corbelled vault or a stone beam could not bridge a wide span and resulted in narrow, single-storeyed structures.

At first sight Angkor Wat appears to have been built of sandstone, but in fact this stone is mostly used for facing slabs or specific architectural elements. Trenches cut into the monument to study the stability of its foundations have found that they consist of layers of sand and small sandstone boulders covered with thick slabs of laterite – a local soil which can be cut into blocks and hardens with exposure to air. Fewer skilled masons may have been needed and so the bulk of construction could have been carried out by unskilled labour. Thus the ornate terraces of Angkor Wat rest on mundane foundations – making it less of an architectural miracle and more of an illusion of splendour.

Sacred to Vishnu
Angkor Wat has been ascribed numerous functions, including an astronomical

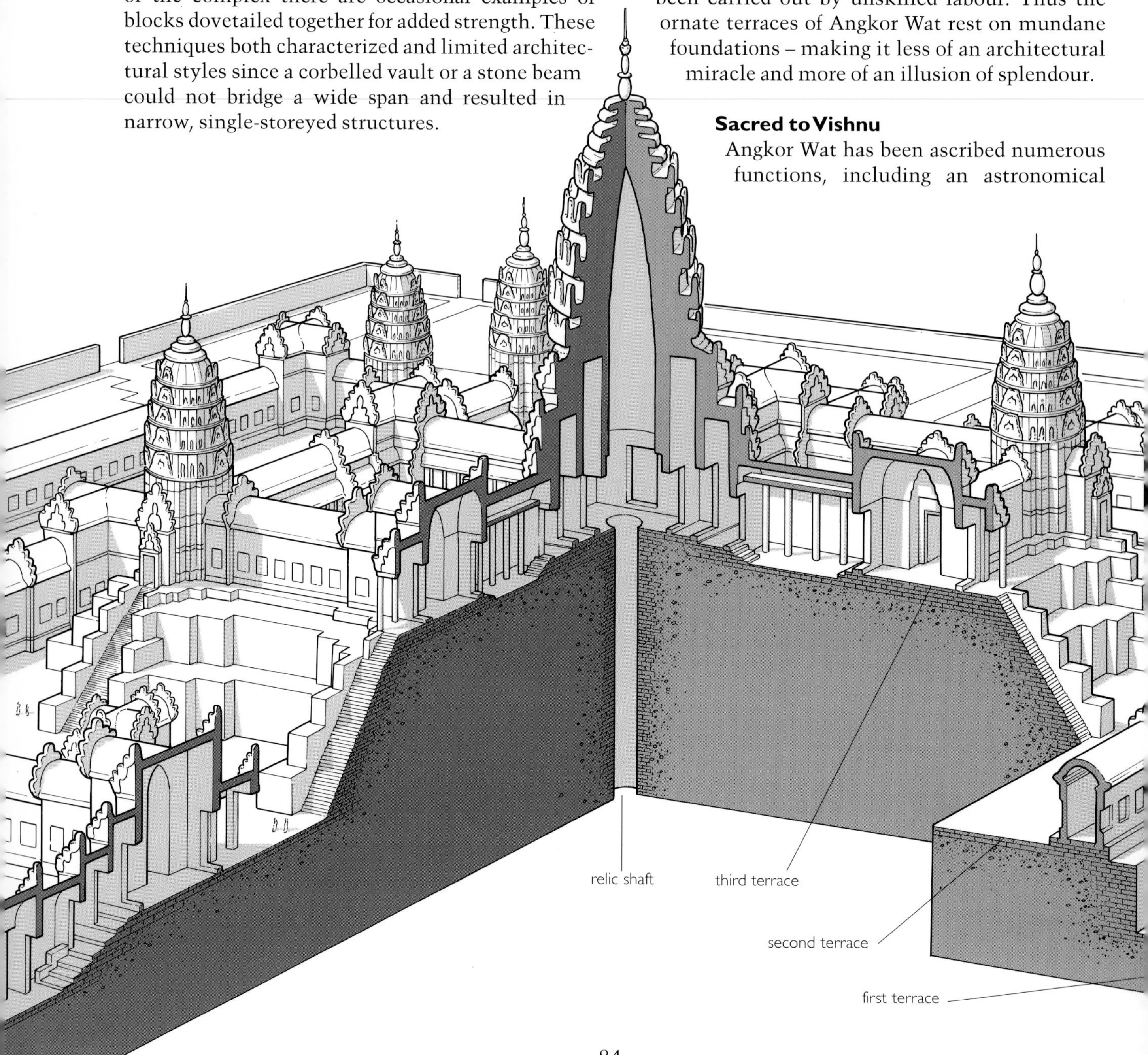

relic shaft

third terrace

second terrace

first terrace

84

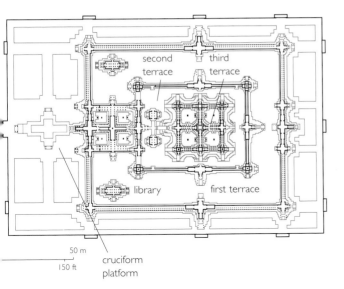

Above **Plan of the central monument.** *Below* **Simplified cut-away section through the central monument.**

observatory, a representation of the four ages of Hindu belief and even a model of Indra's celestial stables. It is now generally accepted, however, that it is a temple-mausoleum, as are the city's other step-pyramids. While some Khmer rulers were devotees of Siva, Indra or the Buddha, Suryavarman II dedicated his monument to Vishnu and it has been suggested that this explains its unique western orientation since this direction is associated with Vishnu. Indeed, after his death Suryavarman was known as Paramavisnuloka or 'one who has gone to the supreme world of Vishnu' and his monument became the centre for his funerary cult – his cremated remains probably having been deposited in the central shrine.

Cult activities at Angkor Wat were conducted by large numbers of officials supported by lesser functionaries, forming a city within a city. Although we do not know the size of the staff at Angkor Wat, an inscription at the Ta Phrom, a smaller temple-mausoleum erected between AD 1181 and 1219, records that it had been provided with 80,000 individuals. Perhaps the apparent open spaces within Angkor Wat's outer courtyard would have contained perishable structures for such people, as only the gods could have dwellings of stone.

Angkor Wat is more than an enormous temple-mausoleum, it is also a microcosm, representing the temple, country and entire universe. Indeed, a number of scholars have suggested that the statue in the central shrine-room represented not only Vishnu but also Suryavarman II himself, and that the 19 statues of Vishnu's avatars, or subordinate lords, in the smaller shrine-rooms represented Suryavarman's 19 provincial governors. Others have proposed that the monument is also a model of the universe: the moat and outer wall stand for the primeval sea and *cakravala*, or range of mountains, which surround the universe, and the central tower and four subordinate towers represent the five peaks of Mount Meru – the centre of the universe – on which rests the city of the gods. This interpretation relies on a knowledge of Hindu tradition – a knowledge demonstrated by the bas-reliefs which depict the underworld, the creation of the universe, the Ramayana and the Mahabharata.

Angkor Wat clearly advertised the splendour and power of Suryavarman II and his personal deity. But the construction of this wonder of the world exhausted the economic wealth of the state and was to have drastic consequences for his successors.

Temples & Shrines

MONUMENTS TO BELIEF constitute some of the greatest and most famous products of human energy. Where institutionalized religions have taken hold, rulers have channelled the efforts of whole populations into the building of temples. The temples of Karnak in Egypt, or the Aztec Great Temple in Mexico City, are statements of faith intended to impress both gods and humans. Rulers who organized such works may have been acting on behalf of their peoples, but they were also seeking the favour of the supernatural, proclaiming their own piety. And the temple to a god, bearing the devout ruler's name, also serves to commemorate that particular ruler: his or her legitimacy, power and achievement. The ultimate step is for the rulers to proclaim themselves gods and have temples built in their honour in their lifetimes. Nobody gazing on the colossal statues which adorn the temple of Abu Simbel in Egypt can be in any doubt that it is the pharaoh Ramesses II who is the divinity here.

Such temples are memorials of royal power, but religious beliefs can by themselves unite people and inspire them to major undertakings. Stonehenge, for example, was the work of a society without powerful rulers or centralized control. Strength of purpose led to the realization of a common aim, pursued perhaps over many generations. Centuries after Stonehenge was built, privileged individuals were still keen to be buried within sight of the stones; whether they viewed the monument as something especially sacred, guarding a tradition that it had

The pyramids of Teotihuacan, near modern Mexico City, illustrate by their sheer size the prominent place of religious beliefs in the life of this major Mesoamerican metropolis.

been built by their ancestors, or whether they understood it as a magical creation, the work of gods or heroes, or even perhaps as some strange natural formation, remains unclear. Whatever their understanding, Stonehenge retained a powerful sense of the exceptional and the mystical.

Temples show us how societies thought of their gods, and also how they thought of themselves. At Newark, Ohio, the astronomical layout of the massive earthworks reveals that for this society, the observation of lunar time cycles had profound importance. Technology was used to create revolutionary effects: the domed roof of the Pantheon at Rome is the largest of its kind ever built. Religious buildings include the greatest expressions of sophisticated architectural traditions, whether it be the mud mosques of Timbuktu in West Africa, the cave-temples of Ajanta in India, or indeed the Parthenon among the colonnaded temples of Classical Greece. On Malta, Ġgantija and other prehistoric temples are equally remarkable in their own way, built of massive blocks by the small island communities.

In the Pyramid of the Sun at Teotihuacan and the Ziggurrat at Ur, we see communities striving to reach the sky, to approach the elevated domain of the gods who controlled their destinies. The temples of Borobudur on Java and Paharpur in Bangladesh were fashioned as models of Mount Meru, the celestial centre of the universe where the king of the gods lived. Orientation is frequently of prime importance, as in the massive Monk's Mound at Cahokia in Missouri, part of a cosmological scheme designed to bridge the divide between humans and the supernatural. Temples might also be shrines, containing sacred relics and demanding a setting worthy of their significance. The Buddhist stupa of Sanchi in India can be seen in these terms, covering relics of the Buddha himself; as can the Lanzón of Chavín in Peru, incorporating elements of a cosmological scheme that showed how humans fitted into the overall conception of things.

Chavín introduces another aspect: the use of technological devices to impress the believer, here by the building of underground galleries to amplify the sound of running water. This serves to remind us that temples were not built as static monuments, to be contemplated from a distance, but as places for ritual, for religious practices, whether public or private, which were laid down by tradition and belief. And if it was, in a sense, the power of belief which built these often extraordinary monuments, it was the monuments by their scale – by their power to impress, by their potency as settings for rituals and ceremonies – which confirmed and consolidated that belief, fixing it in the minds alike of priests, rulers and the secular populace.

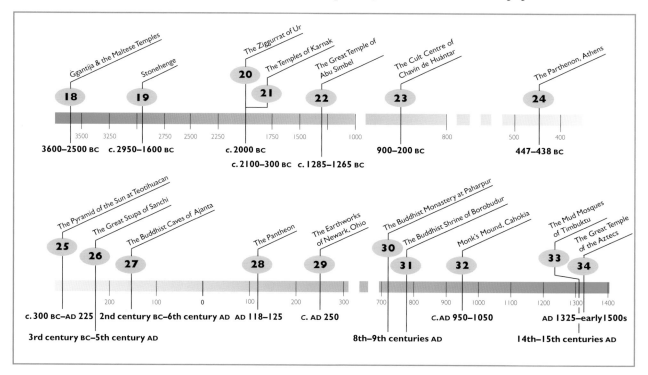

Ġgantija & the Maltese Temples

Time: 3600–2500 BC
Location: Maltese Islands, central Mediterranean

The inhabitants commonly call them towers (torri). They are said to have been piled up by giants;
that is practically all that tradition has to say on the subject.

ALBERT MAYR, 1908

MASSIVE AND MONUMENTAL, the Maltese temples are among the most enigmatic buildings of prehistoric Europe. Small wonder, given the huge size of some of the blocks used in their construction, that the native inhabitants long considered them the work of giants, and one of them still carries the name Ġgantija – 'Giant's House'. Some two dozen temples are known, scattered either singly or in small clusters across Malta and Gozo. After a century or more of archaeological enquiry, we do now know that they were built during the period 3600–2500 BC. Yet the significance of their multi-lobed plan and the striking sculptures they have yielded, including corpulent and sometimes colossal statues, remain difficult to interpret, as do the rituals or activities for which they were intended.

The temples are built of local limestone, which occurs in two distinct varieties: hard coralline and softer globigerina. The former is more difficult to work, but has the advantage that it fissures naturally to yield blocks of building stone, and is very durable and resistant to erosion. Globigerina, on the

Model of the two adjoining temples at Ġgantija on Gozo, illustrating the multi-lobed plan characteristic of the Maltese prehistoric temples.

other hand, would have had to be quarried using antler picks and wooden wedges.

The temple builders well understood the contrasting properties of these two stones and generally chose the hard coralline limestone for external features where weather resistance was at a premium. Globigerina was preferred for internal features, where fine tooling and painstaking carving were added to create impressive, richly decorated interiors. Local availability also played a large part in the choice of stone, and while some was brought from considerable distances, local material was generally (and sometimes exclusively) preferred. To transport stones (weighing up to 20 tonnes) from quarries that might be several kilometres away, wooden sledges

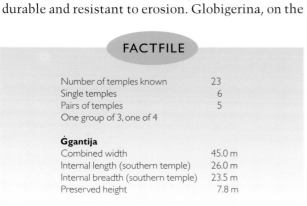

FACTFILE

Number of temples known	23
Single temples	6
Pairs of temples	5
One group of 3, one of 4	

Ġgantija

Combined width	45.0 m
Internal length (southern temple)	26.0 m
Internal breadth (southern temple)	23.5 m
Preserved height	7.8 m

Above **View along the main axis towards the entrance of the larger Ġgantija temple. The doorways are flanked by slabs of globigerina limestone but the walls are of the harder coralline variety.** *Right* **The lower temple at Mnajdra looking out from one of the small rooms formed in the walls.**

or cradles must have been used. Stone balls (found discarded at several temple sites) probably assisted in manoeuvring blocks into their final positions.

Building the temples

Building must have begun with laying out the ground plan and levelling the bedrock where necessary. Floors were generally of *torba* (plaster made of crushed limestone), though in several instances this was replaced by stone pavements or large stone slabs which must have been laid at an early stage. The walls of the temples consisted of inner and outer faces of shaped stone blocks, with earth and rubble infill between. Occasionally, small rooms or niches were formed in the thickness of the walls.

The kind of stone used made a great difference to the final effect. Huge blocks of coralline limestone were carefully jointed in the outer walls of Ġgantija. Yet they appear crude by comparison with the globigerina façade (partially reconstructed) of the Hagar Qim temple, where the regular horizontal courses are notched into the corners of the end-blocks; or with the eastern temple at Tarxien, where the edges of the orthostats fit together precisely, presumably dressed by a lengthy process of trial and error.

Larger blocks were moved into position using a combination of wooden levers and ropes. Many blocks have a notch in the middle of the longer side to take the tip of the lever to ensure it did not slip.

Ropes could have been tied around the stones, or looped through the V-perforations found on some of the blocks.

The temples were designed around a central axis which ran from trilithon entrance to the terminal niche at the back of the temple. Interiors were furnished with altars, screens, niches and threshold slabs of soft globigerina limestone, carved with running spirals or other motifs in relief. In the absence of metal tools, these must have been finished using small flint blades. In some cases, a background texture of circular pits was created by means of a bow drill. This type of decoration was also applied to certain of the major structural elements, for instance the decorated niche in the Lower Temple at Mnajdra. At Ġgantija , where globigerina was not locally available, smooth surfaces were created by applying clay to the rough coralline blocks. A coat of white lime plaster was added to this and painted deep red.

In several of the temples, the upper courses of the inner walls show an inwards slope, which must have been topped by a flat roof of timber and beaten clay. At Tarxien, a stone staircase squeezed into a gap between two temples may have led to such a rooftop. The finished appearance of the Maltese temples is confirmed by the evidence of several contemporary models and rock carvings. With their dark interiors and elaborate decoration, they must have been places of shadowy and mysterious power.

Stonehenge

Time: c. 2950–1600 BC
Location: southern England

The report goeth also, that these were broght from thence [Ireland], but by what ship on the sea, and cariage by land, I think few men can safelie imagine.

WILLIAM HARRISON, 1577

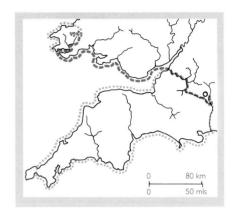

OVER THE centuries, the origin and purpose of Stonehenge have attracted a heady mix of science and speculation. The circle of sarsens, with the taller trilithons towering above and the smaller bluestones clustered around their feet, have long impelled people to wonder just how such a monument could have been built.

To answer that question, we must first recognize that Stonehenge was not built in a single effort. The stones we today regard as the chief characteristic of Stonehenge are in fact a relatively late arrival at the site. Stonehenge

FACTFILE

Date of Stonehenge I	2950 BC
First stone structures at Stonehenge (phase 3)	2550 BC
Modifications to phase 3 continue until	1600 BC
Diameter of enclosing bank & ditch	110 m
Diameter of sarsen circle	30 m
Original number of sarsens	c. 84
Original number of bluestones	c. 82
Length of largest stone (stone 56)	9 m
Estimated weight of stone 56	40 tonnes

Sarsens
30 sarsen uprights, 17 still standing, 8 fallen/fragmentary
30 lintels, 6 in position, 2 fallen
4 station stones, 2 in position
15 stones of 5 trilithons, 2 intact, 1 re-erected, 2 fallen; i.e. 9 stones in position, 6 fallen
2 stones: 1 Heel Stone, 1 lost
3 stones: 1 Slaughter Stone, 2 lost

Total: *c.* 84 sarsens, of which 52 extant & 36 more or less in position

Bluestones
11 in circle, 8 fallen or fragmentary, 10 stumps; original total 60
6 in horseshoe, 2 fallen or fragmentary, 3 stumps; original total 19 plus Altar Stone
Original double circle setting = c. 82 bluestones

Top **Alternative routes proposed for moving the bluestones from their source in the Preseli Hills, South Wales.**
Above **Stonehenge phase 1: a circular bank and ditch with the 'Aubrey Holes' around the inner edge of the bank.**

began as a more modest structure: a simple bank and ditch, roughly circular in plan and about 110 m (360 ft) across (Stonehenge 1: *c.* 2950 BC). Just within the bank was a ring of post-holes known (after their 17th-century discoverer) as the Aubrey Holes.

The chalk-cut ditch soon began to silt up, and the bank to erode, but new, timber structures were built: this was Stonehenge 2. Traces survive only as post-holes cut into the chalk and it is difficult to reconstruct what kind of structure they represent since not all need have been in use at the same time; there could well be several successive settings. Furthermore, the crucial central area of Stonehenge has been heavily chewed about by later interventions, not least the erection of the bluestones and sarsens. But the mortises and tenons – jointing techniques more appropriate to carpentry – of the stones of

Stonehenge 3 may provide a clue. They show that it was modelled on a timber structure, and perhaps Stonehenge 2 was just such a timber structure, with timber uprights jointed to horizontal lintels.

Stonehenge 3 begins *c.* 2550 BC with the arrival of the bluestones and then of the massive sarsen stones. And while it is relatively easy to envisage how the bank and ditch of Stonehenge 1 and the timber buildings of Stonehenge 2 might have been constructed, Stonehenge 3 was an amazing engineering achievement.

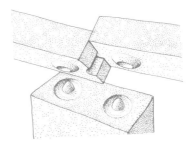

The carpentry origins of the Stonehenge stone settings are revealed by the techniques used to fix the sarsen lintels on the uprights – here a kind of mortise and tenon joint.

Transporting the stones

The first challenge was bringing the stones to the site. This question was given an added importance in 1923, when it was discovered that the bluestones originated in the Preseli Hills of southwest Wales, 240 km (130 miles) away. Though still disputed by some geologists, the Preseli Hills as the source of the bluestones is now generally accepted. Why they were brought to Stonehenge we still do not know, but how they were brought we can tell from experiment and conjecture. Weighing in at around 1.5 tonnes, the bluestones are the smaller stones of Stonehenge, the largest of them (around 2 m or 6.5 ft long) a little taller than a person. From experiments conducted in the 1950s we may picture them, strapped to a wooden sledge, hauled overland down to Milford Haven, then transferred to a timber raft for transport up the Bristol Channel and the River Avon. Some 3 km (2 miles) more of overland haulage would have brought them to Stonehenge itself.

Transporting the huge sarsens was an altogether different proposition. In comparison with the bluestones they did not have far to come (from the Marlborough Downs, 30 km or 18 miles north of Stonehenge), but the largest of them weigh 40 tonnes and are up to 9 m (30 ft) long. Careful preparations would have been needed to haul such enormous blocks across the uneven terrain between the Marlborough Downs and Stonehenge. A 1994 experiment used a railway of parallel beams set into the ground. The 'stone' (a concrete replica of the correct size and weight) was lashed securely to a timber sledge with a central keel designed to fit between the wooden rails; this ensured that the stone could not veer off

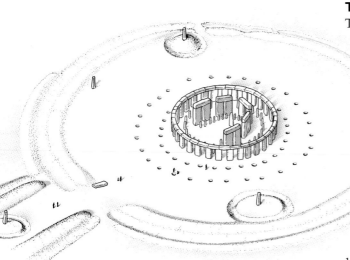

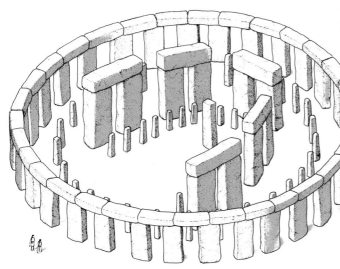

Top **Stonehenge phase 3, showing the central stone settings and (bottom left) the Avenue with the Heel Stone in its own ring ditch.** *Above* **The central settings of phase 3 in their final configuration, with the so-called 'Altar Stone' in their midst.**

course when it was pulled. With grease applied to the rails and runners, a team of 130 people were sufficient to move the stone, even where an incline of 1 in 20 was involved. Moving all 80 or so of the sarsens by this method would have still been an enormous undertaking. We should not be surprised perhaps that medieval chroniclers attributed Stonehenge to the magic of the legendary Merlin.

Raising the stones

Raising the stones was no less of a feat than transporting them. Experiments have shown, however, that using the right techniques, the job can be done by a team of under 150 people. One recent experiment used a ramp and counterweights to raise a replica sarsen upright. The massive sarsen was pulled up the ramp until its foot hung directly over the hole which had been dug to receive it; the stone counterweights were then slid along the top of the sarsen until it began to tilt and slipped gently into position, exactly vertical. Success depended on the

proper shaping of the hole and close and careful control during the lowering of the huge monolith.

Next, the 10-tonne lintels had to be raised to the top of the uprights and placed in position. This may have been achieved using a ramp, but an alternative method is the timber 'crib' or scaffold. In this, the lintel is laid alongside the uprights, and raised step by step with levers. At each stage timbers are propped underneath the stone, forming a scaffold that grows steadily higher until the stone is level with the top of the uprights. At that point some difficult manoeuvring would have been needed to slide the lintel sideways until the two mortise holes cut in its under surface engaged with the projecting tenons on the uprights.

Above **A recent experiment used a system of counterweights or 'tilting stones' to raise a replica of the largest sarsen into position. With the foot of the 'sarsen' projecting over its socket the tilting stones were dragged along till it tipped over.** *Right* **The central settings of Stonehenge survive today in a ruinous condition, if indeed they were ever fully completed.**

We do not know which of these methods – crib or ramp – was actually used to raise the lintels at Stonehenge. The ramp method would have been very labour intensive – not so much for hauling the stone, but for the many hours required to build and then dismantle the ramp itself. We must remember that the centre of Stonehenge is relatively small, and would have provided only a cramped space for such an ambitious engineering project. If the pulling was done from the outside, then the ramp must have filled a large part of the interior. The crib method is much simpler, and the timbers could have been reused. Whichever method was used, there must have been a lengthy period during which the centre of Stonehenge resembled a construction site, with scaffolding timbers, ropes and ramps, antler picks for digging the stoneholes and hammers and mauls for dressing them to shape.

Shaping the stones

At first sight the stones of Stonehenge may seem to be only roughly shaped. Certainly, they are not regular, but closer inspection – especially in oblique light – shows that they were carefully worked. Where weathering has not removed them, the stones are still covered in hundreds of small facets, produced mainly by pounding their surfaces with rounded or spherical stone mauls and hammers.

The builders incorporated a number of subtle features in the final design. The edges of the sarsen

uprights, for example, are not parallel but bulge and taper inwards: a version of the 'entasis' used by later Greek architects to avoid the optical illusion of an outward lean in a tall column. Nor were the lintels – at least, not those of the sarsen circle – mere rectangular blocks. They had curved outer and inner faces, and were jointed at the ends (using a groove-and-tongue technique borrowed from carpentry) to give a continuous smooth circle. Carpentry was also of course the origin of the mortise-and-tenon technique used to secure the lintels in position on top of the uprights. Stonehenge was no mere jumble of stones but a shaped and sophisticated structure.

Sighting the heavens

During the 1960s, the idea gained ground that Stonehenge was some kind of astronomical observatory, planned around a whole series of lunar and stellar (as well as solar) alignments that would have allowed it to be used as an eclipse predictor and for all sorts of calendrical calculations. Most of this has been shown to be untenable, but the significance of the midsummer solstice remains a key feature of the monument. The builders of Stonehenge must have watched day by day throughout the early part of the summer as the sun rose ever further to the north on the eastern horizon. Then, at its most northerly point, they fixed their line, raising the bluestone and sarsen structures around this solar axis. The mystical and romantic appeal of the midsummer sunrise continues to draw crowds to Stonehenge every year.

Left **A Stonehenge lintel being raised into position using long wooden levers and a timber scaffold or 'crib'.** *Below* **Moving the Stonehenge sarsens: in a recent experiment a replica sarsen attached to a timber sledge was dragged along well-greased timber rails.**

The Ziggurrat of Ur

Time: c. 2000 BC
Location: Ur, Iraq

On the summit there is a spacious shrine, inside which there is an exceptionally large bed, richly decorated, with a golden table beside it. No statue of any kind is erected there, and no one occupies the room at night except a single woman whom the god, so the priests say, has specially chosen for himself. They also say that the god comes to the room in person and sleeps on the bed. I do not believe it myself.

HERODOTUS, *c.* 440 BC

THE ZIGGURRAT or temple-tower of Ur is the finest surviving example of Sumerian religious architecture; once every major Sumerian city had something similar. Herodotus was in fact writing about Babylon, much later, but his words probably apply no less to Ur, where the priestess was traditionally a daughter of the king. The ziggurrat, reaching dramatically for heaven, was an appropriate setting for the nuptials of Nanna, the Moon-god.

From village shrine to temple tower

The ziggurrat of Ur has stood since about 2000 BC, when Ur-nammu (variously dated, for example 2112–2095 BC or 2018–2001 BC) and his son Shulgi, kings of Ur, dominated southern Mesopotamia and used the resources of their empire to rebuild the ancient city. Buried within the ziggurrat, however,

The base of the restored central ceremonial staircase of the ziggurrat of Ur.

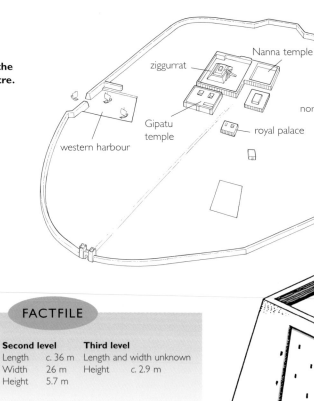

The city of Ur, with the ziggurat in the centre.

Labels: ziggurat, Nanna temple, northern harbour, royal palace, Gipatu temple, western harbour

are almost certainly the remains of other temples, going back thousands of years.

The earliest would have been the simple house of a village god, built perhaps of reeds, regularly repaired, and superseded by a building of sun-dried mud-brick. With each reconstruction incorporating the ruins of its predecessor, the level of the ground gradually rose, the sacred enclosure expanded, and eventually the decision was taken to build something altogether more grand at its heart.

The construction

The ziggurat is roughly rectangular in plan, with the corners orientated on the points of the compass. The walls slope slightly inwards as they rise and are decorated all around with shallow buttresses. Three levels, or stages, decreasing in size, were surmounted by a shrine on top. The structure is essentially solid but ventilation holes reach deep into the core. This consists of mud-bricks laid in regular courses, both flat and on edge. Around the outside is a skin, 2.5 m (8.2 ft) thick, made of baked bricks laid flat. Like other baked bricks throughout the ziggurat, they were set in waterproof bitumen mortar.

At ground level the ziggurat measures 62.5 × 43 m (205 × 141 ft): Mesopotamian architects relished mathematical precision, and these proportions are very close to 3:2. The first stage is 11 m (36 ft) high;

its surface was paved with baked bricks and surrounded by a low parapet. In its centre stood the second storey, now poorly preserved but measuring roughly 36 × 26 m (118 × 85 ft), a proportion of about 4:3. Its height has been calculated as 5.7 m (18.7 ft), and that of a lost third storey as 2.9 m (9.5 ft), so that each of the upper storeys was around half the height of the one below. Nothing is known of the shrine.

Access was by the northeastern face, where three staircases of baked brick led from the sacred enclosure below to a gatehouse between the first and second storeys. The central staircase must have been for ceremonial processions. The two others were probably for domestic use: there was even a large kitchen at the base of the northern one, since gods, like everyone else, required refreshment.

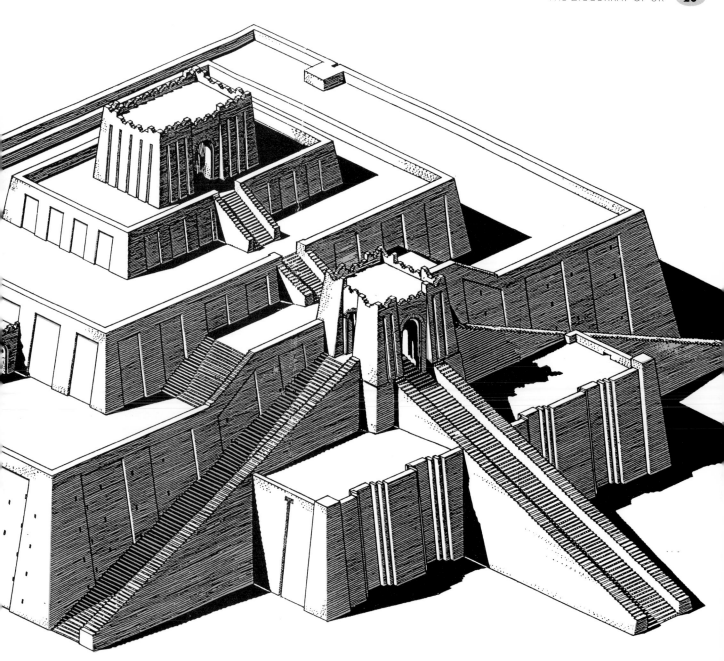

A reconstruction of the original appearance of the ziggurrat, based on the work of Sir Leonard Woolley.

The remaining faces are not straight but, as in some Greek architecture, curve slightly outwards in the centre. The impression of solidity which this feature provides is accentuated by a slight and perhaps deliberate bulge in the brickwork above ground-level.

Venerated for 1500 years

Ur-nammu's ziggurrat stood, with periodic repairs, until Nabonidus of Babylon (555–539 BC), a keen antiquarian and devotee of the Moon-god, entirely restored the staircases and upper storeys. While some blue glazed bricks found in the debris show that Nabonidus was interested in improvement as well as restoration, the general effect was probably much the same. Ur was declining, however, for the city's prosperity depended on the River Euphrates, and this was changing its course. Finally the ziggurrat was left marooned in the desert, its very isolation saving it from marauders.

The Temples of Karnak

Time: c. 2100–300 BC
Location: Luxor, Egypt

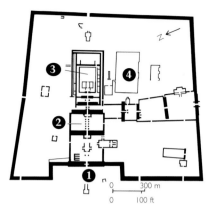

You have to ... walk among these gigantic structures to understand.... The columns are over 30 feet in circumference, so that a man looks [tiny] beside them. The blocks that lie scattered all around are so huge that, even without considering how they were cut, it is impossible to imagine how they were brought here and put in their places.

DAVID ROBERTS, 1838

K ARNAK WAS the religious centre of New Kingdom Egypt and its vast ruins cover an area of over 1.5 × 0.8 km (*c.* 1 × 0.5 mile) just north of modern Luxor. More than just one temple building, it is a whole complex of temples, ancillary religious structures, storage magazines, service quarters, workshops, gardens and processional routes grouped into and around three enclosures. The central precinct is the most important as it housed the cult centre of Amun-Re, the state god of Egypt from the Middle Kingdom onwards. The Amun-Re enclosure is trapezoidal and huge, each side being around half a kilometre in length.

The main temple was not a single construction project: it was considered each king's duty to build or aggrandize the temples of the gods, and the importance of Amun-Re ensured that most kings left their mark somewhere at Karnak. The small Middle Kingdom shrine rapidly expanded outwards as pyloned gateways, columned halls and subsidiary temples were built around it and adorned with relief decoration, statuary and obelisks. The temple must have been a building site for much of the 2000 years it was in use: the main pyloned entrance was still under construction when it was abandoned so that even now one enters through an unfinished façade. Today, the ruined temples provide a wealth of infor-

FACTFILE

Area covered by Karnak antiquities	*c.* 1 sq. km
Area of Amun-Re precinct	*c.* 0.26 sq. km

Hypostyle Hall of Seti I

Date of construction	*c.* 1306–1280 BC
Length	*c.* 104 m
Width	*c.* 52 m
Area of hall	*c.* 5400 sq. m
Maximum height	*c.* 24 m

Enclosure wall of Amun-Re precinct

Date of construction	*c.* 370 BC
Length	*c.* 2 km
Width	*c.* 12 m
Height	*c.* 25 m
Number of mud bricks	*c.* 70,000,000

mation on the techniques used by the ancient Egyptians to build freestanding stone structures.

Building techniques

The general principle employed by the Egyptians in erecting large buildings was to use very substantial blocks of stone to form massive walls, columns and solid stone elements such as pylons. Even larger blocks were used as architraves and roofing slabs: columns had to be placed close together as the distance which can be spanned with stone slabs is limited. The structure was therefore essentially held together by gravity.

Possibly the most impressive example of this building technique at Karnak is the hypostyle hall built by Seti I (c. 1306–1290 BC) and finished by his son Ramesses II. The hall is vast (c. 104 × 52 m or c. 341 × 170 ft – the size of a Gothic cathedral) and is densely packed with 134 massive columns. The columns are tapered and have plant-form capitals which slightly lighten their appearance, but the overall impression is one of solidity. At 22.4 m (73

ft) high, the columns flanking the central axis are larger than the rest and support a raised ceiling with clerestory windows: each is a grille painstakingly carved from slim blocks of sandstone.

Stone was brought to Karnak from quarries all over Egypt. Most of the standing structures are built of sandstone, which is relatively easy to work with metal tools and more durable than limestone, which was used at Karnak in the Middle Kingdom. Harder stones such as granite were used for obelisks (p. 263), statuary and occasionally for doorways, and in the early 18th Dynasty there was a fashion for carving small shrines out of stones rarely used as building materials, such as black grandiorite, red quartzite and 'Egyptian alabaster' (travertine).

The Egyptians performed elaborate foundation ceremonies when a new project was initiated. These

Plan (opposite) **and artist's reconstruction of Karnak:**
1 Entrance to the Amun-Re precinct via unfinished pylon.
2 Hypostyle Hall of Seti I.
3 Sanctuary.
4 Sacred lake.

The Hypostyle Hall of Seti I. The columns are built of stone drums piled up and dressed *in situ*. The clerestory window consists of two grilles carved from sheets of sandstone.

included laying out the building, digging foundation trenches and filling them with a layer of clean sand for symbolic purification. The sand also had a practical function as it provided a stable base for the foundations. By modern standards Egyptian foundations seem very minimal, but it is now thought that in most cases they were adequate: after all, many ancient Egyptian buildings are still standing several thousand years after they were built, and much of the damage they have sustained is the result of earthquakes rather than subsidence.

The blocks used for building are large, although nothing like as massive as the monoliths used for obelisks (p. 263) or colossal statues (p. 267). Even columns and engaged statues were built of manageable blocks. Massive ramps of mud-brick, rubble and sand were used to drag these blocks to their final positions: the remains of such a construction ramp still survive inside one of the towers of the first pylon. The blocks were levered into position and then dressed to ensure that each section fitted perfectly. Walls, columns, architraves and ceilings were all painted in the bright colours favoured by the Egyptians, although most of the paintwork has now been lost.

Mortar was used between blocks – as well as being a binding agent it filled gaps and acted as a lubricant for sliding blocks into position. Cramps and stone dowels were regularly used to hold blocks together, particularly higher up walls and in architraves and roofing slabs. These cramps were usually carved from wood but copper and bronze examples are also found, occasionally cast *in situ*. Such precautions are generally thought to have been unnecessary given the thickness of the walls and the size of the blocks. However, earthquakes have always been a threat in Egypt and the use of cramps and dowels to tie together the upper parts of structures greatly reduced the potential damage caused by blocks being shaken out of position.

Cramps are also used in solid masses of masonry such as pylons. At Karnak, the pylons consist of carefully constructed and dressed ashlar shells with cores of roughly laid stone blocks. These blocks are often remains of previous structures that had been dismantled and are frequently decorated: whole shrines and courtyards have been reconstructed

from the kit of parts removed from inside pylon towers in the course of modern consolidation. Reused blocks also frequently come to light in the foundation trenches of later structures.

A revolution in building technique

One of the most fascinating developments in Egyptian building technique took place in the reign of Akhenaten (*c.* 1353–1335 BC). Known only as 'the heretic' to his successors, he abandoned the traditional gods of Egypt and proclaimed the visible sun-disc or Aten to be the one true god. Not content with restructuring the country's religion, he also brought in new styles of art and literature and even initiated new building methods. For the first time in Egyptian history stone blocks were cut to a standard size, each one about 50 cm (*c.* 20 in) in length and easily handled by a single man. The blocks were laid into relatively thick layers of gypsum mortar which bonded the blocks firmly.

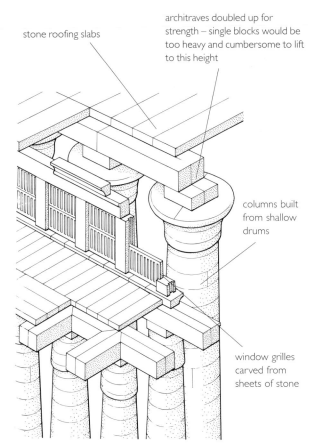

architraves doubled up for strength – single blocks would be too heavy and cumbersome to lift to this height

stone roofing slabs

columns built from shallow drums

window grilles carved from sheets of stone

Above **Construction of the clerestory and roof of the Hypostyle Hall.**

This new method allowed buildings to be put together quickly and efficiently. As the blocks could be lifted easily by hand, scaffolding rather than ramps could be used, which saved both time and man-power, and masons were no longer needed to dress the blocks when in position. Despite the clear advantages of such techniques, Akhenaten's constructional reforms were abandoned along with his religious ones, and his buildings were destroyed. At Karnak, thousands of decorated blocks from his temples have been recovered from the foundations and cores of structures built by his successors.

Enclosure wall

Each of the three enclosures at Karnak is surrounded by massive mud-brick walls and these are extraordinary structures in their own right. That of the central enclosure dates to around 370 BC and replaces a rather less substantial earlier wall. It is built of sun-dried mud-bricks set in mud mortar and reinforced with reeds and timber lacing. It is around 2 km (c. 1.25 miles) long, 12 m (39 ft) wide, and 25 m (82 ft) high. It contains somewhere in the region of 70 million bricks. The bricks are laid in sections

Remains of a mud-brick construction ramp inside the unfinished first pylon. The pylon was abandoned before the blocks had been dressed and the ramp dismantled.

with alternate concave and convex beds giving a distinctive wavy pattern to the wall: this seems to have had a symbolic significance in representing the primeval waters around the temple but may also have been a practical measure to prevent the wall cracking during earthquakes.

Restoration at Karnak

The Hypostyle Hall at Karnak is justly one of Egypt's most famous structures and admirably illustrates the prowess of the ancient architects and builders. The temple as a whole must have been an extraordinary sight in its heyday but much has been badly damaged and it is often difficult to appreciate the jumble of ruins and displaced blocks in the inner parts of the temple. Thankfully a dedicated team of French and Egyptian specialists has been carefully consolidating the existing structures and slowly piecing together the thousands of displaced decorated blocks in an attempt to reconstruct the history and original appearance of this fascinating site.

The Great Temple of Abu Simbel

Time: c. 1285–1265 BC
Location: Abu Simbel, Egypt

This morning I finally reached Abu Simbel. Carved on the mountain face are four colossal human figures in a seated position.... The beauty and size of the temple are not surpassed by any other Egyptian monument, even the Theban sanctuaries.

DAVID ROBERTS, 1838

THE GREAT TEMPLE of Ramesses II at Abu Simbel is one of the most impressive and best known of all Egyptian monuments. With the exception of the outer courtyard walls and a small solar chapel, the entire temple is carved from solid rock. Thanks to its remoteness and solidity, it is remarkably well preserved, despite its dramatic rescue from the rising waters of the Aswan dam. The façade is dominated by four colossal seated statues of the king, *c.* 22 m (*c.* 72 ft) high, while the entrance between them leads to a series of inner chambers penetrating deep into the cliff.

Building the temple

Work on the temple began early in the long reign of Ramesses II and was completed around year 24 (*c.* 1265 BC). It is dedicated to the three major state gods of Egypt, Amun-Re, Ptah and Re-Horakhty and to Ramesses himself who was deified here and worshipped during his own lifetime. Many of the carved reliefs show historical scenes commemorating Ramesses' battles in Syria, Libya and Nubia, while further scenes show his piety before the gods. A smaller rock-cut temple stands about 120 m (400 ft) to the northeast. It is contemporary with the Great Temple and is dedicated to the goddess Hathor and Ramesses' chief wife Nefertari.

The temple lies in Nubia – beyond the traditional boundary of southern Egypt but well within the zone controlled and administered by Egypt at this time. The site was probably chosen because the rock face was unfissured and of good sandstone suitable for creating a rock-cut monument. The temple

The interior of the temple at Abu Simbel, excavated from solid rock. The colossi and wall reliefs represent Ramesses II.

faces the rising sun and twice a year, in February and October, the sunlight penetrates right into the inner sanctuary and illuminates the cult statues on the back wall. Experts are divided on whether this illumination was intentional but, if it was, the orientation of the original rock-face must also have been taken into consideration in the choice of site.

We have almost no textual evidence relating to the construction of the temple, but some information can be gleaned from the site itself. The temple must have been extremely carefully planned and the dimensions of rooms and positions of pillars worked out in advance as mistakes would have been difficult to rectify. Stone-cutters must have roughly carved the colossi to the dimensions of the draftsmen and hollowed out the interior in much the same manner as the tombs in the Valley of the Kings (p. 56). A large team of skilled sculptors will have been needed to dress the façade and to give the colossi their final shape (p. 267). Inside the temple, another team will have dressed the walls and plastered them to fill any cracks in the rock. Then the decoration will have been drawn on to the prepared surfaces by master draftsmen and carved by sculp-

tors before the finishing touches were added with brightly coloured paint. Much of the relief carving is actually rather crude, but the liveliness of the scenes distracts the attention.

Restoration and conservation

Most of the visible damage to the temple seems to have happened soon after construction. The upper part of the second colossus fell during an earthquake

Above **The interior of the Great Temple.** *Right* **The Great Temple is carved directly into the rock face. The colossal figures of Ramesses II are 22 m high. The upper part of the second colossus fell in an earthquake soon after completion.**

about 10 years after the completion of the temple and has never been restored. More minor damage incurred during the same earthquake was restored by the king's officials: their repairs can still be seen under the arm of the third colossus and inside the temple.

In the 1960s Abu Simbel became the showpiece of the UNESCO campaign to save the monuments of Nubia threatened by the construction of the Aswan dam. Between 1964 and 1968 both the temples of Abu Simbel were dismantled and reassembled 65 m (213 ft) above their original site. As the temples were carved from solid rock, they had to be cut into manageable pieces: the Great Temple was cut into 807 huge blocks, averaging 20 tonnes each. These blocks were reassembled on a reinforced concrete skeleton within an artificial mountain at a cost of around 40 million US dollars.

The Cult Centre of Chavín de Huántar

Time: c. 900–200 BC
Location: north-central highlands, Peru

It was a huaca or sanctuary, one of the most famous … like Rome or Jerusalem among us; a place where the Indians come to make offerings and sacrifices, because the demon in this place declared many orders to them, and so they attended from throughout the kingdom.

ANTONIO VÁSQUEZ DE ESPINOSA, 1616

AGAINST THE backdrop of a sacred mountain, confluence of rivers and alignment with the heavens, stands the massive, flat-topped mound known as Chavín de Huántar. Construction of this important monument began *c.* 900 BC, and by its heyday, *c.* 400–200 BC, Chavín had become the centre of a powerful oracle and religion whose art style inspired works in cloth, metal, stone and ceramics disseminated throughout much of the central Andes.

The Old Temple

One of Chavín's earliest ceremonial constructions, known as the Old Temple, lies on terraced and levelled land overlooking the Mosna river. Its earthen and rock core is sheathed by polished slabs of locally quarried granite, sandstone and limestone. Long thought to be the oldest construction at the site, a recent mapping project located seams in the structure indicating that the Old Temple in fact conceals even earlier building stages.

Its layout recalls the sacred, U-shape of the coastal centres that had flourished centuries earlier. A central platform and smaller and larger wings embrace a sunken circular courtyard. The arms or wings represent the opposing and yet complemen-

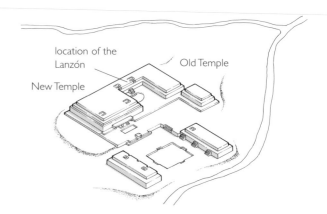

The temple at Chavín de Huántar, located at the confluence of two rivers in the north-central highlands of Peru.

tary forces of the cosmos and society; the plaza between these arms mediated between the opposing powers and the building at the apex of the U represented the synthesis of the forces. Some 10 m (33 ft) above the temple floor on the central platform, large, projecting stone heads were tenoned to the façade at intervals. They depict fearsome, fanged, half-human creatures that some scholars believe represent drug-induced shamanic transformations.

The temple appears to be a solid construction, lacking doorways and windows. Yet its interior is honeycombed with chambers and passageways, known as galleries. Stairways, vents and drains connected these galleries, forming a labyrinth that bore the stress of the temple's rubble core. Conduits provided air to the dank passageways, and stone-lined canals drained rainwater from the flat-topped summit. The network of drainage canals and air ducts, around 500 m (1650 ft) in the Old Temple, far exceeded the demands of simple engineering. Some

FACTFILE

Old Temple

Height of central platform	11 m
Height of southern platform	16 m
Height of northern platform	14 m
Network of drainage canals and air ducts	500 m
Settlement surrounding temple precinct	42 ha
Population c. 500 BC	3000

Above **A view looking west, with the temple of Chavín de Huántar in the foreground and the sacred, snow-covered peak of Huantsan in the distance.**
Left **The Lanzón, a granite monolith and cult image that graced one of Chavín de Huántar's galleries deep within the temple.**

Left **A sculpted panel depicting a mythical jaguar decorates the sunken circular courtyard in front of the Old Temple at Chavín de Huántar.** *Below* **The eastern façade of the New Temple at Chavín de Huántar and its black-and-white portal.**

scholars have suggested that worshippers, gathered in front of the temple, associated the sound of water rushing through the canals, amplified by the opening and shutting of vents and drains, with the thunder-like roar of Chavín's oracle.

A flight of steps in the central platform led to a gallery entrance and the Old Temple's main object of worship, perhaps its earliest oracle: the 4.53-m (15-ft) high granite monolith known as the Lanzón. Facing east, the Lanzón commands the end of a dank, cross-shaped gallery, and is one of the few Chavín sculptures still to occupy its original position. It portrays a human-like form, whose feet and hands end in claws. It sports heavy ear pendants and its thick-lipped mouth is drawn back in a snarl, displaying fearsome upper canines. The Lanzón's notched top reaches through the ceiling into an unexplored gallery above, from which the temple's priests, acting as the voice of the oracle, may have spoken to supplicants.

The New Temple

Chavín's growing prosperity is reflected in the remodelling and enlargement of the temple precinct into the structure known as the New Temple, which thrived from around 400 to 200 BC. The New Temple incorporated part of the Old Temple, and its builders enlarged the south wing, doubling its size, and the precinct grew to the east as well.

At the base of the New Temple's central platform builders added a portal with two elaborately carved columns depicting crested eagles, topped by a carved lintel. The portal led into a square patio or court 20 m (66 ft) wide, decorated with sculpted panels. From there, a monumental stairway of black limestone and white granite led into the New Temple's main plaza. Measuring 105 × 85 m (345 × 279 ft), this sunken, rectangular plaza enclosed a smaller, sunken court 50 m (164 ft) on a side.

Exotic imagery found on sculpture, for instance caymans, jaguars and snakes, prompted some scholars to posit a tropical-forest origin for Chavín de Huántar. Research, however, has shown that, although its religion may have borrowed animal imagery and cosmology from tropical-forest societies, Chavín's architecture has more in common with coastal styles while its subsistence economy is typically highland. Just as Chavín's architects drew on coastal traditions for the design of the temple, so its sculptors fused sacred imagery from the coast, and perhaps Amazonian cosmology from the tropical lowlands, into their stone carvings.

The Parthenon
at Athens

Time: 447–438 BC
Location: Athens, Greece

It is as if some ever-flowering life and unaging spirit had been infused into the creation of these works.

PLUTARCH, 1ST CENTURY AD

THE PARTHENON in Athens is not only an outstanding and innovative architectural achievement, it is also a symbol of Greek independence, culture and pride. It arose from a scene of devastation. In 480 BC the Persians swept down and attacked Athens. They destroyed public works and monuments, massacred Athenians, plundered temples and set fire to the citadel. It took some 30 years before peace was achieved and Athens began to restore itself through an ambitious programme of renewal and rebuilding promoted by the politician Pericles. The pinnacle of this programme is the Parthenon, begun in 447 BC, which stood prominently on the Acropolis on the remains of an earlier temple. It served as much as a celebration of Athens and her achievements as it did as a centre to worship the goddess Athena.

Designed by the architects Ictinos and Callicrates, the Parthenon combines many architectural elements in a manner previously unknown. It measures 69.5 × 30.88 m (228 × 101 ft) at its *stylobate* (base) with 8 Doric columns on the ends and 17 on the flanks. The main room or *cella* was divided into two. It has been suggested that the western end was a treasury while the larger eastern end housed a massive chryselephantine statue of Athena by Pheidias, the greatest Greek sculptor of the day (p. 33). Access was through a Doric 6-column porch.

The Parthenon in its present ruined state.

111

FACTFILE

Foundation

Architectural member	Number of units	Length	Width	Height	Weight
Stereobate		78 m			
Building stones	8000				2 tonnes
Crepidoma		72.31 m	33.68 m		
Stylobate		69.5 m	30.88 m		
Building stones	130				5 tonnes
Corner stones	4				7 tonnes

Exterior

Architectural member	Number of units	Length	Width	Height	Weight
Columns	46		1.91 m	10.43 m	
Drums	506				5–10 tonnes
Capitals	46				8–9 tonnes
Architrave					
Building stones	138	4.3–4.7 m			up to 10 tonnes
Doric Frieze				1.35 m	
Triglyphs	100		0.845 m		
Metopes	92				
Cornice				0.6 m	
Roof (marble)					
Under & over tiles	8480				20–50 kg
Decorative tiles	377				

Cella

Architectural member	Number of units	Length	Width	Height	Weight
Ionic frieze		160 m			
Columns	46			13.5 m	
Walls					
Upright blocks	231				2.7–7 tonnes
Coursing stones	3690				1.5 tonnes

West Chamber

Architectural member	Number of units	Length	Width	Height	Weight
Ionic column				12.5 m	

A perspective view of the Parthenon, cut away to show the inner main room or *cella*, with its gold and ivory statue of Athena.

The sculptures

One of the Parthenon's most outstanding features was its sculptures, which fall into three groups. First, there were the boldly carved figures of the triangular pediments at either end. Second, the 92 'metopes' or square panels carved in more shallow relief which, alternating with plainer 'triglyphs', ran around the exterior of the entire structure just below the eaves. Last but not least was the continuous frieze, 160 m (525 ft) long, placed high up inside the colonnade, around the top of the *cella*.

Not surprisingly for a temple of such splendour, built at such expense, the Athenians turned to Pheidias to design and supervise this sculptural scheme. Perched high above the ground on timber scaffolds, Pheidias and his team worked for five or six years (c. 438–432 BC), carving and colouring the sculptures which for later generations came to represent the highest achievement of Classical Greek art. They include the famous 'Elgin Marbles', removed from the Parthenon in 1801 and brought to England.

Quarrying and transporting the stone

Apart from timber roof supports, the whole superstructure of the Parthenon – including the roof tiles – was built of marble cut from the quarries at Mount Pentelicon, 13 km (8 miles) northeast of Athens. The foundation belonged to the earlier temple and is composed of blocks quarried near Piraeus.

The process of building the Parthenon began in the quarry. A system of iron wedges and levers, mallets and sheer manpower was used to pry blocks from their beds. Where possible, natural lines of cleavage were exploited, making the task of remov-

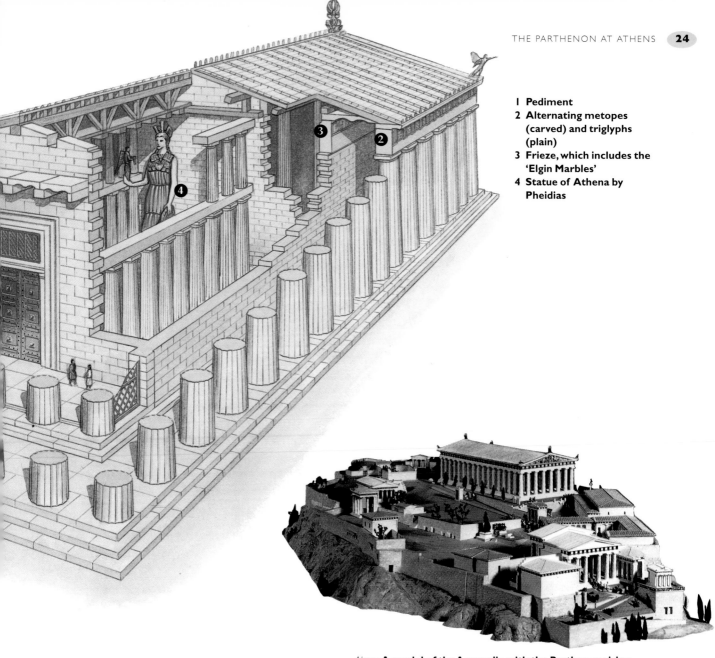

1 **Pediment**
2 **Alternating metopes (carved) and triglyphs (plain)**
3 **Frieze, which includes the 'Elgin Marbles'**
4 **Statue of Athena by Pheidias**

Above **A model of the Acropolis, with the Parthenon rising above the other buildings.** *Below left* **A detail from the North Frieze of the Parthenon: part of the parade of cavalry.**

ing the stone easier. Wedges were inserted into sockets at the edge of the desired stone and hammered in with mallets. Meanwhile, levers worked by teams of men increased the force acting on the stone until it broke free. A minimum of four men with wedges and four with levers would have been needed. However, the more massive blocks for the 5–10-tonne column drums and the 8–9-tonne capitals would have required greater numbers.

Sledges were probably used to haul massive stones out of the quarries: levers raised the blocks just enough so that beams could slide underneath to form the sledge. For an average-size column drum,

113

Quarrying the stone, using wedges and levers.

entablature and long walls of the *cella* incline inwards from the vertical. Corner columns also incline inwards, but on the diagonal. The total effect is a structure full of life and strength; without these refinements the structure would appear top-heavy and as if about to topple on the spectator.

Skilled masons finished only the lower surface of column drums and the parts of the building stone that would be seen. Bosses, small deliberate projections on the stone, provided handles for moving and lifting the stones and were cut off once stones were in place. Additional masons then finished dressing the stones. Capitals, however, were completed before being hoisted into position.

The Parthenon took nine years to build and used well over 230,000 tonnes of stone. This means that more than 70 tonnes of stone were quarried, transported, dressed and moved into place each day. In fact, this figure should probably be much greater as it does not allow for holidays or religious festivals. Nor does it account for materials other than marble. We know that iron clamps were used to secure both building blocks and sculpture, wood was used for the roof and paint to colour the sculptures and architectural details. Moreover the pediment sculptures have not been accounted for. It is clear that even with this extremely conservative estimate, multiple teams of labourers were required.

One or more teams moved building stones from wagons to work areas; others raised blocks into position. Teams finished the various architectural members both on the ground and once in position. For an average column drum, a minimum of 28 men was needed to move the stone on a sledge from the wagon to the appropriate work area. One mason dressed the drum on the ground while a second completed the dressing once it was positioned. Addi-

approximately 28 men would have been required to haul the load on a sledge out of the quarry to a wagon waiting to transport it to Athens.

Literary evidence tells us that wagons and mules were used to transport blocks from the quarry to the Acropolis. Wagons would have had to be sufficiently strong to withstand weights of more than 10 tonnes. To haul the average-size column drum, a minimum of 33 mules and one man to guide the team were required, the numbers increasing to cope with larger blocks and any incline encountered.

Dressing the stones

If stones were not shaped in the quarries, this job was done on site according to their purpose and placement within the overall plan. As a result, no two stones are alike. Slight angles and curves were introduced according to a predetermined mathematical proportion. These served both to counteract settlement and movement within the total structure and to correct any visual imperfections. All horizontal lines curve upwards to form slightly arched surfaces. The exterior columns,

Diagram showing the angles of inclination and rise of horizontal lines in the Parthenon.

tional men were needed to hoist the block by crane and shift it into place.

It has been estimated that the wagon journey from the Pentelicon quarry to the Acropolis would have taken a full day. If each wagon carried one column drum of 70 tonnes, a minimum of 9–14 wagons, more than 300 mules, 250 transport men, 18–28 masons and hundreds of other men to quarry and raise loads were required. Indeed, Athens was drained of almost all available labour and craftsmen. Men who had suffered long years of battle and devastation were provided with work and a sense of purpose and an opportunity to reassert Athenian strength through state propaganda; the sheer size and scale of the Parthenon reinforced the wealth, power and glory of the Athenians.

A stone being lifted into position on the Parthenon. The reconstruction by Manolis Korres is based on a crane described by the Roman engineer Vitruvius.

The Pyramid of the Sun at Teotihuacan

Time: c. 300 BC–AD 225
Location: central Mexico

at a place called Teotihuacan ... the people raised pyramids for the sun and for the moon ....
There is a hollow where they removed the stone to build the pyramids. And they built the pyramids ...
very large, just like mountains.

THE FLORENTINE CODEX, C. 1569

THE MONUMENT known for the last 500 years as the 'Pyramid of the Sun' should actually be called the Pyramid of Time, because according to an ancient Mexican legend it marks the place where time began. The pyramid was erected nearly 2000 years ago as a memorial to this long-ago event, as a place to worship the great gods, and perhaps as the tomb of the ruler who had it built. Rising 60 m (*c.* 200 ft) above the plain of the Teotihuacan valley in the cool arid Central Highlands of Mexico, the pyramid is the finest architectural achievement at Teotihuacan, ancient Mexico's first great city.

Teotihuacan began unpretentiously in the 1st millennium BC, as one of two substantial towns in the Valley of Mexico, each on a lakeshore plain with a backdrop of mountains. Several hundred years BC, volcanic eruptions imperilled Teotihuacan's rival, finally burying it under a lava flow. Refugees found a new home in Teotihuacan, where they and their descendants worked on ancient Mexico's largest

FACTFILE

Stage I
Built sometime between 300 BC and AD 1
Base a low platform directly over cave's inner chamber
Smaller platform to its west lay above and east of the cave entrance

Stage II
First substantial pyramid, c. AD 100
Base c. 184 m on a side
Height c. 46 m

Stage III
Final pyramid c. AD 150–225
Base c. 226 m on a side
Height c. 75 m including now-destroyed temple on top

public works projects: two immense pyramids (of the 'Moon' and of the 'Sun'), a massive ritual causeway (the 'Avenue of the Dead'), a set of huge compounds (the 'Ciudadela', or Citadel, and the 'Great Compound'), and, finally, their own homes, the apartment complexes. Teotihuacan thus grew to surround the Pyramid of the Sun with a densely settled urban grid covering 20 sq. km (8 sq. miles) and housing over 100,000 people.

Teotihuacan's effigy mountains and caves

Scholars think that the refugees worked on these projects voluntarily, supervised by Teotihuacan's rulers and in service to the city's sacred spirits.

Believing in a spiritually charged landscape, they would have regarded mountains and caves as sacred and powerful, and the Teotihuacan valley provided an auspicious conjunction of such features. In the middle of the future city, a cave faced west, orientated to where the sun set on certain astrologically and agriculturally important days. A shrine built over this cave in the 1st century BC was the earliest construction at the site of the Pyramid of the Sun, and consisted of several large mounds above the cave's entrance and its interior chamber.

A view along the Avenue of the Dead, from the Pyramid of the Moon. The Pyramid of the Sun is on the left.

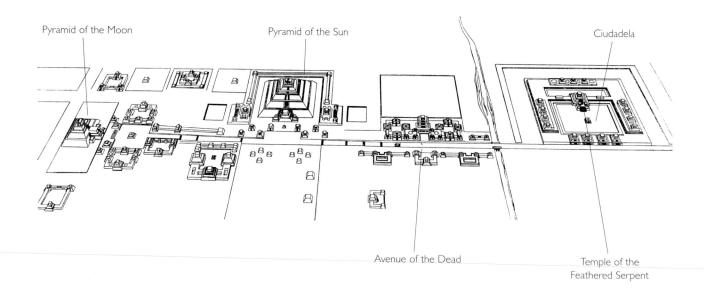

Pyramid of the Moon   Pyramid of the Sun   Ciudadela

Avenue of the Dead   Temple of the Feathered Serpent

The main buildings of Teotihuacan's ceremonial centre.

Standing at the cave entrance, but looking north, exactly perpendicular to the western line of sight, the notch atop the city's sacred mountain was visible. Early in the 1st century AD, Teotihuacan's workforce laid out the causeway now called the Avenue of the Dead, its southern end at the cave entrance, and its northern end at the base of the mountain, where they built the Pyramid of the Moon, the city's first great monument.

Towards the end of the century, work focused on expanding the cave shrine into the Pyramid of the Sun. Construction stages are poorly understood, and further excavations may finally resolve the question of how many rebuildings the pyramid has undergone. We do know, however, that the pyramid's platform was a huge square, 349 m (1138 ft) on a side. Within this, the penultimate version of the pyramid arose from a square base *c.* 184 m (600 ft) on a side, to a height of about 46 m (150 ft). A core of chunks of compacted volcanic ash, sun-baked mud-bricks and volcanic gravel was coated with a thick layer of mortar made from more volcanic gravel, and finished with lime stucco and paint. The pyramid was topped by a temple, or possibly twin temples, to the city's two principal deities, the Storm God and the Great Goddess. Teotihuacan's ceremonial centre was expanded in the 2nd century AD; the causeway was extended south and flanked by huge squares.

Sometime before AD 225 the Pyramid of the Sun reached the form we see today, notwithstanding subsequent destruction of the summit and surface.

The completed pyramid measured about 226 m (739 ft) across the base, slightly less than that of Egypt's Great Pyramid of Khufu (p. 21). The height, including the shrine on top, was about 75 m (245 ft), half that of Khufu. Adding to the first pyramid involved structural bracing, now visible because of surface destruction. Vertical stone buttresses extend up towards the top; the gaps between them would have been filled, and the whole surface covered with a layer of masonry 7 m (23 ft) thick, a layer of pounded volcanic gravel, and finally lime stucco and paint.

Moving materials, building the monument

Clearly, massive amounts of materials were needed: where did they come from, and how were they transported? Bulky materials like pumice, gravels and blocks of compacted volcanic ash may have been mined from underneath the pyramids. Recent studies of the cave system underlying Teotihuacan have found that many caves once thought natural are in fact quarry sites later used for ritual purposes. The sacred cave under the Pyramid of the Sun was itself elaborated by cutting and filling.

To transport building materials, the rulers and planners used the swollen population of Teotihuacan citizens, who probably worked most intensively at times of year when they were not needed at the irrigation-system farms extending from the city down to the lake. If we conservatively estimate that an adult commoner could work on construction projects 100 days each year, then the city's population of 100,000 by *c.* AD 100 would have contributed

A Teotihuacan-style mask.

tens of thousands of work-days each year, transporting materials in baskets and performing other tasks.

How long did it take to build the Pyramid of the Sun? The pyramid's volume of over 1 million cu. m (over 35 million cu. ft) amounted to roughly 30 million basketloads. If each worker made five trips a day from source to site, 6 million work-days were required, and 6000 labourers could finish basic construction in 10 years. The entire surface of over 50,000 sq. m (*c.* 550,000 sq. ft) was then stuccoed, first with mud and volcanic gravel, finally with lime plaster brought in from adjacent valleys. This taste for quality cost the Teotihuacanos dearly, because lime processing consumed whole forests and irrevocably altered the valley's ecology, triggering erosion still visible today.

The city's rulers finished the Pyramid of the Sun with a temple (or temples) on top of the broad summit, and redesigned the entry platform over the cave entrance. This addition bore the distinctive architectural design that would become Teotihuacan's architectural signature: platform walls of long horizontal panels atop sloping bases, known as *talud-tablero* style, and not otherwise seen at the Pyramid of the Sun.

After completion of the Pyramid of the Sun, work ceased on further enhancements to the city's civic-ceremonial centre. Teotihuacan's early tradition of powerful rulers gave way to a more collective style of leadership, presumably the representatives of the denizens of the apartment complexes, which remained occupied for another 400 to 500 years.

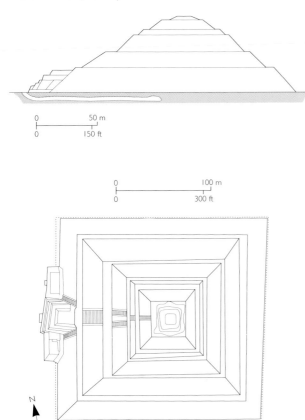

| 0 | 50 m |
| 0 | 150 ft |

| 0 | 100 m |
| 0 | 300 ft |

N

Opposite **The western façade of the Pyramid of the Sun, with entry platform and stairways.** *Above* **Pyramid of the Sun, profile and plan, showing the location of the cave.**

The Great Stupa of Sanchi

Time: 3rd century BC–5th century AD
Location: Madhya Pradesh, India

The gift of Dhana, the wife of the brother of the householder Patithiya from Tubavana.

INSCRIPTION ON THE NORTHERN ENTRANCE TO THE GREAT STUPA

SANCHI IS ONE of the best-preserved com-plexes of freestanding Buddhist architecture in South Asia. A variety of stupas, temples, monaster-ies and pillars were built here, on the summit of an isolated sandstone ridge in central India, between the 3rd century BC and the 12th century AD, but dominating all is the 16.5-m (54-ft) high Great Stupa. Around the base of the stupa runs a proces-sional pathway with a stone railing. At the cardinal points stand four tall ceremonial gateways deco-rated with exquisitely carved bas-reliefs depicting scenes from the life of the Buddha, from previous births of the Buddha and from the early history of Buddhism. The stupa dome rises on a plinth as a truncated hemisphere 36.6 m (120 ft) across, sur-mounted by a rectangular stone railing enclosing a triple stone umbrella. The mass of the stupa and the intricate carving of gateways and railings creates a striking contrast, but the original impact would have been still more powerful. The dome and plinth were coated with white lime concrete, the railings and gateways were coloured a translucent red, the surface of the stupa was painted with swags and gar-lands, and the umbrellas on the summit were gilded.

FACTFILE

Overall			Ceremonial entrances	
Height	16.5 m		Height	8.5 m
Diameter	36.6 m			
			Plinth	
Outer railing			Height	5 m
Number of posts	120		Width at base	1.75 m
Height of posts	3.2 m		Height of railing	1.5 m
Upper railing			**Umbrella**	
Height	2.1 m		Height	2.1 m

An imperial foundation

The monument we see today is the result of several centuries of building and embellishment. The Great Stupa was founded by the Mauryan emperor, Asoka (272–235 BC) in the middle of the 3rd century BC. The first brick structure was only half the size of the present stupa, and probably contained remains of the Buddha himself. Asoka also raised a 13-m (42-ft) high commemorative pillar of polished sandstone next to the stupa, and had inscribed on it an edict forbidding schisms within the Buddhist order. Asoka's stupa is thought to have been damaged by the first ruler of the following Sunga dynasty, Pushyamitra (184–148 BC), but it was then remod-elled and enlarged during the reign of his son Agnimitra, or the latter's successor, Vasujyeshtha. The gateways were added a hundred years later during the reign of the Satavahana ruler, Satakarni II (50–25 BC). In contrast to its royal foundation later phases were carried out not by kings but by hun-dreds of individuals – monks and nuns, merchants, bankers, masons – who inscribed records on the fea-tures they donated.

The building of Sanchi

Asoka's original brick stupa was an object of sanc-tity so that rather than level it, the builders of the second phase encased it within their new construc-tion. They cut foundations down through the Mauryan terrace, and built a new larger dome of uneven horizontal masonry over a thick core of rubble, constructing the plinth and other features separately on shallow foundations. The 40-tonne

View of the eastern ceremonial gateway and stone railing with the Great Stupa behind.

Asokan pillar had been quarried at Chunar on the Ganges and rafted to a nearby river, but the later materials were obtained locally. The casing was of sandstone cut from the ridge on which Sanchi stands, the railings were of a finer sandstone from a neighbouring outcrop, and the ceremonial gateways from an outcrop 6.4 km (4 miles) away at Udayagiri.

Quarrying involved sinking depressions along the desired line of fracture, filling them with water and then setting a fire above. The resultant blocks were rough-dressed with a pointed hammer and claw tool, and decorative elements were carved with steel chisels and files before being smoothed with river sand. While the casing was laid in dry horizontal courses, the elements for the railings used mortise and tenon joints, a technique derived from woodworking. The cross beams were even given a lenticular shape in imitation of bamboo.

Early estimates suggested that the monument had taken over a hundred years to construct, but a much shorter build-time of five to six years is now thought more likely. It was none the less a considerable technical achievement.

Stupas are one of the earliest types of Buddhist monument, and were originally raised in various locations over the ashes of the Buddha (c. 563–483 BC) when they were divided up following his Maha-parinirvana, or great passing away. Mounds of brick, earth or stone, they became objects of veneration in their own right in the reign of Asoka. It is highly likely that the Great Stupa at Sanchi was built over remains of the Buddha himself, since the smaller stupas (Stupas 2 and 3) contained relics of his disciples and their successors. The Great Stupa remained the focus of the Buddhist shrine for almost 1400 years until the site was abandoned to the jungle.

Conjectural cut-away section through the Great Stupa showing the original Mauryan brick-built core.

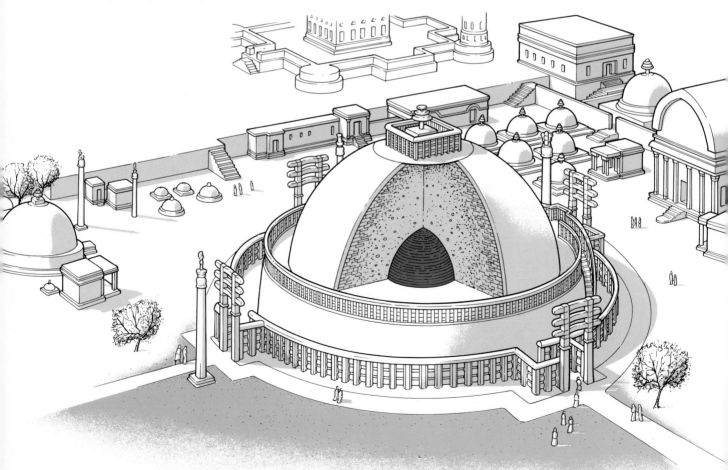

The Buddhist Caves
of Ajanta

Time: 2nd century BC–6th century AD
Location: Maharashtra, India

Whoever makes an image of Jina [Buddha] becomes complete in beatitude, auspiciousness and good qualities and his splendour is brilliant through virtues and physical organs and is delightsome to the eyes.

INSCRIPTION IN CAVE 27, 5TH CENTURY AD

THE TEMPLES and monasteries of Ajanta, 320 km (200 miles) northeast of Bombay, are the finest examples of Buddhist rock-cut architecture in South Asia, decorated with a series of outstanding murals depicting scenes from Buddhist tradition. They offer a unique opportunity to study the early development of Buddhist architecture since most other examples of this period were of wood and have long since perished.

At Ajanta, 30 caves were cut into the cliffs of a narrow gorge above the Waghora river in two separate phases, the earliest between the 2nd and 1st centuries BC, and the rest between the 5th and 6th centuries AD. They were originally reached by rock-cut stairs from the floor of the gorge, some 30 m (98 ft) below. The caves can be divided into stupa sanctuaries and monasteries. Both are adorned with rich murals depicting the Buddha, Bodhisattvas or enlightened beings, and important incidents from the life of the Buddha and the Jatakas or previous births of the Buddha. The five sanctuaries have elaborate façades with an entrance doorway topped by a horseshoe-shaped window. Inside, there is a central chamber with a vaulted ceiling and apse surrounded

The elaborate rock-cut entrance façade to stupa sanctuary 19 with its entrance portico and horseshoe-shaped window above.

Overall

Height of cliff	76 m
Height of caves	10–30 m
Number of caves	30
Number of sanctuaries	5
Number of monasteries	25

Stupa sanctuary 19

Width	7 m
Length	18 m
Height	7.6 m
Stupa diameter	2.7 m
Stupa height	6.7 m
Number of pillars	17
Height of pillars	3.6 m

Monastery 1

Verandah

Width	18 m
Length	2.7 m
Number of cells	2

Pillared hall

Width	18 m
Length	1 m
Number of pillars	20
Number of cells	14

Antechamber

Width	5 m
Length	3 m

Shrine

Width	5 m
Length	5.7 m

Most of the Ajanta caves were cut during the ascendancy of the Vakataka dynasty which ruled much of the western Deccan in the 5th and 6th centuries AD. The Vakataka rulers themselves followed the Brahmanical (Hindu) religion, but the Buddhist monuments at Ajanta were constructed by their ministers, wives and subjects as well as by passing merchants and pilgrims. Thus an inscription in Cave 16 records the donation of Varahadeva, a minister of King Harishena (AD 475–500) and Cave 17 records a donation from a subordinate princeling of the same king.

Ajanta's location, close to the busy trade routes into the Deccan, attracted pilgrims and traders who might, like the merchant Ghanamadada, dedicate a cave in the hope of success for their expeditions. Not all the caves were endowed and dedicated by a single individual, however. Cave 9 records four separate donations, and Vasithiputra's donation of a house door to Cave 10 suggests that the appearance of some caves was the result of numerous stages and modifications.

by a circumabulatory side-aisle separated by pillars. The focus of the structure, the stupa, is located in the centre of the apse.

The monasteries, the second category of cave, differ greatly in size; Cave 6 even has two floors, connected by staircases. Each monastery has a congregation hall surrounded by dwelling cells, and later examples also contain an image shrine. Although both sets of monument are cut into the cliff, they are carved with architectural features normally encountered in wooden structures – carved ribs, rafters, brackets and even stepped merlons.

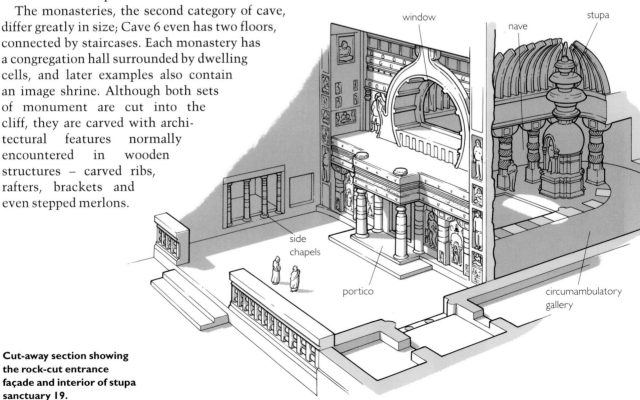

window nave stupa

side chapels

portico circumambulatory gallery

Cut-away section showing the rock-cut entrance façade and interior of stupa sanctuary 19.

Carving the shrines

Six of the caves were never completed, and these allow us to study the initial steps in their construction. The first stage was to select an area of the soft, coarse-grained basalt cliff without visible flaws or cracks. The façade was then marked out and excavation with iron tools began. The ceilings were cut first, and work proceeded downwards so that scaffolding was not needed. While cutting downwards, long working alleys were excavated, leaving the rows of pillars blocked out in the intervening walls to be cut through later. In the case of the monasteries, central halls were excavated first, followed by the residential cells – many of which were never completed. Once the rough cutting had been completed, sculpting and polishing could begin.

Early scholars estimated that some caves must have taken over 100 years to complete – Cave 11

A mural in monastery I depicting one of the previous births of the Buddha in which King Mahajanaka ritually cleanses himself before renouncing his wife and kingdom and becoming an ascetic.

involved the removal of over 350 cu. m (12,360 cu. ft) of solid rock. More recently, Vidya Dehejia has suggested that 15 years would have been sufficient. The rough surfaces of the new chambers were smoothed by application of a thick layer of earth mixed with rock grit or sand, vegetable fibres, paddy husks and grass. This surface was then sealed with limewash and finished off with the lavish murals. The outlines were drawn with charcoal, and the background filled before the detailed foreground was painted. The paints were ground natural materials bound with animal glue. Red and yellow were provided by ochre, white by kaolin, black by lampblack and blue by lapis lazuli.

Ajanta had a dual function as a residential monastery and a cult centre. Despite its secluded location, it attracted patronage from wealthy local rulers, court officials and commoners.

The murals, illuminated only by lamp light, allowed layfolk and the younger monks to be taught Buddhist traditions, and prepared them for the cycle of rebirth and death mirrored in the wonderful paintings of forests, cities, palaces and heavens.

People could only hope to obtain release from this cycle by meritorious actions. Such was evidently the hope of Charya of Sachiva, in his commendable gift of Cave 10: 'may whatever merit is in this, be for the release from miseries of all sentient creatures.'

A view of the Buddhist caves of Ajanta cut into the steep cliff face above the Waghora river.

The Pantheon at Rome

Time: AD 118–125
Location: Rome, Italy

Disegno angelico e non umano [a design of angels and not of man].

MICHELANGELO, 16TH CENTURY

FEW BUILDINGS in the western world have aroused such enthusiasm, or so much controversy, as has the Pantheon in Rome. Although the apparently simple combination of a spherically domed rotunda rising behind a grand temple façade has inspired countless buildings, from Palladio's *Il Redentore* in Venice to Thomas Jefferson's house at Monticello, Virginia, none has ever completely recaptured the dramatic impact of the original. Because of its enormous span the dome itself was also an object of emulation by ambitious archi-

Above **The Pantheon before the removal of the 17th-century bell towers in 1882.** *Below* **A remarkably accurate study by the late 19th-century architect Georges Chedanne.**

tects such as Sir Christopher Wren. The dome of Wren's St Paul's Cathedral in London is, however, only some 35 m (115 ft) in diameter compared with the Pantheon's 44 m (144 ft). In fact, the Pantheon remained one of the largest single-span domes until

A circle of light from the central oculus illuminates the coffered interior of the dome. The perspective effect of the receding stepped sides of the shallow coffers makes them appear deeper, but they have been shown to have no structural function.

the 20th century, well justifying its claim to be the greatest surviving masterpiece of Roman construction as well as of Roman architecture.

Although the Pantheon was to become, according to the plaque erected there by Pope Urban VIII in 1632, 'the most celebrated edifice in the whole world', it is only rarely mentioned in the ancient sources, and these are ambiguous about its appearance and function. The monumental inscription on the façade claims that it was built by Agrippa, the emperor Augustus' right-hand man, but the building we see today was the third Pantheon on the spot,

constructed by the emperor Hadrian (AD 117–138). The archaeological evidence for the earlier buildings is far from clear, but our literary sources speak of caryatids and bronze capitals from Syracuse which have no parallel in Hadrian's Pantheon.

As to its function, we have to rely on Cassius Dio, Roman consul in AD 229, who tells us that it was called the Pantheon either because it contained statues of all the gods or because its vaulted roof resembled the heavens (LIII 27), and that Hadrian used to conduct public business there (LXIX 7); he also tells us that the original Pantheon contained

Porch

Dimensions	34 × 20 m
	(115 × 67.5 Roman ft)
Height of columns	14.2 m (48 Roman ft)
Height of granite shafts	11.8 m (40 Roman ft)
Lower diameter of shafts	1.48 m (5 Roman ft)

Rotunda

Internal diameter	44.4 m (150 Roman ft)
Thickness of walls	6 m (20 Roman ft)
Height from floor to oculus	44.4 m (140 Roman ft)
Diameter of oculus	8.8 m (30 Roman ft)

statues of Julius Caesar and Augustus. Modern scholars are still undecided: temple to all the gods or dynastic monument to Augustus, imperial audience hall or symbol of the cosmos – the 'visible image of the universe', as the poet Shelley later called it – all are possible. Even in the Roman Republic it had been common for the Senate to meet in various temples, and the emperors continued this tradition. Neither was it unusual to place the emperor's image among the gods, or to associate it with cosmological symbols representing the emperor's place within the divine ordering of things. But the elusive quality of the interior space under the vast, centrally lit dome encourages each of us, like Michelangelo, to look for some mystical, ideally irresolvable, mystery at the heart of Rome's greatest building.

The dome

The structure of the Pantheon is as enigmatic as its function, and despite recent advances there is still no real consensus on how the dome was built or why it still stands. The whole of the 6-m (20 Roman ft) thick drum of the rotunda and its dome are made of high-quality Roman concrete, and sit on a ring of dense travertine concrete, 4.5 m (15 Roman ft) deep, which in turn rests on deep clay. The dome, 44 m (150 Roman ft) in diameter, is semicircular in shape on the interior and springs at a height of 22 m (75 Roman ft) above the floor, the lower two-thirds being decorated with five concentric rows of 28 coffers. On the exterior the profile is much shallower, because the drum of the rotunda continues to rise to a height of *c*. 30 m (*c*. 100 Roman ft), while the lower part of the emerging dome is further thickened by seven stepped rings, producing the familiar saucer-shaped profile which is such a land-

mark in modern Rome. The result is that the thickness of the dome reduces from 6 m (20 Roman ft) at its springing to 1.5 m (5 Roman ft) at the central oculus (the circular opening at the apex of the dome). The whole building also becomes lighter as it rises through the grading of the fist-sized pieces of aggregate, from travertine and tufa at 1750 kg per cu. m, to brick, and finally to very light tufa and pumice in the upper part of the dome, the unit weight there being 1350 kg per cu. m.

Early theories about how the dome worked imagined that it was an artificial monolith, like a giant teapot lid, and thus exerted no outward thrusts on the rotunda. According to this theory the changes in the make-up of the aggregate and the coffers were designed to reduce the downward pressure on the drum. The discovery in the 1930s of a series of vertical cracks in the lower part of the dome, which were clearly ancient, suggested instead that the dome was indeed tending to burst outwards under the influence of tensile stresses, and that the extra bulk of the outside of the rotunda and the stepped rings on the dome were designed as giant reinforcement hoops to prevent the base of the dome splaying outwards under its own enormous weight. The various attempts to lighten the upper part of the structure now became understood as ways of reducing the outward, rather than the vertical, thrust. Recently these theories have been put to the test by Robert Mark. Using a computer simulation, Mark tried to answer the question of how the Romans imagined the structure to work, concluding that the builders expected the dome to crack and treated it as a series of arches. The stepped rings were important elements in achieving stability by adding extra vertical loads, rather in the manner of Gothic pinnacles and flying buttresses, while lightening the dome reduced the outward thrust. The coffers, however, turned out to be purely decorative.

It is likely that the cracks in the dome, along with others lower down in the structure, developed during the construction process. One of the problems caused by the pozzolanic nature of Roman concrete is that it gives out heat while curing (like concrete made with modern Portland cements), thereby producing thermal stresses in the structure. The numerous hollows within the structure of the rotunda suggest that the Roman engineers had at least some understanding of the problem. As well as the seven columnar exhedrae (alcoves) and the doorway which divide the lower level of the rotunda into eight piers, each pier has a semicircular (or 'key') chamber concealed at its core, and this pattern is repeated in both the central attic zone and in the upper zone where the dome begins to rise. Hollowing out the structure in this way allows the drum to cure more quickly and evenly, without significantly reducing its capacity to support the dome.

The problems faced in erecting the dome also included that of providing wooden formwork to carry the weight of the concrete dome until it had developed enough strength to support itself. Some scholars imagine a whole forest of large timbers rising from the floor of the building, others a sophisticated and complex set of trusses cantilevered out from the cornice of the attic zone. In both cases the dome is imagined as rising in horizontal rings, requiring all the formwork to be in place at once. An alternative theory, inspired by the vertical cracks in the dome, is that it was put up in vertical segments, allowing a smaller amount of formwork to be moved horizontally once each segment could stand on its own.

A perfect compromise

While most of the interest in the construction of the Pantheon has centred on its dome, a recent theory has revealed how problems in the supply of materials may also have affected the overall appearance of the building. Ever since the Renaissance, architects have been troubled by the awkward juxtaposition of the relatively low porch, with its exceptionally high pediment, the rectangular intermediate block, and the rotunda. The giant granite columns of the porch, with their 11.8-m (40-Roman ft) shafts, may seem impressive today, but if replaced with shafts of 50 Roman feet all the difficulties and disjunctions in the façade would disappear. Columns of this height are much rarer, but were being used at the time of the Pantheon for the Temple of Deified Trajan, Hadrian's adopted father. Given that the columns came from the distant quarries of Mons Claudianus and Aswan in Egypt, it is easy to imagine a shortage in supply, or a disaster at sea along the way bringing one or other project to a halt. Piety seems to have won the day, leaving the Pantheon's architect to bring off a triumph of compromise to produce 'the most celebrated edifice in the whole world'.

The Pantheon dome appears quite shallow when seen from above, despite its semicircular profile inside. The extended drum and seven stepped rings add extra loads to the haunches of the dome which help ensure its stability.

The Earthworks of Newark, Ohio

Time: c. AD 250
Location: Newark, Ohio, USA

No despoiling hand has been laid upon them; and no blundering, hearty traveller has, to my knowledge, pretended to describe them.

CALEB ATWATER, 1820

CIRCLES AND SQUARES, octagons and causeways – the earthworks built by the Hopewell people of eastern North America bewilder the eye, especially when seen from the air. The Hopewell folk, named after a farm of that name in Ross County, Ohio, are best known to archaeologists for their flamboyant burial customs. Simple farmers, they devoted enormous communal resources to building earthworks and elaborate burial mounds. Some complexes, like that at Mound City, Ohio, covered areas equivalent to several New York City blocks, and greater than the base of the Pyramid of Khufu in Egypt (p. 21).

The Hopewell people cremated most of their dead, reserving lavish inhumation burial for prominent families, who wore finely decorated garments and ceremonial masks. In one Ohio mound, a man and woman wearing artificial noses fashioned of copper sheet lay side by side. The woman wore a robe adorned with thousands of fine shell beads. Hopewell artisans crafted magnificent hammered copper silhouettes of people and animals, and made superb ceremonial artifacts of mica and other exotic materials. Many of these artifacts were exchanged as ritual gifts with neighbouring leaders, as prominent individuals living near and far forged ritual and economic bonds that formed reciprocal ties of lasting significance.

In about AD 250, the Hopewell people living near the modern city of Newark, Ohio, embarked on a major earthwork construction project. Over several generations (the duration of construction is uncertain), they laid out an intricate maze of mounds, including an octagon, square and circles over 10.4 sq. km (4 sq. miles) of countryside. From the air, the Newark earthworks seem like a jumble which defies ready explanation, especially since much of the site now lies under a golf course. Fortunately for science, Victorian archaeologists Ephraim Squier

FACTFILE

Area	10.4 sq. km
Octagon dimension	24 ha

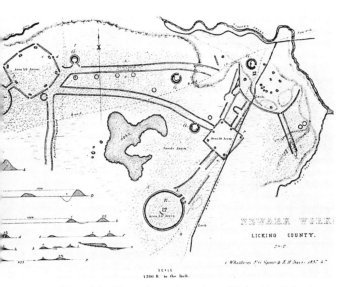

Above **Plan of the Newark earthworks, published by Ephraim Squier and Edwin Davis in 1848. Much of the site now lies under modern Newark, so this plan is a valuable source of information on the original layout of the earthworks.**
Below **Aerial photograph of the Newark octagon and a general view of the site, much of it now occupied by a golf course.**

and Edwin Davis surveyed the earthworks in the 1840s, when they were still largely intact. In recent years, physicist Ray Hiveley and philosopher Robert Horn have produced an accurate map of the much-disturbed monument. They found that the enclosures and mounds display great precision, with exact corners and precise astronomical orientation. For example, the Newark octagon, which covers 18 ha (44 acres) and has openings at each angle, was built with the aid of the diameter of the nearby circle. The 321.3-m (1054-ft) diameter 'Observatory Circle' is connected to the octagon. Hiveley and Horn studied the diameters of the circles, the sides of the octagon, and diagonals, in addition to the sides of the square, and calculated that the builders used an exact unit of measurement.

Astronomy at Newark

The Hiveley and Horn survey also provided clear evidence that the Newark earthworks were aligned with the heavenly bodies. Using astronomical tables, the two scholars calculated the azimuths for the rising and setting of the sun and moon in AD 250, the estimated building date. They compared these azimuths with earthwork features, axes of symmetry and special points such as the centres of earthworks, and found no evidence for solar alignments. However, the Newark octagon fits the northern and southern extremes of the rising point of the moon on the horizon, with a cycle of 18.61 years. The long walls of the octagon, 1.7 m (5.5 ft) high, would have allowed an observer to define precise azimuths within a quarter of a degree. Hiveley and Horn drew up tables which show that the axis of the avenue between the Newark octagon and a nearby circular earthwork marked five of the eight extreme lunar points with an accuracy of a half a degree, the observation points for these alignments being at four vertices of the octagon.

The Newark lunar alignments were probably accurate enough to be able to predict years with lunar eclipses near the winter or summer solstices. They also permitted the Hopewell inhabitants to monitor the monthly and 18.6-year lunar cycles. Some experts believe the octagon and square reflect a Hopewell concern not only with the burials of revered ancestors in mounds within the earthwork complex, but also with seasonal rituals governed by astronomical phenomena, as if the Hopewell people arranged their earthly environment to mirror the heavens.

The Buddhist Monastery at Paharpur

Time: 8th–9th centuries AD
Location: Paharpur, Bangladesh

The most remarkable ruin … an immense steep heap of bricks covered with bushes and crowned by a remarkably fine tree.

BUCHANAN HAMILTON, 1812

T HE 'MAHAVIHARA' or great monastery of Somapura at Paharpur is the largest single Buddhist monastery in South Asia and one of the greatest achievements of Buddhist brick architecture. Founded by the second Pala ruler, Dharmapala (AD 770–810), who ruled much of present-day Bengal and Bihar, its location, some 40 km (25 miles) west of his capital at Mahasthan, may be explained by the presence of earlier sacred structures. A 5th-century AD foundation inscription of a Jain monastery was found, as well as fragmentary structures below the central shrine and reused 5th-century AD Brahmanical stone images. Evidently this was already a site of special sanctity when Dharmapala decided to build his 'Somapura' or 'city of the moon' here.

Paharpur was planned and built as a single block, uniting residential cells with a central devotional focus. There are three main elements: the vihara (monastery), its courtyard and the central shrine. The vihara forms a hollow square measuring some

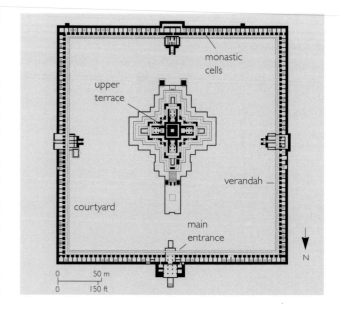

307 m (1007 ft) on a side, with 177 individual cells opening on to a verandah. Access is through the monumental entrance in the middle of the northern wall, a feature mirrored by similar monumental blocks in the other three walls. The second element, the courtyard, covers an area of 9 ha (22 acres) and contains a mass of structures ranging from models of the central tower, stupas and shrines to kitchens, refectories and residential buildings.

Near the middle of the courtyard stands the central shrine, originally towering 22 m (72 ft) above the surrounding buildings. It has a cruciform plan with recessed projecting corners and rises on a series of three massive terraces. Around it are galleries and halls containing images. Staircases lead to upper and lower levels within the shrine, but the summit is badly eroded. The heart of the shrine was a 22-m

FACTFILE

Overall		First terrace	
Present height	22 m	Height	3 m
Estimated height	30 m	Area	4825 sq. m
Area	9 ha		
Volume	34,155 cu. m	**Second terrace**	
		Height	4 m
Vihara		Area	2620 sq. m
Outer wall	307 × 307 m		
Number of cells	177	**Third terrace**	
		Present height	15 m
Courtyard		Estimated height	22 m
Area	9 ha	Area	400 sq. m
Central shaft			
Depth	22 m		
Area	12 sq. m		

Left **Plan of the Somapura monastery.** *Above* **View of the central shrine from the southeast corner of the courtyard. The four structures in the foreground are votive stupas.**

(72-ft) shaft sunk in the centre of the uppermost terrace, which once must have contained the relics over which the whole vast edifice was raised. Terraces and galleries are ornamented and enhanced by around 3000 terracotta plaques, while the lowermost wall is decorated with 63 stone reliefs of Brahmanical deities, a richness of decoration which bears witness to the importance of the monument.

Although largely the work of a single phase, the original monument was augmented by a series of remodellings, and many of the features in the courtyard are later additions. Some changes are connected with new devotional activities, but others indicate widening patronage. Royal patronage remained crucial, however, and when the new Sena rulers of Bengal withdrew their support from Buddhist establishments in the 12th century AD, the site was abandoned and slowly eroded to resemble a natural hill in the otherwise flat landscape.

Building in brick

The central shrine of Paharpur is a marvel of medieval engineering, being built entirely of bricks in mud mortar. Stone is almost unobtainable in the lower flood plain of the great rivers, the Ganges and the Brahmaputtra. Experiments in brick construction had already been attempted at Mahasthan in the preceding century. There, at the site known as Lakshindarer Medh Gokul, a height of 14 m (46 ft) had been reached by superimposing terraces, constructed of earth-filled brick cells set in mud mortar. These base units offered a cheap and effective substructure without running the risk of making the monument too heavy and unstable on the soft alluvial soil. This technique was perfected at Paharpur, where the three massive terraces reached a total height of some 30 m (98.5 ft).

Paharpur was not only a place of cult activity but also a place of learning. The decorative terracotta plaques of Paharpur may have had a particular teaching function: representing deities, plants and animals, and men and women, they offered a portrayal of the universe. Indeed, we can interpret the entire tower complex as a model of Mount Meru, the celestial centre of the universe, home of the king of the gods. Did Dharmapala hope to establish himself at the centre of such a perfect world with the creation of his own Meru? Certain it is that the Pala concept of a stepped or terraced tower-sanctuary at the centre of a square enclosure reached its florescence not in South but in Southeast Asia with Angkor Wat some four centuries later (p. 81).

The Buddhist Shrine of Borobudur

Time: 8th–9th centuries AD
Location: central Java, Indonesia

It resembles a badly-risen cake, of which the extent of its failure to rise is matched only by the overembellishment of its decoration.

ALBERT FOUCHER, 1909

OROBUDUR IS a spectacular step-pyramid, over 30 m (100 ft) high, consisting of nine superimposed terraces embellished with Buddha statues, perforated stupas, miniature stupas and bas-relief panels. While the first six terraces are square and diminish in size with height, the sixth acts as a plateau on which are set a further three circular terraces, on the uppermost of which is a small bell-shaped stupa. Richness of decoration and idiosyncracy of design conspire to make this a uniquely impressive monument to Buddhist belief in island Southeast Asia.

Built between the 8th and 9th centuries AD, the structure stands on the summit of a low hill at the

FACTFILE

Overall height	32 m
Original height of hill	27 m
Number of terraces	9

Decoration
Number of carved stones	1,600,000
Number of Buddha statues	504
Number of perforated stupas	72
Number of miniature stupas	1500

The bas-reliefs
Overall length of bas-reliefs	2.5 km
Number of bas-reliefs	1240

Basal terrace wall
160 scenes from the Karmavibhangga or 'treatise on the workings of the law of cause and effect'

First gallery
120 scenes from the Lalitavistara or life of the historical Buddha
500 scenes from the Jatakas and Avadanas or Buddhist birth stories

Second, third and fourth galleries
460 scenes from the Gandavyuha or pilgrim's progress of Buddhism

Above **Schematic cut-away through Borobudur showing construction details and foundations.**

edge of the Kedu plain in central Java. It is best known for its rich reliefs, which extend for 2.5 km (1.5 miles). The basal terrace wall, sealed by a later revetment, is decorated with reliefs depicting the Karmavibhangga, or 'treatise on the workings of the law of cause and effect'. Above this the four successive square terraces are each enclosed by a balustrade forming a gallery, again decorated with reliefs. The first gallery depicts scenes from the Lalitavistara, or life of the historical Buddha, scenes from the Jatakas and Avadanas, or Buddhist birth stories. The second, third and fourth galleries depict episodes from the Gandavyuha, or pilgrim's progress of Buddhism. Each balustrade is also provided with niches containing Buddha images. Access to the summit is by a series of ten short staircases at the four cardinal points. It has been suggested that originally the entire monument would have been brightly painted, as traces of blue, green, red and black paint as well as gold leaf have been found throughout.

The rival dynasties

Little is known of the history of central Java before the 9th century AD, but it was the core of a largely maritime empire which controlled the Khmer territories of islands and adjacent mainland between AD 760 and 800. Control of the empire was divided between, and probably contested by, two rival dynasties, the Sailendra and the Sanjaya, the former devotees of the Buddha (hence Buddhist), the latter of Siva (Hindu). Epigraphic evidence suggests that when the first phase of Borobudur was constructed in the last quarter of the 8th century AD, central Java was ruled by a Sailendran line but that by its final phase it was ruled by the Sanjaya.

De Casparis has proposed that the site can be identified with the terraced sanctuary founded by the late-8th-century AD Sailendra king Indra. This later received a donation of a village and lands from Queen Sri Kahulunnan, a Sailendra princess married to a Sanjaya king, in AD 842. Dumarcay, on the other hand, believes that the monument was actually founded by Indra's predecessor, Visnu (c. AD 775–784), but was later reconstructed by Indra (AD 784–792) and Samaratunga (AD 792–833), before being lightly remodelled by the Sanjaya dynasty.

Left **Detail of the lattice-work stupas containing Buddha images on the eighth terrace.**

Bas-reliefs from the first terrace, depicting *(above)* **the Buddha deep in meditation, and** *(below)* **an ocean-going vessel with outrigger. Such ships provided crucial links within the island empire of the Sailendras.** *Right* **An aerial view of the monument.**

The development of the shrine

Borobudur was substantially conserved between 1908 and 1911 in an attempt to correct tilting walls and settling floor surfaces. By 1973, however, these problems had reached epic proportions and a campaign was launched by UNESCO to save the monument. The project studied the geological, chemical and hydraulic fabric of the monument, and sank boreholes into it to explore its environment. This work allows us to understand its development and construction. There is now evidence that the hill on which the monument stands is the result of massive artificial reshaping. Originally a weathered core of volcanic rhyolite, 27 m (88 ft) high, it was transformed into a foundation by filling voids with silts, clays and even stone chips – presumably produced during the carving and trimming of building stones. In the process, the builders also constructed a series of partly natural and partly artificial terraces on which to raise their superstructure.

We now also know that although the monument may appear to be the result of a single phase of construction, it is in fact the outcome of four remodellings. During the first phase, *c.* AD 775, two terraces were built but the main superstructure was not completed. Next, in *c.* AD 790 balustrades were erected on the first and second terraces and the width of the staircases to the upper terrace was standardized. Some scholars also believe that a 42-m (138-ft) high stupa was erected on the top terrace. Shortly afterwards a third stage began, during which a revetment of 12,750 cu. m (450,000 cu. ft) was placed over the original base of the monument. This was an attempt to counteract the superstructure's horizontal slumping. During the third phase the stairs and pavements of the first and second galleries were remodelled and the remnants of the central

angles so that they fitted together extremely tightly. Mortise-and-tenon joints were used for the lattice stupas of the first and second circular terraces. A further technique was used on the upper galleries – blocks with uneven joint surfaces were placed intermittently as off-sets, thus further binding the structure. Despite such careful attempts at unifying the fabric, a number of key faults remained. Most crucial was the absence of major structural ties within the floors and walls. This meant that when water collected inside the structure, the fill slumped within the core.

A model of the universe

Borobudur was never intended as an isolated, monumental structure, but was constructed as a ritual focus for an adjacent vihara or monastery. While the remains of this complex have not yet been identified, a number of structures have been found 600 m (1970 ft) to the northwest, and a series of small stupas lies at the eastern foot of the hill. It is also quite possible that Borobudur was part of a major complex which included the nearby shrines of Candi Mendut and Candi Pawon. At one level it can be categorized as a highly ornate Buddhist stupa, but it represents more than a veneration of the Buddha's memory. A number of scholars have attempted to interpret it as a microcosm or model of the universe. From the nature and location of bas-reliefs, they have divided it into the three main zones of Buddhist cosmology. The sealed bas-reliefs of the first terrace and the scenes from the first gallery depict Kamadhatu, or the sphere of desires; the bas-reliefs of the second, third and fourth galleries depict Rupadhatu, or the sphere of (pure) forms; and the circular terraces depict Arupadhatu, or the sphere of formlessness. The central stupa represents the Buddha himself. Thus the monument symbolizes both a physical and a spiritual journey for the devotee.

It has also been suggested that Borobudur had the same microcosmic function as the step-pyramids of the Khmers. De Casparis has argued the name Borobudur can be translated as 'the mountain of virtue on the ten stages of the Bodhisattva' as well as 'the mountain which is terraced in successive stages' and 'kings of the accumulation of earth'. It may thus have represented the universe, Mount Meru and the Buddha, as well as being a powerful dynastic cult centre which symbolized the independence of the Sailendras.

stupa were levelled. In its place a further three elongated terraces, with openwork stupas containing Buddha statues, were constructed. A new central focus was provided in the form of a 10-m (33-ft) high stupa. During the final phase the new base was extended and minor alterations were made to the balustrade of the first gallery.

The monument is constructed of augite-andesite and basalt, stones of volcanic origin. As there are no outcrops in the immediate vicinity, it is likely that water-borne cobbles and boulders from the nearby river bed were used. This may explain the variability of colour, size, shape, composition and permeability of the cubiform blocks. On average they are 20 cm (7.9 in) high, between 30 and 40 cm (12 and 15.75 in) wide and no more than 30 cm (12 in) deep, small enough to be carried by hand. Bamboo scaffolding was used as indicated by circular holes in the pavement.

One of the most striking features is that the monument was built without mortar. In the first phase some blocks were joined by thin stone keys fitting into recessed double dovetail joints cut into adjacent blocks. During the second phase this technique was superseded by the use of blocks with extruding

Monk's Mound,

Cahokia

Time: c. AD 950–1050
Location: Cahokia, Illinois, USA

When I arrived at the foot of the principal mound, I was struck with a degree of astonishment,
not unlike that which is experienced in contemplating the Egyptian pyramids. What a stupendous
pile of earth!

HENRY BRACKENRIDGE, 1814

BETWEEN AD 800 and 1500, a series of powerful chiefdoms, known generically to archaeologists as the 'Mississippian', flourished in the southern and southeastern United States. Only strong religious beliefs, still little understood, linked Mississippian communities and the term 'Mississippian' covers a wide spectrum of societies, from minor chiefdoms to enormous ceremonial centres, the greatest being Cahokia on the eastern bank of the Mississippi near the modern city of East St Louis.

Cahokia lies in a pocket of extremely fertile Mississippi bottomland, where fish, game and wild plant foods once abounded. A series of small settlements coalesced rapidly into a growing ceremonial centre during the 10th century. At the height of its power, between AD 1050 and 1250, Cahokia covered

FACTFILE

Height	30.4 m
Dimensions	316 x 240 m
Area	6.4 ha

more than 13 sq. km (5 sq. miles). Well over 10,000 people lived in pole-and-thatch houses clustered on either side of an east–west ridge over an area of about 800 ha (1975 acres). More than 100 earthen mounds of various shapes and sizes line Cahokia's central precincts, most grouped around open plazas. The largest is Monk's Mound, which dominates the site and surrounding landscape.

Building Monk's Mound

Monk's Mound was built on four terraces, rising to a height of 30.4 m (100 ft). It measures 316 × 240 m (1037 × 790 ft), and covers 6.4 ha (16 acres). To erect this vast tumulus, the builders – probably teams of local villagers – heaped up more than 614,478 cu. m (21,700,000 cu. ft) of earth using simple wicker baskets. The mound was constructed in several stages, c. AD 950–1050, as part of a much larger ceremonial complex. Areas of silty clay were covered with coarser materials, providing internal drainage. Retaining buttresses incorporated into the structure of the mound were also placed externally along the south and west sides. The builders' success can be measured by the fact that for more than a thousand years no collapse occurred despite the instability of the materials and the enormous mass of the mound. Thatched temples may have stood on each stage

before the mound was enlarged. Monk's Mound is more than twice the size of any other Cahokia earthwork, so the building that once stood on its summit was probably the focus of the entire ceremonial complex.

Some of the other largest Cahokia mounds lie in two rows on either side of Monk's Mound, with a central plaza area immediately to the south. Most of these were platform mounds – flat-topped earthworks where important public buildings or elite residences of pole and thatch stood. Excavators believe that on some of the Cahokia mounds there were charnel houses, where the dead were exposed until their flesh decayed and their bones were interred. A large log palisade with watchtowers and gates surrounded the entire 80.9 ha (200 acres) of the central area, perhaps to isolate Monk's Mound and other ceremonial structures and high-status individuals from commoners.

Cosmological significance

Cahokia's layout is the earliest representation of a traditional southeastern native American cosmos, with four opposed sides reflected in the positions of Monk's Mound, lesser earthworks and the central plaza. Ethnographic and archaeological data suggest that the rectangular plaza was a plan of a four-sided

This artist's reconstruction of Cahokia's central precincts around AD 1100 looks northwards between the conical Roundtop burial mound and Fox Mound, a platform thought to have supported a mortuary temple. The two mounds face Monk's Mound and the central plaza.

cosmos with a primary north–south axis, perhaps divided into four quarters. Anthony Aveni believes Cahokia's rulers used the sun to schedule the annual rituals that commemorated the cycles of the agricultural year. This most important of all Mississippian centres was laid out to bring together the spiritual realms of fertility and life and also to validate living rulers, who were intermediaries with the supernatural realm. Cahokia's public rituals

unfolded in a symbolic, humanly created landscape where the bodies of select members of different kin groups were processed, then buried, thereby establishing a link between the living and the ancestors.

By pre-Columbian North American standards, Monk's Mound was an enormous structure and only part of a much larger ceremonial centre. The Mississippian earthworks are all the more stupendous when one reflects they were built by communities using the simplest of technologies. Cahokia's vast size was a reflection of the political and religious authority of its builders, of the fertility of its environment, and its strategic place astride major Mississippi trade routes. For two centuries, Monk's Mound stood at the spiritual and political centre of a complex native American world before fading into obscurity during the 13th century AD.

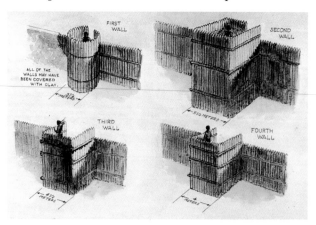

Left **The first version of the Cahokia palisade had round bastions, later reconstructions square ones; L-shaped entrances gave added security. The stockade surrounded the central precincts.** *Below* **Aerial photograph of Monk's Mound, showing the multiple platforms. The now much-eroded tumulus was built in stages, beginning around AD 950.**

The Mud Mosques of Timbuktu

Time: 14th–15th centuries AD
Location: Mali, West Africa

All the houses whereof are now changed into cottages built of chalke, and covered with thatch.
Howbeit there is a most stately temple to be seen, the walls whereof are made of stone and lime.

LEO AFRICANUS, 1600

THIS ADMITTEDLY inaccurate description of Timbuktu (in the modern West African state of Mali) was the first available in Europe and was written by Leo Africanus, a Spanish Moor and Christian convert whose travel narrative was translated into English in 1600. Since then Timbuktu has persevered as a metaphor for the remote, exotic and mysterious in the popular imagination.

Established as a terminus for camel caravans at the beginning of the second millennium, the city prospered through trade and acquired fame in the Muslim world as a centre of Islamic learning – a university city attracting scholars from far and wide. Teaching was focused on the mosques, visible statements of the wealth and Muslim identity of Timbuktu, which are among the finest examples of mud architecture in Africa, if not the world.

The foundation dates of the three main mosques are unclear: the historical sources are vague, and no archaeological research has yet been undertaken. Furthermore, the mosques have been repeatedly rebuilt over the centuries, both as the chequered history of Timbuktu brought changes in who controlled the city, and as congregation sizes and religious requirements changed. The most important mosque and initial foundation is the Djinguereber, which was possibly founded as early as the 13th century. Second in importance is the Sankore, which was the main centre of Muslim learning and was founded sometime between 1325 and 1433, the period of Mande or Malian control. A third mosque, the Sidi Yahya, is also important. It was founded c. 1440 but was extensively rebuilt in 'stone' (a hard

View of the interior of the Sankore mosque. Note the 'Timbuktu stone' wall on the left.

FACTFILE

Djinguereber
Possibly 13th century in origin
Alternatively attributed to Spanish architect al-Saheli and built in 1327
Dimensions
35 m (south wall) × 52 m (east) × 40 m (north) × 44 m (west)

Sankore
Built during the period of Mande or Malian hegemony (1325–1433)
Dimensions
Outer (if squared off) 31 m (south wall) × 28 m (east) × 31 m (north) × 31 m (west)
Inner courtyard 13 sq. m

Sidi Yahya
Built c. 1440 by a Timbuktu chief, Muhammad Naddi and named in honour of his friend the imam, Sidi Yahya.
Dimensions
30 m (south wall) × 31 m (east) × 31 m (north) × 30 m (east)
Minaret 9.3 × 8.4 m

The dominant material used in both the Sankore and Djinguereber is mud-brick – either rectangular and cast from a mould, or rougher hand-made tubes and spheres. These were laid in courses by the masons (although they largely work in mud, this is the locally used term), assisted – until the abolition of slavery – by slave labourers who transported clay in wicker baskets and water in calabashes under the supervision of an overseer. In contrast, the masons, the Gabibi, were freemen and form a distinctive guild or caste. Today repairs on the mosques are the focus of communal effort.

The inner mud-brick core was given a protective rendering of mud which was skimmed to a smooth surface with a trowel. In principle, the infrequent rains wash away this layer, but leave the inner wall intact. However, another historical source, the *Tedzkiret en Nisian*, records that the minaret of the Sankore collapsed in 1678, which was probably not an isolated instance. Excessive rainfall, infrequent maintenance, possibly compounded by an insecure political situation as often prevailed in Timbuktu, sand erosion and dune movement, are all destructive factors which have had to be countered.

'Timbuktu stone' (a hard clay mined in the desert) was also used in the mosques. More frequently, it was used in selected contexts, as in the Djinguereber where it was employed for the mihrab, and parts

clay referred to as 'Timbuktu stone') by the French in 1939 and thus does not really qualify as a 'mud mosque'.

Materials and techniques

Although the plans of the three mosques vary, certain elements recur. All possess the basic features of any mosque: the mihrab (prayer niche) and minaret (formerly used for the call to prayer), and a main prayer sanctuary giving on to a sahn (courtyard). Both the Sankore and the Djinguereber are built in the so-called 'Sahelian' style, with buttressed mud walls and flat roofs. They also have characteristic externally projecting and permanently fixed scaffolding poles, used to facilitate the annual rendering of mud to the usually tiered, pyramidal minaret. In all probability the Sidi Yahya was originally built in this style, as indicated by the core of the original mud minaret preserved within its more recent crenellated and French-built 'Timbuktu stone' casing.

Information on the actual design process is lacking, but one of the local chronicles, the *Tarikh el-Fettach*, tells how a Timbuktu notable, Cadi El-Aqib, who was responsible for rebuilding or restoring all three mosques in the late 16th century, measured the Ka'ba, the central shrine in Mecca, and transferred the dimensions to the Sankore mosque in Timbuktu. He recorded the length and breadth of Islam's holiest shrine on a length of cord; and once in Timbuktu he simply unravelled the cord and marked out the new courtyard dimensions based on the exterior measurements of the Ka'ba.

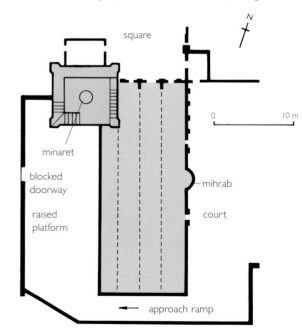

Plan of the Sidi Yahya mosque.

144

of the exterior particularly vulnerable to wind damage. Cut 'Timbuktu stone' was also utilized for the vaulted arches in the Djinguereber – arches which have been called true 'Roman' arches. This use of dressed 'stone' in Timbuktu sets the city apart from others in the region where stone, when employed, is frequently only roughly shaped, as in the stone towns of Mauritania.

Timbuktu's situation on the Sahelian–Saharan fringe means that good building timber is absent and has to be imported from more wooded regions to the south on the River Niger. To compensate for this the wood of the local palm was extensively employed in both the mosques and local houses. Roofs were constructed of split palm trunks, with pieces of wood set across the narrow spaces between the doum palm beams laid longitudinally between the pillars. Over this were

placed mats woven from doum palm fibre and above this in turn was a protective layer of the ubiquitous earth. Drainage from the flat roof was achieved through runnels made from pottery or from split doum palm set into the roof, allowing the water to drain off into the street below. These drains are now more often made of corrugated iron sheets or flattened sections of old oil cans. Lengths of acacia and other available wood were also used for the scaffolding poles set deep into the earthen walls, and timber was utilized for the few internal fittings such as the main door.

The splendour of the Timbuktu mosques lies in their simplicity. They lack the decoration frequently found in mosques elsewhere in the Muslim world – there are no tiles, ornate carved woodwork or massive hanging lamps, and where

Masons applying mud to the Djenne mosque as part of the regular communal maintenance.

145

A

B

C

Decoration on the interior of the Djinguereber mosque.
A **Design on each side of the mihrab;** *B* **design on a pillar
in front of the mihrab;** *C* **decoration around the mihrab.**

**Part of the Djinguereber mosque. The wooden poles are
permanent scaffolding, to facilitate annual maintenance.**

decoration is present it is restrained and simple.
Cast brick might be used to create lozenge patterns,
as in the Sankore mosque, or a plaster rendering was
applied and patterns were incised into this, as is
found in the Djinguereber. Similarly, the apex of the
minaret could be topped with an ostrich eggshell,
a symbol of the unity of Islam. But it is the projecting buttresses and mihrab niches, the pyramidal
minarets with their scaffolding stubble, and the
expanses of smooth or sun-crazed mud which are
the true beauty of the mud mosques of Timbuktu.

The builders themselves are largely anonymous.
Certain patrons or master architects might be
remembered but the generations of masons and
others who have built, rebuilt, renovated and per-
petuated these structures remain nameless. The
mud mosques of Timbuktu present a jigsaw puzzle
of elements old and new, imported and indigenous.
Formerly, too much emphasis was given to their
supposed North African or foreign Arab origins. In
particular, credit for the founding of the Djinguereber was given to a Spanish architect, al-Saheli, who
accompanied the Malian ruler, Mansa Musa, back
from *hajj* or pilgrimage to Mecca in 1327. However,
more critical analysis of the available evidence suggests that these mosques, the Djinguereber included, were indigenous foundations.

Future prospects

The significance of the mud mosques of Timbuktu
has recently been recognized and the city has been
listed as a World Heritage Site. Equally importantly
the mosques are still used as their original builders
intended, as places of Muslim prayer and study.
They are still very much focal points of community
identity and pride and continue to be cared for and
maintained. The centuries old 'evolution' of the
Timbuktu mosques, through repair and rebuilding,
thus continues.

146

The Great Temple
of the Aztecs

Time: c. AD 1325–early 1500s
Location: Tenochtitlan (Mexico City)

In the year after the foundation of Tenochtitlan, the Mexicans established the great and ever-expanding Temple of Huitzilopochtli, and it grew very large, because each succeeding Mexican king added a new layer to it, and so the Spaniards found it, high and strong, and splendid to see.

HISTÓRIA DE LOS MEXICANOS POR SUS PINTURAS, C. 1536

CORTÉS AND HIS men were certainly impressed by the massive Great Temple of the Aztecs (Templo Mayor), the principal ritual structure in the city of Tenochtitlan. It was truly an effigy mountain, a fitting home for gods. The pyramid's base was almost square, about 80 m (261 ft) on a side; its summit, over 30 m (100 ft) above the city, was reached by ascending the 113 steep steps of one of the twin staircases on the western side of the pyramid. On the summit were twin shrines dedi-

The myth of the founding of Tenochtitlan as illustrated in a 16th-century document. An eagle with its prey, perched on a cactus growing on a rock, was the sign given by the gods for the site of the city.

cated to Huitzilopochtli, the city's patron deity, and Tlaloc, a water and fertility god. In front of them, was an open-air space 44 m (143 ft) across, where rituals including human sacrifice were performed.

The pyramid the Spaniards marvelled at is today known as Stage VII because it superseded – and enclosed – a solid block of superimposed structures, beginning with Stage I. This earliest Great Temple was dedicated in the early 14th century, the first building in the newly founded city of Tenochtitlan. The gods had marked the site for the city on a marshy island with the sign of an eagle on a cactus on a rock, now the central motif of the Mexican flag. This was the location of the first temple's earthen platform and thatched shrines, which were enlarged and rededicated in increasingly permanent form.

FACTFILE

Stage I, built at or before dedication of city c. AD 1325
Base significantly less than 17 m E–W, 34 m N–S
Materials probably mud platform with perishable shrine, or shrines, of thatch
Known only from textual references

Stage II, rebuilding c. 1390
Base c. 17 m E–W, c. 34 m N–S
Materials stone facing over gravel and lake mud conglomerate – as in later stages
Only complete version of pyramid extant

Stage III, rebuilding c. 1431
Base c. 40 m E–W, c. 45 m N–S
Only staircases largely intact

Stage IV, rebuildings c. 1454 and c. 1469
Base c. 55 m E–W, c. 60 m N–S
Sculpture of Coyolxauhqui embedded at foot of stairs

Stage V, rebuilding early 1480s
Very few remains

Stage VI, rededication 1487
Base c. 75 m square
Few remains

Stage VII, rebuilding early 1500s
Base 83.5 m E–W, 76 m N–S; height to summit 30.7 m
Only parts of platform paving survive

Left **Stone sculptures of standard-bearers found reclining against the stairway of the Stage III temple leading to Huitzilopochtli's shrine.** *Right* **Reconstruction of the Great Temple.**

I **Shrine to Tlaloc**
2 **Chacmool figure**
3 **Shrine to Huitzilopochtli**
4 **Sacrificial stone**
5 **Coyolxauhqui stone**

Tenochtitlan, the Aztec capital, was the largest city in the Americas in AD 1519 and, as Mexico City, it still is today. In 1519, from the Gulf Coast to the Pacific, millions paid tribute to the rulers of Tenochtitlan, amounting to vast quantities of precious and utilitarian goods and the labour service of hundreds of thousands of commoners. Like great lords everywhere, Tenochtitlan's rulers displayed their wealth ostentatiously, building lavish palaces for themselves and monumental temples and ritual precincts for their gods.

In the centre of Tenochtitlan's quadripartite grid was the main ritual precinct, a huge square roughly 500 m (1631 ft) on a side, crowded with dozens of temples, dormitories and shrines. Major causeways and canals extended from it in the cardinal directions. The Great Temple faced west across this precinct and was the city's civic and ceremonial

At the foot of the main stairs lay a giant circular stone carved with an image of the goddess Coyolxauhqui, sister of the principal Aztec god, Huitzilopochtli.

The temple was continually rebuilt over a period of some 200 years, each new stage completely burying and covering the last. The shrines to Tlaloc (on the left) and Huitzilopochtli (right) dominated the structure.

focus, located on a geographic and cosmological axis that linked the earthly domain with higher and lower levels of the sacred universe as well as with an expanding Aztec empire. South of the precinct was (and is) the city's main plaza, and facing the plaza on the east side was Motecuzoma's palace, now the site of the Mexican National Palace.

Destruction and rediscovery of the Great Temple

After the Conquest in 1521, the Spanish made deliberate efforts to pull down the temple – which they considered a centre of devil worship. Further destruction was caused by the reuse of its stone to build Mexico City, and by the looting of its offerings. The pyramid gradually eroded into a rough mound about 5 m (16 ft) high, known as 'the Hill of the Dogs' because the city's mongrels congregated there during floods. In time, houses were built on the site, and the Great Temple's exact location became a matter of scholarly speculation.

Then, in 1978, utility workers digging in this area happened upon a massive sculpture of Coyol-

xauhqui, the sister of Huitzilopochtli, Tenochtitlan's patron deity. Clearly, this sculpture was part of the Great Temple itself, and modern Mexico was inspired by the unearthing of this important buried cultural treasure. A research team directed by Eduardo Matos Moctezuma and supported by the Mexican nation began a long-term project that has made the Great Temple one of the world's most accessible and impressive archaeological sites.

Design and construction

The pyramid was solid except for small offering cists. This lack of interior rooms simplified the overall design and construction, but caused its own complications. The structure's enormous weight meant that it sank into the spongy subsoil of the island. Archaeological excavation has uncovered some Aztec solutions to the problem. Repeated rebuilding was itself a way of raising the structure's ground level, and Aztec civil engineers stabilized the foundations by driving stakes into the soft ground and surrounding them with small pumice stones, lending strength with less weight.

The Aztecs were innovative civil engineers, designing sophisticated hydrological projects using technology far simpler than that of the Old World. Lacking effective cutting tools of metal, the ancient Mexicans achieved refined results in masonry and

Artist's reconstruction of the Great Temple and other buildings in the ceremonial precinct of Tenochtitlan.

stone sculpture by cutting with tools of even harder stone, and sawing with string, water and sand. Construction materials were transported to the Great Temple by human porters and by canoe, because indigenous peoples of the Americas had no wheeled vehicles, nor were there beasts of burden in Mexico.

Like all Aztec temples, the Great Temple was painted in bright colours. The paint was applied to stucco overlying a layer of cut stone slabs set into aggregate fill made of volcanic gravel and mud from the lake. Stone tenons, embedded into the fill, helped to stabilize the outer sheath of stucco. Beneath these layers was the outer stuccoed surface of the previous temple, and so on.

Life-size terracotta sculpture of an eagle warrior, found in the Stage V temple.

Building stages

The deepest excavation revealed Stage II, surmounted by the surviving wall bases of twin shrines. Stage II may date from the era of the founding of Tenochtitlan's noble dynasty, and divine right to rule was aptly demonstrated by the impressive stone and stuccoed rebuilding of the original perishable temple. At this time Tenochtitlan was still tributary to another town but it rebelled in about 1430, taking over the regional tribute system. Stage III, a substantial rebuilding, may date from 1431 and celebrate Tenochtitlan's power to demand timber, stone, lime and labour crews as tribute payments and gifts to honour the city and its gods.

The 1450s brought floods and famine to the city. Rulers remitted tribute payments and opened the city's granaries, but also used their largesse to fund work on their palaces and temples. Stage IV may date from 1454, a product of these public works projects. Offerings of child sacrifices near the Tlaloc shrine perhaps represent special appeals for the water god's favour. One of the temple's most impressive offerings is a set of near-life-size stone sculptures of standard-bearers, leaning against the Stage III steps up to the Huitzilopochtli shrine, and covered by Stage IV's fill and stone facing.

Stage IVb, a rebuilding of the western side, included the Coyolxauhqui stone, associated with funeral urns perhaps related to the death of Motecuzoma I (AD 1440–1469). By this time Tenochtitlan had become the most powerful city in ancient Mexico, and income was drawn from tribute provinces within and beyond the Valley of Mexico.

Stage V, from the early 1480s, left few remains. Stage VI may date from 1487 and represent a well-documented rebuilding, commemorated by the most elaborate and costly ceremony in pre-Columbian Mexico, when over 80,000 people died on sacrificial altars at the pyramid's summit. The city was at the peak of imperial power and to celebrate the new Great Temple the ruler called for urban renewal of the city's canals and extensive gardens.

Little remains now of the other enlargements to the temple made prior to 1519, but the temple and city impressed all who saw them. Behind the temple pyramid, two snow-covered volcanoes dominated the southeastern sky, and were echoed by the two shrines atop the urban mountain of Tenochtitlan. The city was a verdant marvel of intertwined lake and land, raying out in a turquoise net from the Great Temple that anchored earth in its place.

Detail of the Coyolxauhqui stone, showing the severed head of the goddess, discovered at the foot of the Stage IV temple.

Palaces, Baths & Arenas

PALACES AND PLEASURE play a memorable role in the imaginary ancient world immortalized by the Hollywood epic. It is not surprising that those who ruled over great kingdoms and mighty empires wished to lead lives of comfort in settings of splendour. Yet these were more than simple indulgences. The palace of the ruler was the stage-set in which he or she presented him- or herself to courtiers, visitors and subjects. Such was the purpose of the vaulted hall which survives as the Arch of Ctesiphon, until very recently taller and wider than any other structure of its kind. The mighty vault, and the colossal engineering achievement which it represents, expressed the power and ambition of the Sasanian emperors who sat enthroned beneath it. Most palaces also contained public or semi-public areas, such as courts or arenas. It is often imagined that the bull-leaping rituals depicted in Minoan frescoes were performed in the great courtyards at Knossos.

The planning and decoration of palaces was a crucial element of royal propaganda. It shows us how the rulers wished to be perceived – whether as mighty hunters, indomitable warriors or dutiful servants of the gods. At the same time, such scenes show how the palaces were used. The well-planned propaganda of the Assyrian palace at Nineveh has depictions of torture and execution of rebels in the very rooms where visiting foreign delegations were received. The palace reliefs at Persepolis carry a more peaceful message but equally persuasive: the tribute delegations from every corner of the empire

The ornate podium of the Persian royal palace at Persepolis in Iran, with finely carved reliefs conveying a carefully composed message of imperial power.

bearing local produce and emphasizing its vast extent and variety.

Palaces are not private places though they may contain private apartments, and those of considerable luxury. For early Roman emperors, the ideology of the palace was a contentious theme, and less successful rulers were criticized for the way they shut themselves off from the people. Augustus, the first emperor, forbore to build a palace at all. Later emperors indulged themselves on a lavish scale; the palatial villa of Hadrian near Tivoli extended over no less than 120 ha (296 acres). Yet the emperors also went to great expense to create grandiose settings at Rome itself in which they could appear to their subjects, such as the Colosseum, where each rank in Roman society had its allotted place among the tiers of seats. They also paraded imperial patronage by building luxurious public pleasure complexes such as the Baths of Caracalla.

Not all seats of power conform easily to our modern notions of a palace. Each of the palace compounds of Chan Chan in Peru began as the residence of a Chimú ruler but became his burial place at death, retaining its role as administrative centre of the deceased's extensive estates. Great Zimbabwe in southern Africa falls still less comfortably into our category. Although the impressive enclosures formed part of the Shona capital, it is not possible to say with confidence what each area was used for.

Such massive structures are triumphs of ancient engineering, and have survived rather better than most palaces. For, lacking the sanctity associated with religious structures, and built for this lifetime rather than generations to come, palaces and pleasure domes have fared less well than temples and tombs. Many were reduced to mere piles of mudbrick when archaeologists first came upon them. Yet careful exploration has revealed how they were built and used. Palaces could be at one and the same time storehouses, craft centres, administrative hubs and residences of luxury. They might be home to royalty, courtiers and households of enormous size. They might have gardens attached, or be built in a vast garden setting. The fabled Hanging Gardens at Babylon were one such, as were the gardens of Sennacherib's 'Palace without Rival' at Nineveh. Further east, in Sri Lanka, the great South Asian tradition of palace gardens found early expression around the rock-citadel of Sigiriya. Such structures enter very properly among the greatest examples of human achievement, and challenge us to comprehend how they were created. Technology in the service of elites is no less impressive when directed to palaces and pleasure than to temples or tombs.

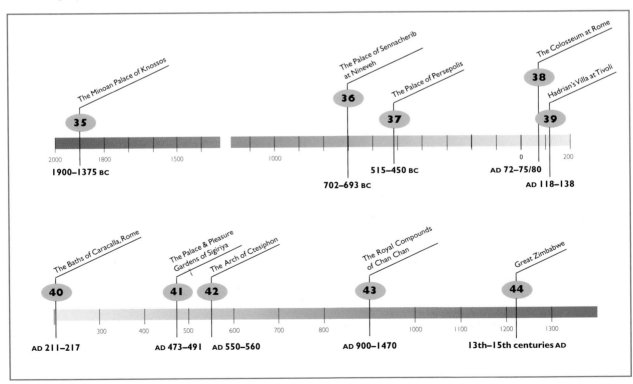

The Minoan Palace of Knossos

Time: 1900–1375 BC
Location: Crete, Greece

…the whole is still inspired with Minos' spirit of order and organization, and the free and natural art of the great architect Daedalos. The spectacle indeed, that we have here before us is assuredly of world-wide significance.

SIR ARTHUR EVANS, 1939

GREEK LEGENDS tell of King Minos, the labyrinth and the Minotaur, but it was only in this century that archaeologists began to put flesh on these bones with the discovery of the palace from which Minos himself might have ruled. The site lies at Knossos, some 5 km (3 miles) south of Heraklion on Crete. With its complicated plan of passages, staircases and hidden rooms, the palace is indeed suggestive of a labyrinth like that in which the Minotaur might have been contained. In sober reality, however, these are the remains of a ritual, residential and administrative complex, whose inhabitants enjoyed accomplished and brightly coloured wall paintings and sophisticated plumbing. It is such features that make the palace of Knossos one of the most outstanding ruins of the ancient Mediterranean, the pre-eminent example of Minoan architecture. Although other large Minoan palaces are to be found on Crete – Phaistos, Mallia

The Grand Staircase at Knossos. Now reconstructed in concrete, the columns with their characteristic downwards taper were originally fashioned from local trees.

and Zakros – Knossos was the largest, covering an area of 20,000 sq. m (215,285 sq. ft), and seems to have held a high degree of supremacy in Minoan religious, administrative and economic affairs.

The first palace was laid out in *c.* 1900 BC on the remains of a Neolithic settlement. It consisted of separate blocks of buildings, which were joined some time during this first phase. What is visible today are the remains of the succeeding period when the palace was rebuilt on an even grander and more impressive scale, beginning around 1700 BC. Skilfully adapted to the naturally sloping terrain, the palace was built on different levels linked by monumental stairways, with light wells, or small sunken courtyards, allowing light and air to circulate throughout the maze-like complex. Another characteristic feature of Minoan architecture was the system of pier-and-door partitions, by which large rooms could be divided or opened out, as desired.

FACTFILE

Before c. 3000 BC	Neolithic settlement at Knossos
3000–1900 BC	Early Minoan settlement
1900–1700 BC	First palace at Knossos built
1700–1450 BC	Palace rebuilt following earthquake
Second Palace Period	
1450 BC	Mycenaean conquest of Knossos
1375 BC	Fall of prehistoric Knossos
Area of Palace	20,000 sq. m

Complex	Location	Approx. no. rooms
Magazines	west, northeast	25
Ritual rooms	west	8
Grand Staircase	southeast	
Domestic quarters	southeast	8
Pottery & stone workshops	north	7

The palace was divided into four distinct sections surrounding a large central court. To the west were storage magazines for items such as oil, wine and grain. Between these magazines and the court were rooms reserved for ritual activities. In the southeast a great staircase led to two upper floors of reception rooms and domestic quarters. To the south was a processional corridor, along which visitors arrived. Pottery and stone workshops were located in the north and in the northeast additional store-rooms and workshops occupied the ground floor, above which was a large reception hall. Frescoes decorated some of these walls, being reserved for the most important rooms.

Above **The Priest King fresco (also known as the Prince of the Lilies) was found in fragments near the southeast entrance to the Palace and was restored by Evans.** *Left* **The North Entrance, reconstructed, and bull fresco.**

Building materials

The entire palace was constructed of either large ashlar stones or rough blocks which were carefully plastered. Large wooden beams framed sections of the wall and were also used in ceilings. Over these stone slabs were laid. The materials used to build the palace were found locally: gypsum and limestone were quarried on nearby hills, cypress wood was abundant, as was clay. Wherever stone was used for building walls it was dressed and fitted tightly or covered with a thick layer of plaster, sometimes painted red. Local limestone was the most widely used stone, in particular a grey-blue variety. It was carved to form pillars, column bases, door and window facings, walls, stairs and pavements. Gypsum was used for similar purposes but because of its solubility in water it was reserved mostly for the interior.

Gypsum was easier to work than limestone and was extracted readily from Gypsadhes Hill overlooking Knossos. Guidelines were marked out and stones lifted from beds with wedges and levers. It was then cut by saw and where exposed covered with a layer of plaster. Thin sheets of alabaster, a variety of gypsum, were used as veneer for facing walls and floors of the most prestigious rooms. It was cut in sheets as large as 1.8 m (6 ft) and as thin as 2.5 cm (1 in). Quarries also produced chalk for the stucco that was used to face rough limestone walls.

Timber was used as a frame to support walls and at the same time helped to absorb shocks caused by earthquakes. It was also used for columns, with their characteristic downwards taper, ceilings, roof beams, the flooring of upper storeys, doors and stairs. Clay secured courses of building stones and in the form of bricks formed walls of upper storeys. A watertight clay was used to protect and seal the roof from rain. Clay was also fired into terracotta pipes, each measuring 60–75 cm (24–29.5 in) and tapered to fit into each other. A lime mortar sealed the joints. These pipes carried water to different parts of the palace and large stone drains carried it out. Drains were laid out early on, at the foundation stage of building.

The whole building operation was organized and methodical. The palace was laid out along grid lines and a standard unit of measurement, the Minoan foot (30.36 cm or 11.94 in), was used to map out façades and central court. Quarrymen, masons, plasterers, woodworkers, bricklayers and general labourers would have been involved. Men to fell and trim trees, transport materials and mix plaster and mortar were also required.

The palace was not built in one phase, but evolved over time. Its architectural history is complicated but it appears that considerable parts of the palace were restored or rebuilt following earthquakes and fire. Knossos survived further changes, but in c. 1375 BC, after a severe destruction, most of the inhabitants abandoned the site, leaving the palace in ruins.

Following the rediscovery of the site in the 1870s, the palace was partially reconstructed by its excavator, Arthur Evans, in the early 1900s. This restored some of the vanished timber elements to give an impression of the elegant features and bright colours of the palace as it was in its heyday, with frescoed walls and tapering columns.

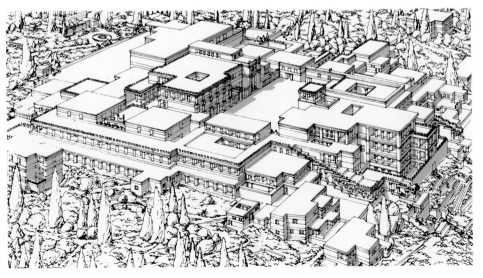

Artist's reconstruction of the palace of Knossos: a large complex of rooms on several storeys arranged around a central courtyard. The whole structure was adapted to the naturally sloping terrain.

The Palace of Sennacherib at Nineveh

Time: 702–693 BC
Location: Nineveh, Iraq

By a rough calculation, about 9880 feet, or nearly two miles, of bas-reliefs, with twenty-seven portals, formed by colossal winged bulls and lion-sphinxes, were uncovered in that part of the building explored during my researches.

A.H. LAYARD, 1853

BYRON'S CELEBRATED description of the Assyrian war-machine – 'The Assyrian came down like the wolf on the fold' – is familiar to many. Fewer know that Sennacherib, king of Assyria (705–681 BC), like many absolute rulers, was a man of outstanding judgment and ingenuity, who set out to unite the Middle East by ideology rather than simple terror. At the heart of his empire was the ancient city of Nineveh, which he transformed into a metropolis whose magnificence was to astonish the civilized world. And at the heart of Nineveh lay the new royal palace.

This palace reflected not only Sennacherib's imperial aspirations but also the peculiarly difficult circumstances he had faced on becoming king of Assyria. His father had just been killed in a frontier war; the empire, laboriously expanded over 40 years and now stretching from central Iran to the borders of Egypt, was threatened by rebellion and external interference. His very position as king was vulnerable. In four years of intensive campaigning, however, he eliminated these threats and by 701 BC was free to concentrate on building the future.

Left **The citadel of Nineveh, with Sennacherib's Southwest Palace at the southern end. Areas shown in brown denote excavated sections.** *Below* **A relief showing the southwestern façade of Sennacherib's palace, with bronze column-bases in the shape of lions and human-headed winged bulls behind.**

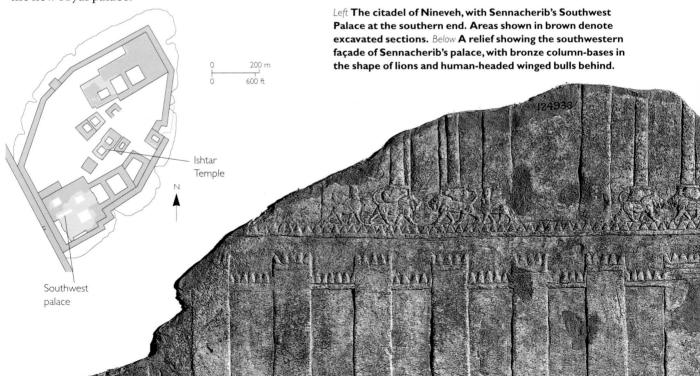

Ishtar Temple

N

Southwest palace

124938

Height of foundation	c. 22 m
Additional height of walls	c. 20 m
Groundplan	503 × 242 m
Number of rooms excavated	approx. 120
Number of rooms unexcavated	at least 100
Number of colossal doorway figures	approx. 120
Weight of largest colossal figures	c. 30 tonnes
Length of carved stone panelling	at least 3 km

Building the palace

By then Sennacherib had acquired innumerable prisoners-of-war from Babylonia, southern Turkey, Palestine and elsewhere. They provided the forced labour without which his projects would have been impossible to realize: they quarried stone, created a vast new city wall and excavated canals many miles long to bring water for the gardens of Nineveh. It was the palace itself, however, that was the crowning achievement. Cuneiform inscriptions, written on memorial documents of baked clay buried in its foundations, give extensive details of how it was built, confirming and amplifying what archaeologists have found there.

A previous palace had stood on the site, and we are given its dimensions in Assyrian cubits. We know that these were slightly over 50 cm (19.7 in) each, and so we can calculate that it measured some 200 × 66 m (656 × 216 ft). This old structure was decrepit: the ferocious rains of the Assyrian spring were eroding its foundations and exposing graves in the adjacent mound. Sennacherib expanded the site, reclaiming land from the adjoining river. As his building records range in date from 702 BC when the palace was little more than an idea to 693 BC when it was finished, we can follow its development.

The problem of floodwater was resolved by a massive foundation of limestone blocks. On this was laid a platform of mud-bricks – clay bricks tempered with straw and left to dry in the sun. Unimpressive as it sounds, this material has remarkable qualities, and even the walls of the palace were built of it. It provides enviable insulation against heat and cold, and with proper maintenance can stand for centuries. By about 697 BC the platform measured some 385 × 212 m (1260 × 695 ft) on its longest sides, and its height was 180 brick-courses, about 22 m (72 ft). This means that somewhere in the region of 107 million bricks were used. This figure is approximate, but it gives some impression of the sheer scale of the operation. Between 697 and 693 BC the site

was still further expanded, to reach a total of 503 × 242 m (1650 × 795 ft).

Appearance and decoration

Sennacherib named his building the Palace Without Rival, and there had been nothing like it in the world before. We can envisage a traveller from the cities of the Levant looking east across the River Tigris, and staring with amazement at the city walls 25 m (82 ft) high with a palace façade towering another 20 m (65 ft) or more above: an Assyrian carved wall panel shows us what the visitor saw. Three main gates punctuated the façade, and in

Left **Artist's reconstruction of the throne room of Sennacherib at Nineveh.** *Below* **Every room in the state apartments had alabaster panels showing the achievements of the king. Here Sennacherib sits on a fine throne in a rocky landscape.**

front of each was a portico supported by a pair of giant columns. Every column-base was bronze, in the shape of two striding lions, and these 12 lions were a wonder in themselves. Traditional hollow-casting by the lost-wax technique was simply unsuitable for things of this size, and Sennacherib himself, or one of his engineers, invented a new technique. Molten metal was poured into a mould and successfully cooled as one solid mass. Two of the columns were also of bronze. Others were single wooden shafts, made from the tallest trees that could be found, cedars cut in the mountains of Lebanon, and transported 800 km (500 miles) over-

land and by river to Nineveh. Elaborately decorated with inlay and overlay of gold and silver, they were crowned by capitals in the Aeolic style. Above, meeting the sky, crenellations gleamed with lines of brilliant blue glazed brick.

Huge human-headed winged bulls of alabaster dominated the façade behind the columns. Magical spirits, these deterred enemies and bad luck, looking aggressively in every direction at once. There were at least 12 of them approaching or flanking the grand façade, and over 100 bulls or sphinxes in other doorways of the palace. The façade examples were about 4 m (13 ft) high and weighed about 30 tonnes

Sennacherib in a rickshaw watches a colossal human-headed winged bull being dragged across country on a sledge for erection at his palace.

apiece. Sennacherib proudly records how previous kings had great difficulty bringing such colossal figures from quarries across the Tigris: it was necessary to wait for the spring floods and even then the workmen hauling the loads were frequently injured. Sennacherib, however, found a similar quarry on the near side of the river.

A series of carved wall-panels in the palace itself shows just how difficult the journey still was. Once a huge block of stone had been excavated by pick-axe, roughly shaped to reduce its weight, and loaded on to a sledge, it had to travel some 50 km (30 miles) across rough terrain to Nineveh. It had then to be hauled 20 m (65 ft) up to the level of the palace. The heavy labour was done by prisoners-of-war, under Assyrian foremen. Some levered up the back of the sledge, others rushed to insert rollers beneath it, hundreds more tugged on ropes at the front. Officials on the bulls shouted instructions by megaphone; Sennacherib himself inspected the work.

Our visitor had then to pass through city and citadel gates before finally entering the palace through the main entrance on the far side. Two or three outer courtyards then followed, which were surrounded by stores and service buildings, minor government offices and quarters for the royal body-guard. Eventually the visitor was confronted, in the innermost courtyard, by the throne-room façade, where Sennacherib presided on state occasions. Behind it was a further elaborate complex of rooms and courtyards, including the main state apartments where an army of bearded officials, eunuchs and aspiring courtiers bullied and prevaricated. To one side lay the quarters of the women of the royal household, with their own guard of eunuchs. No visitor was allowed to enter here.

In every major room brightly painted wall-panels of carved alabaster displayed the campaigns and achievements of the Assyrian king. And if these were not impressive enough, the results spoke for themselves: exotic stones came not from Assyrian quarries but from the far corners of the empire; other colossal figures and wall-panels had been floated downstream from the mountains of the north; gold was everywhere; the doors, ceilings and furniture were made of aromatic woods and ivory; rich carpets covered the floors. Even the plumbing was extraordinary, with water channelled through Archimedean screws. Gifts and treasures were sent or looted from all over the Middle East. For those who saw it this building was not merely the finest of its time; it was the centre of the universe.

Demise and discovery

For 50 years the palace of Sennacherib remained the heart of the Assyrian empire. Then a later king built himself a palace elsewhere, and in 612 BC Nineveh was sacked and the building went up in flames. But its platform and mud-brick walls were immune to fire. In 1850 archaeologists tunnelling in semi-darkness deep in the modern mound of Kuyunjik were guided by half-burnt alabaster wall-panels running like a maze for 3 km (2 miles) or more; half the palace is still waiting to be explored. The carvings found their way to museums the world over, but the solid stone foundations of Sennacherib's palace, built to withstand the spring floods of the 7th century BC, still rest intact beneath the ruins.

The Palace of Persepolis

Time: c. 515–450 BC
Location: Persepolis, Iran

Everything is devoted, with unashamed repetition, to a single purpose, viz. the delineation of majesty in its most imperial guise, the pomp and panoply of him who was well styled Great King.

LORD CURZON, 1892

THE FIRST Persian empire flourished between the 6th and 4th centuries BC. Its dominions stretched from the Indus to the Nile, and in central Iran, at the heart of the empire, stood Persepolis, 'city of the Persians'. Its palaces are breathtaking monuments to imperial self-confidence and vanity. They were also some of the most splendid ever built.

Today the principal ruins of Persepolis appear as a high stone-walled terrace supporting columns and occasional colossal stone doorways, backed by mountains and overlooking a fertile plain; royal tombs are cut into the cliffs and a stone fire-temple stands nearby. Originally the terrace supported a series of buildings most of which were constructed over 60 or 70 years, about 515–450 BC; while there was some evolution, the evidence of substructures such as drainage channels suggests that they largely

follow an original design laid down by the founder, Darius I. The main buildings were columned halls, with mud-brick external walls that have now disappeared. Some stood on platforms of their own, with façades of columned porticoes and stairways.

The most imposing building, and one of the earliest, was the Apadana of Darius I, c. 110 m (361 ft) square and with stone columns 20 m (66 ft) high. It can only have been used for grand formal ceremonies or receptions, since it simply consists of one enormous room, corner towers and a few service apartments. The royal court was resident at the city of Persepolis for only part of the year, and even then the king probably lived in a palace below the terrace. It is possible that the Apadana was the site of a

The Persian king, surrounded by officials of his court, perhaps presiding over the annual ceremony at Persepolis.

single great annual ceremony, when the peoples of the empire brought their tribute to the king. In addition, there were also treasuries and store-rooms on the Persepolis terrace, and quarters for guards. Other large columned halls may equally have been used only on special formal occasions.

Stone carvings on the walls of the platforms and staircases illustrate the delivery of the tribute. The artistic resources of the Persian empire were utilized for the building of Persepolis, and craftsmen came from far afield. Some of their places of origin are listed in ration documents: Egyptians, Ionian Greeks and Carians from what is now western Turkey, Babylonians, and Hittites or Syrians.

The quarry
While some of the finest stone had to be transported 40 km (25 miles), much of Persepolis was built of a grey limestone found in quarries near the site. Tools such as iron picks, punches and sledge-hammers were used to isolate a block with grooves, and it was

Above **The terrace at Persepolis, with the Apadana in the centre.** *Left* **Plan of the palace at Persepolis, with buildings of different phases.**
1 The Apadana.
2 Main stairway.
3 Stairway to Apadana.
4 Offices and store-rooms.
5 Hall of 100 columns.

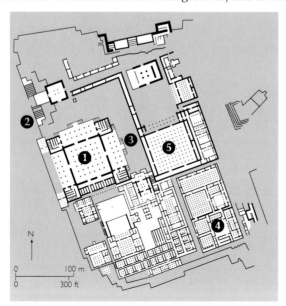

Right **The stairs to the palace platforms are flanked by Persian soldiers, perhaps the 10,000 'Immortals' who formed the royal guard.**

then detached by the insertion of wooden wedges, which were wetted so as to swell and force the block free. Wedges were also used for splitting larger blocks, as the stone was too hard to saw. The blocks were then roughed down to reduce their weight, but projections were left to facilitate moving and to protect the angles during transportation and setting. The blocks and slabs were then hauled to the site, probably on sledges.

The terrace

A low spur of rock projecting into the plain acted as the prime foundation of the terrace and, though partly cut away, influenced its shape. Around the sides stone walls, sloping very slightly inwards, either abutted against the bedrock or had solid fill behind them. Although some of the walls are built of regular rectangular blocks, most consist of rectangular, trapezoidal and L-shaped blocks locking together. This system may have been chosen for strength, clearly demonstrated by the fine state of preservation today, but it also suited the raw material, since the layers in the quarry are very irregular.

The blocks were laid without mortar. Internal surfaces were left quarry-finished but outer faces were carefully worked to meet flush. When building was complete, the face was punched, pecked and chiselled smooth from top to bottom. The uppermost courses, and those of the more regular walls, were secured with dovetail clamps of iron set in lead. Iron clamps also tied together damaged blocks, but a more delicate technique was employed for repairing carved or moulded stones. First a patch of the requisite shape was cut, then fixed in position with gum; the joint was secured from the back by pouring molten lead through small holes drilled in the adjacent stonework.

The decoration

The most extraordinary aspect of Persepolis today is the decoration of the platforms supporting the buildings. Over 3000 human figures, mostly officials, soldiers and people bringing tribute, are carved in low relief. The most startling and ultimately impressive feature of these carvings is not their variety but their sameness. Despite the long period over which most were carved, differences between early and late carvings are trivial and not easily detected. This deliberate standardization is the antithesis of what was happening at the same time in Greece. It emphasized the perfection and permanence of the

Persian empire, which was further expressed in similar carvings on the front of the royal tombs, all of which were virtually identical.

Because some carvings were left unfinished we have considerable evidence for the techniques used in making them. Once the slabs had been fixed in position, the sculptors probably defined the outlines of the figures with lightly incised lines. Tools used included edged and toothed hammers and chisels, narrow chisels and points, which became increasingly fine as the work progressed. Curved chisels may have been used for small deep cuts, and bow-drills with hollow bits for places where metal fittings, such as a king's gold and jewelled crown, were to be attached. Finally the carved surface was smoothed with a paste of abrasive and water, and scratches were removed by polishing with materials such as stone, lead or shark-skin. The work was completed by painting the carvings in bright colours.

The uniformity of some large carvings such as the capitals of columns was ensured by using dividers to define points which the workmen could then use as a guide. At an early stage the location of the deepest points within the block that had to be reached in the final product were established and marked. Then the workmen, as they cut the stone, could rely on measured distances rather than their own judgment alone.

Subjects of the empire bringing tribute, which here includes a humped bull and a Bactrian camel, are carved on the platforms of the palaces.

A predetermined plan for the shapes and positions of the figures must have been laid down by the designers in overall charge of the operation. No canon of proportions has been identified – there may have been model sketches or templates, but experienced craftsmen seldom need such aids. Two or more teams of workmen were active at the same time on adjoining stretches of wall, and some left mason's marks to distinguish their areas of responsibility. Despite the overall uniformity of every figure in one sequence, for instance a row of soldiers, the foreman of each team tended to have his own characteristic style, and tiny differences are visible in details such as items of equipment or the treatment of the hair. Demarcation lines between teams were maintained when a motif such as a chariot and horses crossed them, so two teams might carve parts of a single animal, but any such junctions were fluently disguised.

Retribution

Building continued sporadically at Persepolis, until the city was captured by Alexander the Great in 330 BC. One night some weeks later, during a drunken party, an Athenian who was present suggested that the place should be set alight, in revenge for the Persian burning of Athens 150 years earlier. The idea appealed to the king, he led the way throwing torches into one of the palaces, and he changed his mind too late. Ironically the destruction, by sealing the lower parts of the buildings underneath debris, probably helped preserve them.

The Colosseum
at Rome

Time: begun c. AD 72–75, dedicated AD 80
Location: Rome, Italy

Let barbarous Memphis speak no more of the pyramids, nor Assyrian toil boast of Babylon; nor let the soft Ionians be extolled for Artemis' temple; let the altar of many horns say nothing of Delos; nor let the Carians exalt to the skies with extravagant praises the Mausoleum poised in empty air. All labour yields to Caesar's Amphitheatre. Fame shall tell of one work in place of all.

MARTIAL, 1ST CENTURY AD

THERE IS A prophetic quality about these words of the poet Martial, written for the opening of the Flavian Amphitheatre in AD 80; for under another name – the Colosseum – this vast structure was to become the symbol of the power and endurance of pagan Rome to the medieval mind. We tend nowadays to associate the Flavian Amphitheatre most with the bloody wild beast hunts and gladiatorial games that took place there. Martial reminds us, however, that it was equally famous as an extraordinary feat of construction, one to rival the Seven Wonders of the Ancient World. In his day, nothing on this scale had been built before in Rome, and even in the 4th century AD, when there were the great imperial bath complexes and temples such as the Pantheon to compare with it, the Colosseum retained its place as one of the major wonders of the city.

The Colosseum was begun by the emperor Vespasian sometime in the early 70s AD, and largely completed by his son Titus, though the underground structures were left to be completed by the last Flavian emperor, Domitian. Rome's first permanent amphitheatre in the Campus Martius had been destroyed in the great fire of AD 64. The emperor

The upper three zones of the Colosseum's travertine façade. The supports and sockets for the *velarium* are clearly visible.

FACTFILE

Overall	156 × 189 m (c. 530 × 640 Roman ft)
Height	52 m (c. 176 Roman ft)
Arena	48 × 83 m (163 × Roman 280 ft)
Area of arena	3357 m
Length of outer perimeter	545 m (1835 Roman ft)
Number of arches in each level	180
Estimated capacity	50,000–80,000 spectators

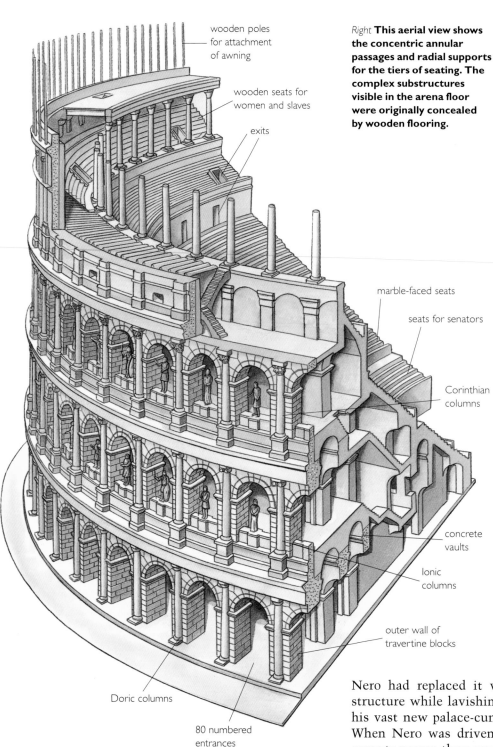

wooden poles
for attachment
of awning

wooden seats for
women and slaves

exits

Right **This aerial view shows
the concentric annular
passages and radial supports
for the tiers of seating. The
complex substructures
visible in the arena floor
were originally concealed
by wooden flooring.**

marble-faced seats

seats for senators

Corinthian
columns

concrete
vaults

Ionic
columns

outer wall of
travertine blocks

Doric columns

80 numbered
entrances

Above **The intersecting radial and annular passages are
visible in this reconstructed section of the Colosseum.
The superimposed rings of arches, each pushing against
its neighbour, resisted any outward thrust from the raked
vaulting which supported the seats.**

Nero had replaced it with a temporary wooden
structure while lavishing most of his attention on
his vast new palace-cum-villa, the Golden House.
When Nero was driven to suicide and Vespasian
came to power, the new emperor made a shrewd and
brilliant political gesture by building his amphitheatre, the new venue for popular entertainment,
in the very gardens of Nero's Golden House. He also
paid for it out of the spoils of war rather than from
the public purse.

The building

Although the design of the Colosseum was based on established motifs long used in Roman theatres and amphitheatres, the end result was an exceptional building. The immensely tall façade was divided into four horizontal bands, consisting of three storeys of superimposed arcades, 80 in number, framed by half-columns of the Doric, Ionic and Corinthian orders, and surmounted by a masonry attic decorated with Corinthian pilasters. The arches reflected the inner structure of radial stairways and annular passages designed to provide access to the seating around the oval arena. Audiences, estimated variously at between 50,000 and 73,000, were controlled outside the building in an area bordered by bollards. They held tickets corresponding to the 76 numbered arcades on the ground floor, allowing spectators to reach their allotted section of seating quickly and easily. The sections of seating themselves were supported by concrete

169

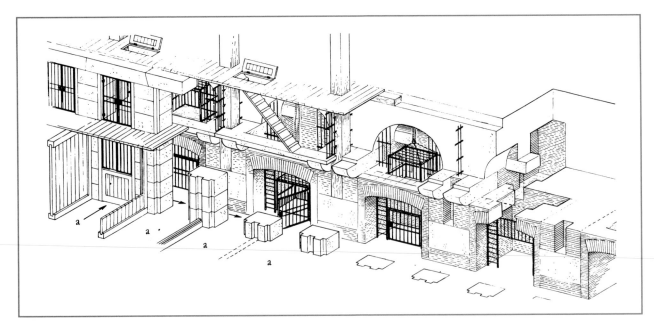

Reconstruction of the animal cages and lifts by which the wild beasts were made to appear in the arena. The cages were raised to the upper level by a system of counterweights.

vaults in three tiers, with wooden stands right at the top. The arena was cut off by a fence and a high platform carrying marble chairs for officials, including boxes for the emperor and magistrates, who had their own entrances.

The Colosseum was built on low-lying land over the site of the lake of Nero's Golden House. It sat on a great concrete and stone foundation raft, on average 13 m (44 Roman ft) thick, laid on a massive bank of clay. The façade and outer ambulatories, as well as some of the main piers at the ground and first floor levels, were of travertine, a strong hard limestone of volcanic origin. Many of the radial walls were of softer, lighter tufa, another volcanic stone, while much of the upper levels and the vaults were of concrete.

An astonishing 100,000 cu. m (over 3,500,000 cu. ft) of travertine were needed for the building, probably the largest single employment of this material ever in ancient Rome, and one of the last. It had major implications for labour requirements at the quarries some 20 km (12.5 miles) east of Rome, and simply getting the material to the building site would also have created huge logistical problems. All 240,000 tonnes of the travertine had to be brought to Rome in barges down the Anio and the Tiber, then unloaded on to ox-carts for the final trip

to the site, a distance of 1.5 km (nearly 1 mile) even if the closest wharves were used. Over 8 years of construction, one cart carrying one tonne of travertine would have left the Tiber wharves on average every 7 minutes for 12 hours of the day and 300 days of the year; larger blocks needed multiple-yoked carts which were slower and more difficult to handle. Carts carrying materials for public building works were among the very few allowed in the city during the day, and the steady stream of heavily laden vehicles through some of the busiest parts of Rome must have been a constant concern to the inhabitants, as well as a constant reminder of the project in hand.

The use of ashlar on this kind of scale also had implications for the construction process. Travertine is a relatively hard stone which requires a high level of labour to work under any circumstances; small wonder that dressing was kept to a minimum, except where visible, as on the façade, and that no attempt was made to keep the courses of stone at a uniform height. The horizontal faces were however levelled with great care to ensure the stability of the structure, and the joints were further strengthened with 300 tonnes of large iron tie-rods set in lead.

Further problems were posed by the need to raise large blocks of stone to great heights and to manhandle them into place. Concrete construction required only relatively light scaffolding for workmen and small quantities of materials, but ashlar blocks must be raised by crane on to more solid platforms, and the cranes themselves must be firmly fixed. As well as the men providing the lifting power, extra labour was needed to guide the blocks as they were raised and to move them into position. It is therefore no surprise that the amount of travertine used in the Colosseum decreases as the building rises, so that at the fourth tier only the façade is in travertine.

It was once believed that the whole structure was erected first as a travertine skeleton supporting a series of raking arches so that the work of finishing could continue at different levels simultaneously, but it is very hard to imagine how a 25-m (80-ft) vertical wall of travertine – the upper two levels of the façade – could be erected without the stability provided by the radial walls and vaults. In addition the vaults would have provided the platforms for setting up the cranes and other heavy lifting equipment. Altogether, it now seems more likely that the whole edifice went up stage by stage, and that the travertine piers were located at points of particular stress concentrations within the structure.

Engineering entertainment

The opening of the amphitheatre was celebrated by lavish games lasting a hundred days. Martial, who gives us the best description of these games, praises the spectacular 'special effects'. The arena floor was not solid but made of timber, covering an amazingly complex underworld. Here a system of narrow runs, cages and lifts worked by counterweights allowed up to 64 wild beasts to appear simultaneously in the arena, while other mechanical devices allowed mountains and similar scenery to appear and disappear in the centre of the arena and provide a background for the ensuing slaughter.

The attic or uppermost storey provides the best evidence of one of the amphitheatre's most spectacular amenities, the great awning (*velarium*) which protected the spectators from the weather. Between the pilasters were large projecting travertine corbels, three to each bay, and directly above each corbel the cornice is pierced by a vertical hole, square in shape. These are thought to have supported the 240 tall masts which provided the supporting framework for the awning. How this worked is much disputed, although the fact that 1000 sailors from the Roman fleet on the Bay of Naples were stationed in Rome specifically to erect the *velarium* gives some clues. One theory is that the masts carried ropes attached to a central oval ring within the arena, and to capstans fixed in the bollards at ground level outside the building; as the ropes were tightened by means of the capstans, the ring was hauled up into position and the actual awnings rolled out over the network of ropes. Others imagine the masts supporting horizontal or inclined spars extending inwards over the seating area, with the awnings stretched between them. Whatever the precise system used, the sheer size of the Colosseum must have made its *velarium* an exceptional feat of engineering, as great in its way as the building itself. But the *velarium* is long gone, and only the gaunt travertine and concrete shell remains as a permanent symbol of the Eternal City.

Terracotta models of Roman gladiators. The fights staged in the Colosseum were set against a background of movable scenery.

Hadrian's Villa at Tivoli

Time: AD 118–138
Location: Tivoli, Italy

[Hadrian] built the villa at Tivoli in a marvellous fashion, in such a way that he could inscribe there the most famous names of provinces and places, by calling [parts of it] such things as the Lyceum, the Academy, the Prytaneum, the Canopus, the [Stoa] Poecile, the Vale of Tempe. And, in order to omit nothing, he even made an underworld.

AUGUSTAN HISTORIES, *LIFE OF HADRIAN*, 4TH CENTURY AD

H ADRIAN'S PALATIAL villa at Tivoli is the most splendid architectural testimony to the opulence and luxury of the Roman imperial court. Stretching across acres of gentle hillside, this rich collection of baths, pavilions and water features in a garden landscape gives us, even in its ruined state, a taste of the glories of the imperial palaces of Rome itself, above all the lost 'Golden House' built by Nero some 70 years before.

FACTFILE

Major dimensions

Overall area (estimated)	120 ha
Overall maximum length (estimated)	2 km

Island Villa

Diameter of enclosure	44.2 m (150 Roman ft)
External diameter of canal	34.3 m (116 Roman ft)
Diameter of island	24.5 m (83 Roman ft)

Piazza d'Oro

Overall	59 × 88 m (200 × 300 Roman ft)
Central court, external	59.7 × 51.6 m (200 × 175 Roman ft)
Central court, internal	36.9 × 46 m (125 × 156 Roman ft)
Vestibule, diameter	10.3 m (35 Roman ft)
Main pavilion	22.1 × 22.1 m (75 × 75 Roman ft)

Canopus canal

	121.4 × 18.65 m (410 × 63 Roman ft)

Serapeum

Internal diameter	16.75 m (57 Roman feet)

Known water features
Aqueduct
12 large fountain display pieces (nymphaea)
30 single fountains
6 grottoes
19 pools, basins & channels
6 bath complexes
10 cisterns
35 lavatories

Nine of the 20 years of Hadrian's reign (AD 117–138) were spent travelling, from Britain to Egypt and the Levant, making him the first emperor to visit the whole of the empire. He was highly educated, bilingual in Greek and Latin, trained in philosophy and rhetoric, and he had a strong interest in, if not an actual talent for, architecture. His reign was notable for a whole series of major building projects in Rome, above all the Pantheon (p. 127) and the massive (now ruined) Temple of Venus and Rome. These were public buildings, but for his own indulgence and relaxation he built a remarkable and extensive villa at Tivoli (ancient Tibur), some 28 km (17 miles) from the city.

Tivoli had long been a choice location for the villas of wealthy Romans who wished to escape the oppressive heat of summer in the capital. These country villas were not simply summer retreats, however, but had other essential roles to play. Originally the country villa had been a working unit, the centre of an agricultural estate. Later it became the focus of leisure time (*otium*), that part of life not given over to business or affairs of state (*negotium*). Under the influence of the luxurious palaces of the

Aerial view of the central part of the complex, with the 'Stadium' garden and residential quarters in the centre foreground, and the circular 'Island Villa' and great pool of the 'Poecile' behind.

Hellenistic east, and especially the royal palace of the Ptolemies at Alexandria, Roman villas and suburban estates (*horti*) were given baths and dining rooms, gymnasia and libraries, formal gardens decorated with topiary and exotic fruit and artificial wilderness haunted by equally exotic animals and birds in gilded aviaries, all lavishly decorated and often whimsically named after the famous places of the fabulous east. The site was often chosen for its views, and the terrain enhanced by the use of terraces and earthworks. Water was essential to the design – whether as part of the natural setting or within artificial channels. Fishponds supplied fine fare for the table, aqueducts fed the baths, fountains cooled the air and refreshed the mind with their murmurings.

The villa at Tivoli

While Hadrian's Villa was very much in this established tradition, it was on an exceptional scale and incorporated remarkable buildings. Given that the emperor's *otium* was only relative, allowance had to be made for the court to move with him. That Hadrian conducted business at the villa is shown by copies of an official letter that he sent from Tivoli in the late summer of AD 125. Recent estimates put the area of the Villa at roughly 120 ha (300 acres), or the size of Kew Gardens in London, almost twice the size of even quite substantial Roman towns like Pompeii or Ostia. In some ways it resembled a town, with its temples, baths, theatre and warehouses, but it lacked the muddle of residential and commercial properties of a town; all were housed there strictly at the emperor's pleasure.

At present only half the area has been excavated, so it is often difficult to understand the relation between individual or groups of buildings. Still, it is clear that the structures were developed with the potential of the site firmly in mind; by emphasizing changes of level, many areas which are separated physically are connected visually. Sometimes the physical separation itself is more apparent than real: an extensive 'underworld' of service corridors and tunnels links the whole site together.

Many of the standing structures have been named – somewhat arbitrarily – after famous sites in antiquity under the influence of the passage in the *Life of Hadrian* quoted above. Such names were common in antiquity and should not be dismissed as mere fancy. Given Hadrian's attachment to the cities of

Simplified plan of the excavated area of the villa.

the east, it would not be at all surprising if he had named one garden area after the groves of Plato's famous academy in Athens; after all, even the late Republican orator Cicero had an 'Academy' in one of his villas. If the Academy, Lycaeum, Poecile and Prytaneum recall Athens, the Canopus is a reminder of another of Hadrian's favourite cities, Alexandria, and its famous canal.

Water, in fact, is one of the dominant motifs of the whole Villa. The setting allowed Hadrian to tap into some of the major aqueducts supplying Rome, fed by the upper reaches of the Anio above the town, thus providing an excellent head of water and avoiding the need for water-lifting devices. The water entered from the southeast and was channelled across the whole site by a sophisticated system of pipes and cisterns. Every group of buildings had its water feature, with over 100 identified, from the vast pool of the so-called 'Poecile' to the water organ in the Small Baths. Typical of the degree of sophistication is the 'Serapeum', really a semicircular dining room surrounded by water where guests reclined on a C-shaped bench (*stibadium*) under a vaulted canopy. A channel in front of the diners served as a table for floating dishes, and they looked out over a small reflecting pool to the open water of the 'Canopus' canal. The water was

Above **Umbrella-vaulted entrance vestibule to the Piazza d'Oro complex.**
Left **A model of the villa illustrating the co-ordinated terraces and the impact of the major water features such as the 'Poecile' pool and the 'Canopus' canal (lower and middle right).**

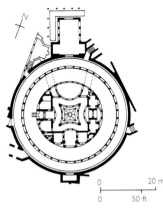

Above **The complex circular geometry of the 'Island Villa' is clear from this plan.** *Left* **The long pool of the 'Canopus' provides a stunning prelude to the domed dining pavilion of the 'Serapeum' in the distance.**

brought in from the high ground behind the vault, allowing for spectacular fountains somewhere in the ensemble, while behind the diners was a water grotto, lit dramatically from above.

An ambitious architecture

One of the most distinctive features of Hadrian's Villa is the number of halls and pavilions of curvilinear plan, ranging from the relatively simple circular or semicircular spaces of the 'Serapeum' to the intricacies of the 'Island Villa' or the main pavilion of the 'Piazza d'Oro'. Many of these were roofed with complex concrete vaults, divided into concave segments like umbrellas, and decorated with glass mosaic to reflect light and water. In some cases the ground plan of the design seems deliberately to challenge the ingenuity of the builders and the capabilities of Roman concrete to roof it; the results where still visible, as in the Small Baths, continue to impress today.

Other examples suggest a source of inspiration not in the pumpkins which ancient sources tell us Hadrian was mocked for drawing, but in the tents and marquees of the Persian and Hellenistic courts. The very slender columns originally set at the interior angles of the vestibule of the 'Piazza d'Oro' must have seemed like tent poles holding down its billowing roof, not merely applied decoration to a solid concrete shell. The decoration of the vestibule vault is now lost, but was probably a glass mosaic intended to reinforce the tent-like effect. The patterns and rich colours of the mosaic may have been inspired by the silken fabrics of the Near East, and such fabrics were used for awnings across the Colosseum in Rome on state occasions. Indeed, the long controversy over whether the main pavilion of the 'Piazza d'Oro' was roofed or not, and how, may only be resolved by imagining a temporary, lightweight construction of timber and cloth set up as and when necessary to protect the diners from the worst of the summer sun.

Other ambitious structural devices were also used to maintain the impression of airiness and lack of solidity. Column spacings normal to timber architraves but generally impossible in stone, were achieved by using iron tie-bars in tension to support flat concrete lintel arches, anchored to the columns by distinctive wedge-shaped blocks which are the only traces remaining today. This 'reinforced' construction was masked by a veneer of marble, making it seem yet again as if the Roman builders had somehow defied nature. The Villa as a whole demonstrated how daring Roman architecture had become in this age of confidence and innovation.

The Baths of Caracalla, Rome

Time: AD 211–217
Location: Rome, Italy

Among his works at Rome he left the magnificent baths which bear his name, and architects say of it that the construction of the cella solearis *cannot be imitated. For the whole ceiling is said to be entrusted to lattices of bronze or copper set over the room, the span being so great that experienced engineers say it could not have been done.*

AUGUSTAN HISTORIES, *LIFE OF ANTONINUS CARACALLA*, 4TH CENTURY AD

IN THE 4th century AD one ancient tourist to Rome marvelled at the 'baths built like whole provinces'. The Roman baths were already recognized as one of the wonders of the city; and the greatest of all were those built by the emperor Caracalla. Marcus Aurelius Antoninus, better known as Caracalla, enjoyed only a brief reign from AD 211 until his assassination in AD 217. Detested in antiquity for his cruelty, he was particularly notorious for the murder of his younger brother and co-heir, supposedly in their mother's arms. Nevertheless, he left two enduring monuments: universal Roman citizenship for all free men within the empire, and the stupendous baths in Rome which bore his name.

The baths of imperial Rome

By the time of Caracalla, public baths had been an integral feature of Roman towns for at least three centuries. The essential elements of the early baths

Aerial view of the central bathing block, with the *caldarium* and other heated rooms in the foreground.

FACTFILE

Principal dimensions

Precinct maximum	412 × 383 m
Internal	323 × 323 m
Central block overall	218 × 112 m
Swimming pool	54 × 23 m
Frigidarium	59 × 24 m; height c. 41 m
Caldarium	35 m diameter; height c. 44 m
Internal courts	67 × 29 m

Quantities of materials

Pozzolana	341,000 cu. m
Quicklime	35,000 cu. m
Tufa	341,000 cu. m
Basalt for foundations	150,000 cu. m
Brick pieces for facing	17.5 million
Large bricks	520,000
Marble columns in central block	252
Marble for columns and decoration	6300 cu. m

Estimated average labour figures on site

Excavation	5200 men
Substructures	9500 men
Central block	4500 men
Decoration	1800 men

were a dressing room and a communal hot tub in a heated room (*caldarium*), reached through a slightly warmed room (*tepidarium*). Some also had one or more dry sweating rooms like saunas and a cold room with a plunge pool (*frigidarium*). These baths were domestic in scale, poorly lit and simply decorated, reflecting their utilitarian function to provide a hygienic facility for the town's inhabitants.

Ostensibly fulfilling the same function, the baths created by the emperors in Rome were in reality very different. The largest of them – like the Baths of Caracalla – were the size of small towns, with a vast bathing block set in a garden precinct surrounded by libraries, lecture halls, art galleries and sports tracks. The bathing facilities were on a correspondingly massive scale, with Olympic-sized swimming pools and cavernous *frigidaria* 200 Roman ft (59 m or 194 ft) long, brilliantly lit by huge glazed windows. Everywhere the floors and walls gleamed with precious marbles from all over the empire, and the glass mosaic of the niches and vaults reflected the abundant water. Statues looked down on the bathers at every turn, like the colossal 4-m (15-ft) high representation of Aesclepius, the Roman god of healing, whose gilded features presided over the Baths of Caracalla. Surrounded by these splendours,

Artist's reconstruction of the central block. The cutaway shows the large swimming pool (*natatio*), the central *frigidarium* and the great domed *caldarium*.

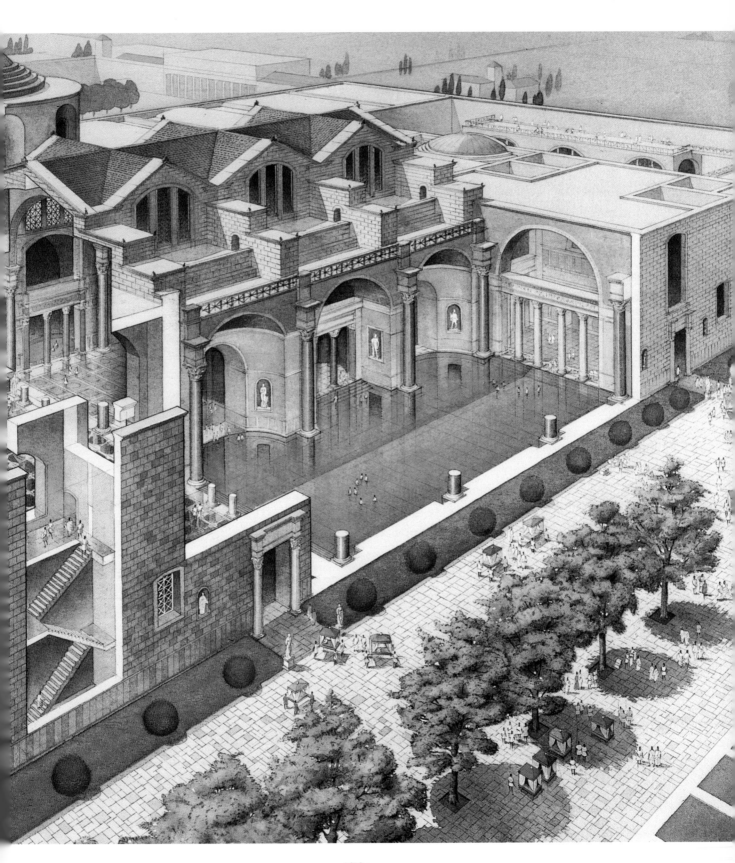

the ordinary Roman could not help but be impressed with the overwhelming power and divine status of the emperors who gave the baths their names.

Building the Baths

Today the stark ruins of the Baths of Caracalla are the best preserved of the great imperial baths. This was one of the largest single building projects ever undertaken by the emperors in Rome itself, consisting of a vast artificial platform roughly 323 m (1080 ft) square supporting the symmetrically planned central bathing block, measuring 218 × 112 m (c. 730 × 370 ft), plus the projection of the circular *caldarium*, three-quarters of the diameter of the Pantheon.

The basic building material for all the walls and vaults was a mortared rubble of fist-sized pieces of soft volcanic tufa. These were contained in a thin skin of brick which formed a permanent formwork for the rubble core. The mortar was one part high quality well-slaked lime and two parts pozzolana, a volcanic sand – this is the legendary 'magic ingredient' which gave Roman mortar its great strength and hydraulic properties. In the foundations the tufa was replaced by basalt for solidity, and in the upper parts of the vaults by pumice for lightness.

There are logistical advantages in this type of construction. Relatively little highly skilled labour is needed either in the production of materials or in the actual construction, and, apart from mixing the mortar, all the materials could be prepared off-site and in advance; the individual elements in the construction were also small and could be put in place by a single worker.

Preliminary works

While this type of construction facilitated large-scale works, we must remember that the entire substructure and central bathing block were completed during Caracalla's six-year reign. Such rapid construction required the marshalling of exceptional resources of materials and manpower, and the solving of complex logistical problems impressive even by modern standards.

The first step in preparing the site for construction was the reshaping of the natural ground surface into terraces, into which were dug the foundations, some 6.5 m (22 ft) deep under the central block. For these earthworks 500,000 cu. m (17,650,000 cu. ft) of clay had to be removed, and all of it, as far as we know, by hand using picks and shovels, and baskets for removing the spoil – there is no evidence that the Romans ever used the wheelbarrow.

Above the foundations were 8-m (27-ft) tall solid walls which supported the superstructure, pierced

Above **A victorious athlete carrying a crown and palm, from one of the mosaic floors.** *Below* **The two remaining piers of the circular *caldarium* still tower 34 m (112 ft) over the site.**

through and connected by maintenance passages and drains, while in the area of the open precinct service galleries wide enough to take two carts side by side were built – some 6–7 km (3.75–4.4 miles) of tunnels and passages altogether. All of this had to be built up by hand and all the voids filled with inert materials, so that only after three years of building and the expenditure of almost three million man-days of labour, could work commence on the baths proper, rising to a minimum height of 22 m (75 ft), with the *frigidarium* and *caldarium* at 44 m (150 Roman ft) towering above the rest.

The problems of scale

For the entire building to have been finished in the six years, however, the whole central block must have gone up together. Thousands of bricklayers working side-by-side, as many as 4500 at peak periods, must have been employed. Simply co-ordinating such large numbers of masons would have been difficult. The surviving remains reveal something of how this was done.

Although the overall standard of workmanship is extremely uniform and the hands of individual workmen difficult to detect, differences in details such as the location of drains, the construction of staircases, and the distribution of materials, show that the site was divided into two halves, each under the supervision of a different 'master-builder' who followed his own particular tradition. Vertical progress could be regulated through the horizontal courses of *bipedales*, large flat bricks 2 Roman ft square; because these courses were carefully set at 4.5 Roman ft (1.32 m) apart, window sills, door lintels, terraces and the springing of vaults could be established at the correct level without the need to measure from the ground. Laying the brick courses also provided a break in construction while the top of the wall was levelled and the builders checked that the walls were true; often a new level of scaffolding was erected at the same time. The speed of construction depended very much on the creation of efficient systems like this.

A building project of this size also created problems of access to the superstructure. Due to the height of the building, complex pole scaffolding had to be used, tied to the walls with short horizontal supports (called putlogs) which have left tell-tale holes in the fabric. Altogether some 100,000 poles were needed, just one of the many hidden materials which went into making the Baths of Caracalla.

Roman soldiers on Trajan's Column construct a fort using simple tools and baskets – also used for building the Baths.

Sophisticated and large-scale cranes were required for lifting the large timber formwork on which the great concrete vaults of the *frigidarium* and *caldarium* were laid, or moving the 12-m (40-ft) granite columns of the *frigidarium*, each weighing nearly 100 tonnes, into place.

Providing manoeuvring space for large columns and formwork timbers created other logistical problems. Building joins show that the central block was built in sections and materials were stored in the large internal spaces – *frigidarium*, swimming pool and the two exercise courts – and that temporary openings were left in walls. The colonnaded terraces of the internal courts were added only at the last minute, the stability of the lightweight vaults being achieved through the use of iron tie-rods anchored in stone blocks built into the walls at terrace level at an earlier stage of construction – a precocious anticipation of modern reinforced concrete.

That there were even more exceptional uses of metal in the Baths is suggested by the description of the mysterious '*cella solearis*' (most likely the *caldarium*) quoted above, probably a decorative gilt bronze lattice which the 4th-century writer had simply failed to understand. Whatever the system was, the sense of awe it inspired in later generations is indisputable.

Altogether, the huge scale and the daring feats of construction show the Roman builders of the Baths of Caracalla pushing technology to its limits and at the same time making a spectacle out of the process, which carried an unmistakable message about the power of imperial Rome.

The Palace & Pleasure Gardens of Sigiriya

Time: AD 473–491
Location: Sigiriya, Sri Lanka

He betook himself through fear to Sihagiri ... he built there a fine palace, worthy to behold,
like another Alakamanda and dwelt there like Kuvera.

CULAVAMSA, XXXIX.2–5

THE 5th-century AD palace and pleasure gardens at Sigiriya form one of the most spectacular early medieval residences in Asia. Centred on an almost sheer rock outcrop around 200 m (656 ft) high, surrounded by elaborate gardens predating Mughal experiments by many centuries, it is a unique monument – all the more striking as it was created in Sri Lanka's dry zone.

The entire complex covers no less than 40 ha (99 acres), comprising an outer courtyard, inner courtyard and citadel. Around the outer courtyard runs a moat and wall. Once inside this, an avenue leads through a complex of symmetrical water gardens with cisterns, fountains, ponds and island pleasure pavilions. The inner courtyard is raised on a series of terraces studded with pavilions, caves and plastered boulders. Finally, the citadel on the summit of the

FACTFILE

Overall		**Outer courtyard**	
Height	182 m	Outer moat	35 m wide
Area	40 ha	Outer rampart	9 m wide
		Inner moat	25 m wide
Gardens		Inner rampart	9 m wide
Pleasure garden			
Length	120 m	**Inner courtyard**	
Width	201 m	Area	4 ha
Fountain garden			
Length	160 m	**Lion platform**	
Width	24 m	Length	66 m
		Width	33 m
Gallery			
Length	146 m	**Citadel**	
Height	12 m	Area	1.2 ha
Private chambers		**Main rock-cut cistern**	
Area	168 sq. m	Length	24 m
		Width	21 m
		Depth	4 m

rock outcrop is reached by a long flight of steps, opening on to a decorated gallery running along the cliff face, which in turn leads to a terrace on the northern side of the rock. Although badly eroded now, the cliff was fashioned with the brick head and paws of a huge lion – hence the name Sigiriya, or 'rock of the lion'. Entry to the citadel was by a staircase which passed through the lion's mouth. It is hard to imagine a more graphic portrayal of royal power. The summit was covered by buildings, courtyards and cisterns on artificial terraces. On the highest terrace were the private royal chambers, though 1500 years of erosion have taken their toll.

A place of refuge?

Sigiriya was only occupied for a single reign, that of Kassapa I (AD 473–491). According to the Culavamsa chronicle, Kassapa murdered his father, Dhatusena

The royal citadel on the central rock outcrop towers over the water gardens in the foreground, with ponds and channels.

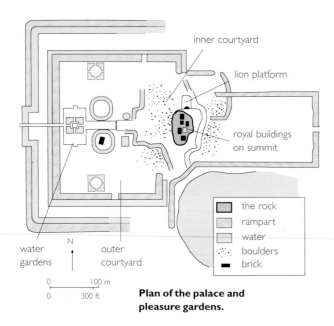

Plan of the palace and pleasure gardens.

Legend:
- the rock
- rampart
- water
- boulders
- brick

Labels: inner courtyard, lion platform, royal buildings on summit, water gardens, outer courtyard, N, 0 — 100 m, 0 — 300 ft

sluices, the supply pipes led through the higher ponds and down towards the more complex pools, channels and limestone-headed fountains at the western entrance where the water pressure was at its greatest.

Heaven on earth

Sigiriya represented more than a sumptuous residence, it was also an attempt to create heaven on earth. By combining archaeological and textual sources it is possible to identify Sigiriya with Alaka-manda, the palace of the god Kubera on the summit of Mount Meru at the centre of the universe. The mountain is so bright it is called the 'mirror of the damsels of heaven'. Kubera's palace, reached through the Himalayas, is on the shore of Lake Ano-tatta, close to the pleasure garden, Caitraratha. The palace is built of marble and its inhabitants enjoy unlimited wealth and are untroubled by human ills.

Elements of this celestial topography are recognizable at Sigiriya, which is also located on the shore of its own reservoir, close to the pleasure gardens. The citadel complex, paved with crystalline limestone, is reached by climbing through the plastered boulders of the inner courtyard, evoking Himalayan snow, and along the gallery known as the mirror-wall with murals above depicting princesses of lightning and damsels floating on clouds. In the words of Sri Lankan archaeologist S. Paranavitana, Sigiriya was 'intended to be a miniature Alakamanda and, residing there, Kassapa proclaimed himself to be Kubera on earth.'

(AD 455–473), and forced his brother, the heir-apparent to the island kingdom, into exile. The chronicle records that Kassapa moved his palace from Anuradhapura (the traditional capital) to Sigiriya because he feared his brother's return. More likely, Kassapa wished to establish a new dynastic centre at Sigiriya, so monumental in form that none would question his position. After 18 years, during which Kassapa atoned for his crimes, his brother, Moggallana, returned. When Kassapa died, the new ruler moved back Anuradhapura, abandoning Sigiriya to the jungle.

Improving on nature

The spectacular complex was created through the manipulation of local topography. The numerous pavilions and palaces in the citadel and inner courtyard were constructed on artificial terraces made of gneiss chippings held in place by retaining walls of ashlar or brick. These walls were secured by keying them into stepped cuts in adjacent rocks and boulders. The gravity supply for the water gardens similarly used local topography and is itself an outstanding feat of medieval hydraulic engineering. Rainwater on the summit of the rock outcrop was collected in cisterns, and the excess was channelled down towards the water gardens. Vertical transfer of water was either through downpipes made of limestone bound by metal straps, or along gullies cut into boulders; and horizontal transfer used brick or stone conduits set in puddled clay. Regulated by

Detail of a mirror-wall mural depicting a lightning princess attended by a cloud damsel.

The Arch of Ctesiphon

Time: c. AD 550–560
Location: Ctesiphon, Iraq

As the quivering sun rose in unclouded splendour, the palace was transformed into a vast arcade of enormous arches resting upon columns and masses of masonry … until the ruin assumed the shape of a tower reaching to the sky, and pierced from the base to the summit by enormous arches.

A.H. LAYARD, 1853

UNTIL VERY recently the Arch of Ctesiphon was the highest and widest parabolic arch in existence. Still today an extraordinary sight, it lies in modern Iraq, south of Baghdad. It bears the name of the Sasanian ruler for whom it was built: Taq Kisra, the Arch of Khusrau. The arch is in fact a vault, and beside it remains one half of the façade of the palace of which it was the centrepiece. Within this vaulted hall the Sasanian emperor once sat in state, surrounded by Byzantine marble panelling and by mosaics showing the capture of Antioch. Over his head was a magnificent crown, far too unwieldy to wear, that was suspended from the vault by a golden chain. At his feet was a carpet representing a garden; it was made of gold and precious stones, and was at least 25 m (82 ft) square.

The best of both worlds

In AD 540 Khusrau (Chosroes) I, after fundamental reforms to the chaotic empire he had inherited, was strong enough to lead his army west against the Byzantines. Victory took him to the great Greek city of Antioch, which he duly captured. He carried away, besides the entire population and innumerable fine architectural fittings, ideas about a new palace, to stand in his winter capital of Ctesiphon. It would be bigger and better than anything that had existed beforehand in his own country, and would give him a reputation to rival that of neighbouring contemporary rulers in Byzantium and India.

Experts sent by the emperor Justinian helped with the construction of the palace, which amalgamated several traditions. Its basic plan was Sasanian but it

The Arch of Ctesiphon was the throne room of Sasanian kings. The arch itself was flanked by columned façades, one of which still survives.

FACTFILE

Height of vault	35 m
Span of vault	25 m
Length of vault	50 m

incorporated columned façades of a Greco-Roman type that had been introduced, from west to east, centuries previously. Its most impressive feature, however, was a soaring vault built in the pitched-brick technique. While the skills necessary to build a vault on the scale of Ctesiphon were probably brought by Justinian's experts, the technique was originally Mesopotamian. Its antecedents can be traced back to 2500 BC or earlier, when it was used for much smaller roofs of unbaked mud-brick.

No need for centering

The vault was and remains the most impressive feature of the palace. It is some 35 m (115 ft) high and 25 m (82 ft) wide, and originally covered a hall 50 m (164 ft) long, the eastern end of which was left open. In shape the vault is not semicircular but parabolic, with the inner faces of the lower walls converging slightly upwards from the base to the impost. This reduced the area to be spanned.

The entire structure is built of bricks, about 30 cm (12 in) square and 7.5 cm (3 in) thick, which were laid in a quick-drying gypsum cement. For the lower walls these bricks were laid horizontally; for the vault, however, they were laid on edge, an essential feature of the pitched-brick technique. In fact they were laid at an angle of about 18 degrees from the vertical, so that those at the far end of the hall rested partly against its back wall, and the successive rings of bricks rested against those laid previously.

There is a significant difference between this technique of vaulting and that traditionally used for the standard freestanding arch. The latter has to be supported during construction by centering, a temporary wooden framework that holds the heavy structural elements in place until the arch is complete and self-supporting. In contrast, as the cement of the Arch of Ctesiphon dried rapidly, the bricks adhered to those which had already been laid and were taking part of their relatively light weight. The whole formed a solid mass and there was no need for internal scaffolding. This was not merely advanta-

geous in a country where wood was scarce: it would have been virtually impossible for Khusrau to build a vault of this size in any other way.

While the crown of the vault is only 1 m (3.25 ft) thick, the side-walls carrying the thrust reach a width of 7 m (23 ft) at their base. A number of wooden beams built into the lower brickwork may have helped alleviate the stresses caused by differential settling. In any event the structure, though long robbed of its external decorations, remained largely complete until it partly collapsed during a serious flood in 1888.

The most beautiful of palaces

The Arabs captured and looted Ctesiphon in AD 637, using Taq Kisra as a mosque, but they found the surrounding country too marshy for their liking, and the city was gradually abandoned. Yet even two centuries later the palace of Khusrau was still described as the most beautiful ever made of brick. While most of those bricks eventually found their way to other buildings, the arch was too difficult to remove. Even modern high-explosive bombs, falling in the vicinity, have so far failed to demolish it.

Opposite **Although the back wall has collapsed, the Arch still dwarfs its visitors.** *Below* **Diagram showing the construction of a parabolic arch. As the arch is built, successive rings of brick rest on those already laid.**

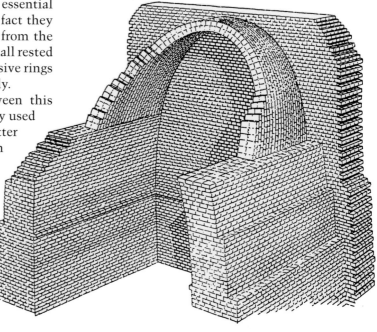

The Royal Compounds of Chan Chan

Time: c. AD 900–1470
Location: north coast, Peru

The valley of the Chimo took its name from a powerful lord and when the Inca occupied it they regarded it highly and esteemed its lords and its people. In it are found great tombs where much treasure has been taken.

ANTONIO DE HERRERA, 1610–15

THE MASSIVE PALACE compounds of Chan Chan served as the residences of the lords who ruled the great Peruvian kingdom of Chimor (Chimú) from the 10th to the 15th centuries AD. They are the most remarkable structures of their kind in South America.

Construction began at Chan Chan around AD 900 and the city reached its peak *c.* 1350 when it flourished as the centre of the largest kingdom to dominate the coast of Peru before the rise of the Incas. Its remains sprawl across the desert not far from the Pacific Ocean, near modern Trujillo in the Moche valley. Central Chan Chan is an area of monumental, rectangular compounds called *ciudadelas*. These covered 6 sq. km (2.3 sq. miles) and served as the palace compounds of successive Chimú kings, their families and retainers, and functioned as seats of government and centres for redistributing the wealth of Chimor.

The city as a whole covered some 20 sq. km (7.7 sq. miles), although not all of it was occupied simultaneously. Scattered among the *ciudadelas* lay elite compounds – the residences of lesser nobles – and monumental, terraced *huacas*, or mounds, all built of adobes – mould-made, sun-dried bricks. In addition there were neighbourhoods of small-roomed, cane-walled residences, large cemeteries, and sunken fields – garden plots dug below the valley floor to tap the water table. Five monumental adobe mounds, probably temples, rose above the *ciudadelas*. Today much of the city lies in ruins, its mudbrick walls melted by El Niño rains and its temples and burial platforms ransacked by looters.

Palace compounds

Chan Chan's palace compounds are aligned north–south and surrounded by imposing adobe walls on foundations of stone, some of them towering 9 m (30 ft) high. These high walls effectively screened the Chimú elite from the surrounding populace.

Opposite above **This wooden model of a courtyard may depict a ceremony at Chan Chan when the mummy of a Chimú king was brought out from its burial chamber and received new offerings.**
Right **An aerial view of Chan Chan, the Chimú capital that sprawled across the desert of northern Peru; walled compounds served as palaces of Chimú kings.**

FACTFILE

Overall area of city	20 sq. km
Area covered by palace compounds	6 sq. km
Estimated population c. AD 1350	20,000
Number of palace compounds	9
Height of compound walls	9 m
Largest palace compound approx.	400 m E–W × 500 m N–S

The internal organization of the *ciudadelas* varies, but a standard late *ciudadela* was divided into three sectors: north, central and south. Variations in size – the largest covers and area of 20,530 sq. m (221,000 sq. ft) – or the number of store-rooms they contain, may reflect the rise and fall of the Chimú kings' fortunes.

A single entryway on the north side provided access to the palace compound. Pairs of painted and carved wooden human figures set in niches flanked these entryways, which led into an enormous court edged by low benches, with a raised area approached by a ramp on the southern side. Mud-brick friezes with geometric designs and patterns of birds, fish and mythical figures embellished the entry court's walls. From this court, which appears to have been the most public, corridors led to an area of U-shaped structures, called *audiencias,* that probably served as administrative offices and residences for the nobility. Some *audiencias* apparently controlled access to courts containing store-rooms, while others had administrative functions.

The central area also contained courtyards, *audiencias* and store-rooms, but its primary feature was the burial platform. Surrounded by an imposing wall and built of adobe, the burial platform was honeycombed with cell-like tombs. An I-shaped chamber in the centre served as the principal tomb of the Chimú king. The accounts found in colonial documents of rich treasure and more recent excavations only hint at the wealth that these burial platforms would once have contained: fine pottery, textiles, weaving tools, carved wood and metal artifacts, as well as the skeletons of retainers who may have been ritually sacrificed to accompany the Chimú king to the afterlife.

Periodically, the mummies of the Chimú kings were removed from their burial chambers and lavished with ceremonies. One such ceremony may be illustrated by a small architectural model depicting a compound that resembles those surrounding the burial platforms at Chan Chan. Miniature wooden figures representing musicians and officiants face a ramped structure and shell-inlaid mummy bundles. The scene may illustrate a ceremony marking the periodic opening of royal tombs and the replenishing of offerings to the ancestor-kings buried at one of Chan Chan's palace compounds.

Below **A wooden figure (one of two) flanking an entrance to the palace-compounds at Chan Chan. It would once have held a spear or staff.**

Great Zimbabwe

Time: 13th–15th centuries AD
Location: Zimbabwe, Africa

Great Zimbabwe lies at the heart of Zimbabwe's history and culture. No other place can give a visitor a deeper insight into the path of the country's history and development. Understanding Great Zimbabwe and the interpretation of its past will help us to understand a great deal about Zimbabwe today.

PETER GARLAKE, 1985

FEW IF ANY archaeological sites have generated a larger literature, and a higher proportion of nonsense, than Great Zimbabwe. When first brought to the attention of the outside world in the late 19th century these spectacular stone structures were seen to represent a settlement of south-central Africa by foreigners – even Phoenicians, linked in some unspecified way with the Queen of Sheba. Today, they are regarded as symbolizing indigenous African culture and achievement; they have even given their name to the country in which they are situated.

The monument

Great Zimbabwe is located near the western edge of the plateau country between the Zambezi and Limpopo rivers, now the Republic of Zimbabwe. In the Shona language the name Zimbabwe means 'stone houses' or 'venerated houses' and it is also applied to very many ruins of smaller stone buildings that are widely distributed throughout the region. Although the simple name Zimbabwe has often been applied to it erroneously (particularly in colonial times), the site is now correctly designated Great Zimbabwe.

In its heyday Great Zimbabwe was a large town, covering an area of some 78 ha (193 acres) and with a population plausibly estimated at some 18,000 people. The site comprises two principal stone ruins, with a substantial area covered by remains of lesser structures. On a steep-sided rocky hill, lengths of well-coursed walling link the natural boulders to form a series of enclosures. In the adjacent valley is a series of larger freestanding walled enclosures in some of which stood circular thatched pole-and-

mud houses joined by short lengths of similar walling. One enclosure stands out through its size and complexity, and shows signs of repeated modification and extension. Its outer perimeter wall reaches a height of over 10 m (33 ft), as does a solid stone tower which stands within.

Despite its massive scale and accomplished execution, the Great Zimbabwe stone architecture is basically simple. It was built without the use of mortar from roughly squared and easily transported blocks of granite. This stone probably derives from natural exfoliation of the domed granite hills, *kopjes*, which are a prominent feature of the local landscape. The narrow doorways were roofed with lintels of stone or, rarely, wood, supporting the upper courses of stonework. The open tapered entrances through which today's visitor enters the Great Enclosure are the result of inaccurate reconstruction in the early 20th century, replacing lintelled doorways which had collapsed. There is no evidence for the use of detailed plans, mensuration or the plumb-bob; there were no domes or arches. Other structures were skilfully made of puddled mud, sun-baked to great hardness and durability. Despite its size and careful construction, Great Zimbabwe has the same stylistic and technological features as numerous other stone buildings in southern Africa.

Left **Sections of walls link the natural boulders: the doorway retains its original stone lintel.** *Below* **The Great Enclosure from the hill; remains of similar domestic enclosures are also visible.**

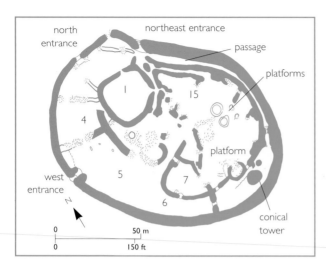

Recent research gives us a view of Great Zimbabwe in the context of southern African history during the past two millennia. The earliest examples of simple stone walling probably date from the 10th century AD. By the second half of the 13th century stone enclosures and platforms were erected, along with pole-and-mud houses. The main period of building, however, was between the late 13th and mid-15th centuries, when all the major structures to be seen at Great Zimbabwe today were erected.

The purpose of the site

There can be little doubt that the inhabitants of Great Zimbabwe were directly ancestral to the modern Shona. This connection has stimulated attempts to determine the uses to which various parts of the Great Zimbabwe complex, particularly the stone buildings, were put. The resultant claims remain controversial, being largely based on oral traditions of uncertain origin and on poorly recorded information from more recent times. Although the potential value of such work is undeniable, it would not at present be wise to rely on suggestions that the main stone-walled enclosure was a place for female initiation, or that a certain area was inhabited by the royal wives.

FACTFILE	
Total area	78 ha
Estimated population	18,000
Circumference of 'Great Enclosure'	255 m
Weight of perimeter wall	15,000 tonnes
Maximum height of surviving wall	10 m

It is, however, clear that Great Zimbabwe was the capital of rulers who controlled major territories, resources and trade. Imported objects such as glass beads, Chinese and Persian pottery, Near Eastern glass, and a coin minted in one of the East African coastal ports are more common here than on contemporary sites elsewhere in Zimbabwe. Gold and copper objects from other parts of the interior have also been found, suggesting that the products of outlying regions were collected at Great Zimbabwe, where exchange for coastal imports was organized.

Great Zimbabwe's period of greatest prosperity coincided not only with its architectural florescence but also with the peak in the export of gold via the Indian Ocean coast. It was the centre of a network of related sites extending from northern Zimbabwe to the coastal plain of southern Mozambique.

It is significant that the development of Great Zimbabwe as a major settlement coincided almost exactly with the decline of an earlier centre further south at Mapungubwe in the Limpopo Valley, close to the meeting of frontiers between Zimbabwe, South Africa and Botswana. For reasons that are not properly understood, but which may have been linked with overgrazing and environmental deterioration, this politico-economic centre appears to have moved late in the 13th century from the Limpopo Valley on to the plateau to the north. The new site at Great Zimbabwe was better placed both for the exploitation of gold deposits and for access to the Indian Ocean coast via the Sabi River.

Decline and fall

The decline of Great Zimbabwe in the 15th century came at a time when political power was transferred to a more northerly site, near the Zambezi Valley, which was then replacing the Sabi as the major route between the interior and the coast. By the mid-16th century the Portuguese had penetrated the Zambezi Valley route to the interior. In central and southwestern Zimbabwe the kingdom of Guruhuswa maintained many of the traditions of Great Zimbabwe, including stone building, and traded with the Portuguese during the 17th and 18th centuries. Archaeology thus serves to confirm the evidence of oral tradition for the essential continuity between the inhabitants of Great Zimbabwe and the modern Shona-speaking peoples.

Opposite left **Plan of the Great Enclosure, the largest and most complex at Great Zimbabwe.** *Opposite right* **Built of solid, well-coursed masonry, the Conical Tower stands within the Great Enclosure and is one of its most impressive features.** *Above* **A soapstone bird – seven complete ones were found at Great Zimbabwe and they are not known from any other site.** *Right* **The 10-m high outer wall of the Great Enclosure, with the stone blocks laid in regular courses.**

Fortifications

THE QUEST for security is a major impetus in human affairs and as technological skill has developed, the solutions have taken ever more elaborate form. Yet the creation of massive fortresses and defensive circuits is not merely a utilitarian concern; towering walls and imposing gateways convey a message of power which goes well beyond any mere military objective. Thus fortifications are not just protection against an enemy, but symbols of status and control.

The need for permanent defensive structures probably first arose among the early settled communities which developed in different parts of the world as populations grew and agriculture became the mainstay of life. The very earliest cities of Mesopotamia may have been undefended but during the 3rd millennium BC virtually all acquired lengthy and impressive circuits of mud-brick wall. In the Near East, this tradition reached its fullest expression in the famous walls built around Babylon by Nebuchadnezzar in the 6th century BC. They feature in several early accounts as one of the Seven Wonders of the Ancient World.

The walls of Babylon were the defences of an entire city, an imperial capital. So too were those of Syracuse, the leading Greek city of Sicily. Built by Dionysius in the 4th century BC, they enclosed not just the city area but the strategic plateau of Epipolae to the north. Within or alongside such city defences, individual rulers often built fortress-palaces, to protect themselves and dominate not

The Great Wall of China was built and rebuilt several times from the 3rd century BC. This section to the north of Beijing in the Jinshan Range was constructed during the declining years of the Ming dynasty in the 16th century AD.

only foreign enemies but also their own subjects. The citadel of Van in eastern Turkey, one of several such fortresses in the region, stood on the edge of an ancient city, and served both to provide the ruler with additional security in the event of foreign attack and to separate him from the ordinary populace. Mycenae and Tiryns, Bronze Age citadels in southern Greece, were likewise accompanied by a lower town in which the ordinary people lived. The powerful citadel rising high above the settlement of the ruler's subjects gave physical expression to the hierarchy present in the society as a whole.

The fortress of Masada in the Judaean desert represents another solution to the quest for security. For here King Herod put his faith in remoteness; Masada is not a citadel rising above the dwellings of his subjects but an isolated desert stronghold, a refuge in times of emergency. The place was chosen for its natural defensive capabilities, and here the problem was not so much to construct impregnable defences – the terrain did most of the work – but to create a royal residence within.

In terms of sheer scale, no ancient fortresses can compete with the enormous linear defences created by early imperial powers. The Roman empire by the 2nd century AD was ringed by fortified frontiers, some along natural barriers such as rivers, others in the shape of ramparts or walls. The most impressive example of this capability is without question the Great Wall of China. Whether such extravagant projects were ever effective in strictly military terms may be open to question; but they did proclaim imperial control in a striking and inescapable manner. No northern nomad arriving at the Great Wall of China could have been left in any doubt as to the power of the empire which could command the work of so many men over so many years.

The extravagant nature of such imperial frontiers brings us back once again to the dual function of great fortifications: both to dominate and to protect. The ambiguity is such that appearances can sometimes be deceptive: the Inca 'fortress' of Sacsawaman may really have been a temple. Many have argued that the hillforts of southern Britain, such as Maiden Castle, were statements of power by local leaders or communities, rather than places of refuge or residence. In the absence of written accounts, it is often difficult to be sure; archaeology rarely provides conclusive evidence for attack. And indeed, it may be that the absence of such evidence is the strongest testimony to the effectiveness of these structures, secure behind the aura of power they projected as well as the height of their ramparts and the breadth of their ditches.

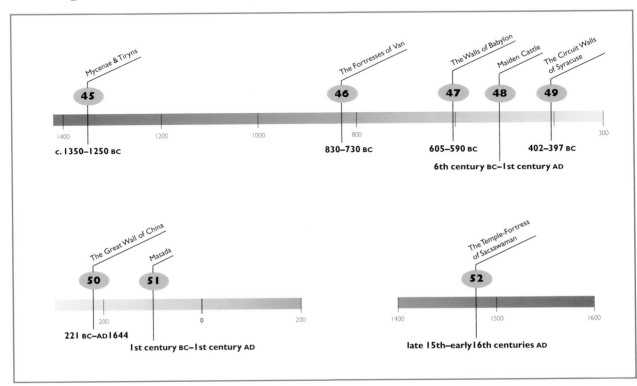

Mycenae & Tiryns

Time: c. 1350–1250 BC
Location: southern Greece

The wall, which is the only part of the ruins still remaining, is a work of the Cyclopes made of unwrought stones, each stone being so big that a pair of mules could not move the smallest from its place to the slightest degree.

PAUSANIAS, *c*. AD 150

MYCENAE AND TIRYNS, Bronze Age citadels in the eastern Peloponnese, are renowned for their massive fortifications built with huge blocks of stone fitted together in 'cyclopean' style. This construction technique was named after the one-eyed Cyclops of Greek legend, because it was thought that only giants could have lifted such massive blocks. Mycenae first came to modern attention in 1876, when Heinrich Schliemann excavated there, believing it to be the palace of Homer's Agamemnon. Schliemann did indeed discover remains of a palace, along with tombs – the famous Shaft Graves – containing swords, daggers and other precious objects. These confirmed his belief that Mycenae was a royal stronghold, and he followed this with explorations at Tiryns, 5 km (3 miles) to the south. Similar sites have subsequently been discovered elsewhere in Greece, but Mycenae and Tiryns remain the most impressive examples of Mycenaean skill in fortification.

The massive fortifications at Mycenae and Tiryns enclose palaces, cult centres, central storage areas and valuable underground water sources. Their ruling elites were buried in large tholos tombs near

The imposing Lion Gate at Mycenae. Lintel and jamb stones weigh well in excess of 20 tonnes.

FACTFILE

Tiryns

Circuit length	1105 m
Preserved height	up to 12.5 m
Width	7.5–17 m
Minimum stone required	145,214.784 cu. m or 14,420 aver. stones
Time to move 1 block using men	2.125 days*
Time to move all blocks using men	110.52 years*
Time to move 1 block using oxen	0.125 days*
Time to move all blocks using oxen	9.9 years*

* based on an 8-hour working day

Artist's reconstruction of the citadel of Mycenae in the final phase of the fortification circuit, when it enclosed both the circle of shaft graves to the west and extended to the northeast. Wall crenellations and building superstructures are purely hypothetical.

the citadels, such as the famous Treasury of Atreus at Mycenae (p. 54). While it cannot be established whether an autocratic state was imposed or an oligarchy governed the sites, there is little doubt that what we are looking at are centres of power. The sheer size of the fortifications illustrates the massive effort involved and the huge numbers of labourers who would have been needed to quarry, transport and assemble these stones.

The first fortifications at Mycenae were built *c.* 1350–1330 BC, at approximately the same time that the circuit wall at Tiryns was constructed. Walls were composed of two faces made up of large limestone blocks, fitted together with smaller stones, and an earth and stone fill between. There was no order to laying the stones: walls were not built in courses, though larger stones tended to be reserved for corners.

This same style of building continued to be used in the next phase of the fortifications, although clay was also employed to fill joints between stones. Building stones became larger, many averaging over 1 m (3.3 ft) in length, and were dressed into shape by the use of stone hammers. Walls were extended to enclose and protect a greater area and massive entrance gates were erected with lintel and jamb stones well exceeding 20 tonnes. At Mycenae, the walls now encircled the shaft graves to the west. At Tiryns, the walls were extended to enclose the whole of the upper citadel rock.

In the final phase of construction at Mycenae, the walls were extended out to enclose the northeast spur of the citadel. By this time at Tiryns there was already a mud-brick fortification enclosing the large, lower part of the citadel rock; this was replaced by a stone construction at approximately

Above **The East Gallery at Tiryns. A number of store-rooms could be accessed by way of this corbelled passage.**

the same time that Mycenae built its northeast extension, *c.* 1250 BC. Blocks are now larger, some up to 4 m (13.2 ft) in length, and walls are substantial, averaging 8 m (26.3 ft) wide at Mycenae and up to 17 m (55.8 ft) wide at Tiryns, where covered passages were built within the walls. By the final phase of building, the fortifications were impressive constructions of massive stones.

Building the fortifications

The quarries were located within 1 km (0.6 miles) of the citadels and it is here that work on the fortifications began. For the larger blocks weighing up to 100 tonnes, such as those intended for the monumental gates, channels were dug and a system of wedges and levers used to free the block from its parent stone. For the smaller blocks, averaging close to 2 tonnes, teams of men worked the limestone with picks, prying stones free from their beds. Sledges and wagons would have conveyed the stones from the quarries, while levers, ramps, ropes and sheer manpower would have raised and shifted building stones into position.

The use of a sledge saved time and energy – pulled by a team of oxen each would have required only one or two men to guide the draft team and load. Sledges were also ideal for moving the massive lintel and jamb stones, the weight of which would have crippled any wagon. Wagons were more commonly used for smaller loads since they were better suited to the terrain and provided greater resilience to uneven roads. Additional oxen were probably harnessed to the teams at the approach to the citadels to assist in the steep climb upwards. Donkeys were also used, but purely as pack animals to convey small stones and clay.

The outer fortification wall of the citadel of Tiryns.

On site, there was little room to manoeuvre blocks into place and so a combination of methods was used. For the largest stones, a system of levers was employed. By wedging up one end of a stone with levers, inserting a block, raising the opposite end and again inserting a block, a platform was created on which the stone could rest. This process was continually repeated until the stone had reached its required height and could be shifted into place. Smaller loads were simply hoisted by ropes running over a support frame or timber horse. For the largest blocks weighing close to 100 tonnes a ramp and oxen power were surely essential.

These walls were not simple in design. At Tiryns, galleries run along the south and southeast sides of the upper citadel. Although argued by some to have served a defensive purpose, there are no embrasures through which defenders could have taken aim on besiegers, nor do the galleries occupy the most vulnerable parts of the walls. Rather, the passages lead to a series of closed spaces that may have served as store-rooms. Embrasures do occur in the final, lower wall at Tiryns and it may be at this time that the site took on a defensive role.

The passage roofs were built using the corbelling technique, with the stones of the walls overlapping slightly on either side of the passage as the walls rise, until they meet in the middle. It would have been necessary to use a support frame to build these 'arches' employing a dry masonry technique. Such a frame would have held stones in place until they could have been secured with the packing of earth and small stones into crevices.

Galleries were also built to give access to vital underground water supplies. At Tiryns, two passages of corbelled arches run beneath the lower fortification wall, and at Mycenae, corbelled construction is used for part of the passage in the northeast leading to a water supply.

The minimum effort to build these fortifications was substantial. At Tiryns, at least 112 oxen and close to 50 men would have been required to build the entire circuit wall. However, these numbers must surely be increased to account for more than one team of labourers working quarries, transporting stones and building various sections of the wall. Moreover, the fortification evolved into its final form through distinct phases, each of which would have demanded additional labourers for the extensive building that was going on within the confines of the walls. Further embellishments to the fortifications – wallwalks and parapets, towers and staircases, and architectural decoration and refinements – would have required yet more resources.

Although there is some evidence of destruction, the sites do not seem to have been sacked. Earthquakes were responsible for some damage and at Tiryns a flood destroyed the lower city mud-brick wall. The enormous effort suggests in fact that these structures were not built for any immediate defensive purpose but were rather part of an offensive, or even suppressive, programme in which the centres displayed their power over the surrounding territories. We cannot doubt their success, for the massive fortifications of Tiryns and Mycenae still convey a powerful message of dominance and control.

The Fortresses of Van

Time: c. 830–730 BC
Location: Turkey, Armenia and Iran

Of the beauty of the site it would be impossible to speak too highly.... The Armenians have a proverb which is often quoted: Van in this world and Paradise in the next.

H.B.F. LYNCH, 1901

MODERN TURKEY, Armenia and Iran meet in a strange landscape: plains, narrow valleys and blue mineral lakes are dominated by mountains, of which Mount Ararat, over 5000 m (16,400 ft) high, is much the most dramatic. Between 850 and 600 BC, this region was home to the powerful kingdom of Van, or Urartu, and the fortresses which controlled it are even today among the most spectacular in the world. In their heyday the plastered mud-brick walls, with massive stone footings and gleaming crenellations, would have drawn the eye from miles away, perching watchfully on precipitous peaks with an ominous and commanding presence – one ancient writer compared them with the stars of the sky. And of all these, the citadel of Van, overlooking the Urartian capital Tushpa, is without question the most impressive.

No site too steep

The Urartians took advantage of the natural terrain, siting their fortresses on hilltops overlooking the main centres of population. That some of these hills were inconveniently long and narrow was no deterrent. The Van citadel is a good illustration: the steep-sided ridge on which it stands is over 1 km (0.6

The gateway of the medieval castle at Van, which was founded on the ancient walls.

FACTFILE

Van citadel (Turkey)	length 1050 m; max. width 125 m
Bastam citadel (Iran)	length 1000 m; max. width 325 m
Armavir citadels and town (Armenia)	length 3500 m; max. width 600 m
Founder of kingdom (?) Aramu	c. 860–840 BC
Founder of Van (Tushpa) Sarduri I	c. 840–825 BC
Expansion of fortress system	830–730 BC

miles) long, but for the most part is only 50 m (165 ft) wide, with a maximum width of around 125 m (410 ft). At another site, the Urartian fortress was separated from the adjoining ridge by a rock-cut ditch 10 m (33 ft) wide.

Sometimes the walls had a substructure of cyclopean blocks laid directly on natural soil, but more often the creation of the walls first entailed cutting into the rock itself along the edges of outcrops. The rock was carved into a series of steps, up to 1 m (3.25 ft) high, on which the bases of the walls were to be laid. The work was done with iron picks and hammers, and innumerable prisoners-of-war probably provided the manpower.

Master masons

The lower parts of the walls were built of stone, unmortared, with a slight backwards slant, and dressed with varying degrees of care. Sawn local stone was the straightforward material, but at Van itself basalt blocks up to 6 m (20 ft) long had been transported from a volcanic mountain 50 km (31 miles) away on the far side of the lake.

While the height of the stonework depended on the location, the walls were generally about 3–4 m (10–13 ft) wide, with regular courses 50 cm–1 m (19 in to 3.25 ft) high. The core was not solid but filled with smaller packed stones. At intervals of about 10 m (33 ft) along the walls were shallow projecting towers or buttresses, about 4 m (13 ft) wide. The top of this structure was level, and was sometimes covered with a course of lime, apparently to protect against rising damp.

It was the superstructure that really defended the fortress, and it was made of the classic Middle Eastern material, sun-dried brick covered with mud-plaster. Sargon of Assyria in 714 BC, describing one Urartian fortress he had probably managed to capture, says that the walls were 120 brick-courses high. Bricks around 15 cm (6 in) thick would give a total height exceeding 18 m (59 ft), to which may be added the height of the stone base and the crenellations. Other strongholds were described as standing 120 m (394 ft) above the plain, perhaps the height of the outcrops on top of which they were built.

Rigorous government control

Some of the fortresses enclosed palaces and temples, while others seem to have functioned mainly as administrative centres and contained store-rooms for the produce of the land, notably grain, fruit,

meat, oil and wine. Internal buildings were placed at different levels on rock-cut terraces or artificial platforms. Visiting Assyrian armies captured staggering quantities of wheat and barley: one fortress had space for about 5000 tonnes. Liquids such as oil and wine were kept in pottery jars with a capacity of 1000 litres (220 gallons) each; there were about 400 of these in one group of store-rooms. We are left with the impression of a very tightly organized

kingdom, and the probably diverse nature of the region's population suggests that this network of fortresses was built more for internal control than against external aggression.

Numerous stone inscriptions list the conquests and public works of Urartian rulers, and we have a few other documents, but there are no good records of the decline. The kingdom finally disintegrated towards the end of the 7th century BC, when nomads such as Scythians from the northern steppe were raiding much of the Near East. Urartu later became part of the Persian empire. The fortresses were later looted and abandoned, but the stone foundations remained viable. Those at Van still today support medieval walls.

The fortress of Van dominates a long and narrow ridge, with a precipitous drop on the far side.

The Walls of Babylon

Time: 605–590 BC
Location: Babylon, Iraq

I built a mighty moat-wall of brick and bitumen, and linked it to the moat-wall built by my father.
I laid its foundations on the underworld. I made it as high as a mountain.

NEBUCHADNEZZAR, *c.* 590 BC

IN 625 BC NABOPOLASSAR expelled the Assyrians from Babylon and established himself as an independent monarch. Within 20 years his empire had expanded to reach from the Gulf to the Mediterranean, and his son, Nebuchadnezzar (605–562 BC), set about converting the capital city into an imperial metropolis of appropriate magnificence.

Nebuchadnezzar's main innovation was the extensive use of baked brick. Sun-dried mud-bricks were traditionally used in Mesopotamia, where stone is scarce; these are simple to make but need constant maintenance. Baked bricks are more complicated to make – furnaces and fuel are required – but then they last virtually forever. Unfortunately the outstanding quality of Nebuchadnezzar bricks

ensured that, in later times, his finest buildings were gradually demolished and the bricks reused.

The bricks were made of the local alluvial soil or clay, which is very fine-textured and needs a liberal admixture of chaff. Herodotus states that the clay was dug from the city's moats and the bricks made on the spot, which makes excellent sense. They are

FACTFILE

Outer wall
Nebuchadnezzar (605–562 BC)
Length at least 12 km
Internal wall mud-brick, 7 m wide, with projecting turrets on both
    faces, 8.37 m wide and 52.5 m apart; height 25 m?
Fill between walls rubble, 12 m wide; height 15 m?
External wall baked brick, 7.8 m wide; turrets? height 20 m?
Moat-wall baked brick, 3.3 m wide; height unknown
Main gates 5

Inner wall
Nabopolassar (625–605 BC) and Nebuchadnezzar (605–562 BC)
Length c. 8.5 km
Internal wall mud-brick, 6.5 m wide, with projecting turrets on both
    faces, 9.5 m wide and 18.1 m apart; height 25 m?
Fill between walls earth?, 7.2 m wide; height 15 m?
External wall mud-brick, 3.7 m wide, with projecting turrets on both
    faces, 5.1 m wide and 20.5 m apart; height 20 m?
Open space between external wall and moat-wall 20 m wide
Moat-wall baked brick foundations, 3.5 m wide
Moat 80 m wide, depth unknown
Main gates 8

The wall alongside the Euphrates at Babylon, with the ziggurrat, the 'Tower of Babel', beyond.

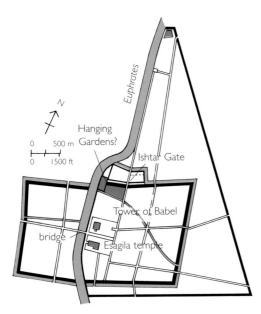

Babylon: the triangular outer wall partly enclosing the rectangular inner wall of the city.

as forming a square, with each side over 20 km (12.5 miles) long, giving a total length of about 85 km (53 miles); later historians reduce the figure to some 60 or 70 km (37 or 44 miles), but this is still far longer than anything found today. The Greek accounts are generally so well-informed that it is difficult to dismiss them as fantasy: one possibility is that, because the city was described as square, the total length was inadvertently multiplied by four.

One side of the outer wall, meeting another at a right angle, can still be traced on the ground, east of the River Euphrates. It is 4.4 km (2.75 miles) long, which would give a square enclosure of about 1936 ha (4784 acres) – half the size of Manhattan island. Scholars usually give the area of Babylon as about 850 ha (2100 acres), as no evidence for the outer wall has been found west of the river; it would still be the largest city in ancient Mesopotamia.

Impregnable defences
Towers at regular intervals and gates covered in bronze punctuated the wall, and there was a moat in front filled from the Euphrates. Ancient descriptions give the width of the wall as some 25 m (82 ft), a dimension confirmed by modern excavations, and its height as 100 m (30.5 ft), which is certainly too much; some ancient writers reduce it to a more plausible 25 m (82 ft), like the wall of Nineveh. On top was a roadway wide enough for four-horsed chariots to turn in; this would have been invaluable for moving soldiers rapidly when danger threatened.

The wall actually consisted of an exterior wall of baked brick and an interior wall of mud-brick, with rubble infill between. The interior probably rose

mostly about 32–35 cm (13–14 in) square and 11.5 cm (4.5 in) thick; many were stamped with the king's name. As many as 40 separate moulds would have been needed for the special bricks representing a variety of animals in low relief which decorated the Ishtar Gate.

No kilns have been found, but they were probably simple structures, consisting of brick walls surrounding the piles of bricks and roofed with clay; the firing temperature would have been about 800–900°C (1472–1652°F). Fuel would have been laid along the base of the structure, and in channels underneath it. Dung, dry reeds and scrub would have been suitable as fuel, but it is difficult to see how sufficient supplies were obtained. Bricks were being made by the million, not only for the walls but also for the huge palaces and other structures, and it seems possible that wood from the mountains was shipped to Babylon down the Euphrates. Bitumen from Hit upstream may also have been used. The bricks were then laid with mud mortar, except in areas vulnerable to water, where bitumen was also used. Reed mats were sometimes laid every few courses.

The giant city
Nebuchadnezzar's own documents mention the fortifications, but the Greek historians describe them most vividly. There were in fact two walls. Herodotus, writing about 440 BC, describes the outer wall

One of the bulls of glazed brick which decorated the great Ishtar Gate through the inner wall of Babylon. The bull was a symbol of kingship.

higher than the exterior, so that attackers had two obstacles to overcome. A comparable arrangement existed on the inner city-wall which surrounded the old residential heart of Babylon. This was a rectangle, with a wall that measured about 8 km (5 miles) long; Herodotus says it was almost as strong as the outer wall itself.

The main entrance through the inner wall was the Ishtar Gate. It probably stood over 25 m (82 ft) high, with foundations 15 m (50 ft) deep and internal joints to alleviate problems of subsidence. Gigantic bronze figures of sacred bulls and dragons flanked the door. Above and below ground-level the walls of the gate-tower and street were faced with moulded bricks showing more bulls and dragons. Those above ground-level were glazed in brilliant blue and other colours. Conservators working in the 1920s had great difficulty reproducing the original technique.

The flaw

The weakness of the walls, however, was the River Euphrates. A lake or marsh upstream of the city guarded against flood, subsidiary walls were built along the river banks, and gratings controlled the points at which water entered the moats and other channels within the city, but nothing could guard against complacency. In 539 BC the Persian king, Cyrus, diverted the river. His troops marched into the city along its bed as soon as the water-level was low enough, and by the time the inhabitants realized what was happening, the city was in Persian hands. It was the end of the Babylonian empire. Although the walls were sometimes used again, they had failed the really crucial test.

The Ishtar Gate, decorated with glazed bricks showing bulls and dragons, was the main ceremonial entrance through the inner city wall of Babylon.

Maiden Castle

Time: 6th century BC–1st century AD
Location: Dorset, southern England

It may indeed be likened to an enormous many-limbed organism of an antediluvian time lying lifeless, and covered with a thin green cloth, which hides its substance, while revealing its contour.

THOMAS HARDY, 1885

MAIDEN CASTLE is one of the largest, and certainly the most impressive, of the 1000 or so hillforts built in southern Britain during the 1st millennium BC, the period conventionally known as the Iron Age. From a distance, it appears like an enormous serpent coiled around a long low hill on the rolling chalklands. Approaching the site, concentric circuits of rampart and ditch become visible, cut and built into the slope of the hill, improving on nature to turn this steep-sided plateau into a strongly defended enclosure. Just over 17 ha (42 acres) of hilltop are enclosed by the defences.

Maiden Castle from the air, showing the complex western entrance. Cutting across the middle of the enclosure is the low bank marking the limit of the original smaller hillfort.

On the north and south of the hilltop, successive lines of rampart separated by ditches provide strong defence. But it is the entrances at the eastern and western ends of the enclosure which give the most striking illustration of the design: outworks and hornworks oblige would-be attackers to wind their way through successive lines of defence to reach the final pair of gateways in the inner rampart.

The southern defences of Maiden Castle, formed by successive lines of ditch and rampart encircling the hilltop.

Constructing the hillfort

The hillfort we see today is the product of construction, expansion and remodelling over 300 years. The first hillfort, built in the 6th century BC, enclosed only the eastern part of the hilltop. Basic building material came from the site itself: a simple dump of freshly quarried chalk from the ditch, faced by a revetment of turf. Root marks suggest that this rampart, 10 m (32.8 ft) wide and perhaps 4 m (13 ft) high, may have been planted with a thorn hedge.

Special attention was paid to the entrances. Either side of the eastern entrance, the ends of the early rampart were reinforced by timber revetment, or may have been timber-framed, with rows of vertical posts front and back tied together by horizontal beams passing through the body of the chalk rampart. The builders must have begun by erecting the timber framework, pinning it together with wooden pegs, before piling the chalk blocks between. The gates themselves were also of wood, probably oak from nearby woodlands. In later phases, these timber revetments were replaced by drystone walling of limestone quarried from exposures near Upwey, some 3 km (2 miles) to the south.

The most significant change in the history of Maiden Castle was the extension of the original

FACTFILE

Area within defences	17.22 ha
Area including defences	45.28 ha
Area of early hillfort	6.47 ha
Maximum depth of defences (western entrance)	190 m
Maximum depth of defences (southern side)	130 m

Reconstruction of Maiden Castle as it may have appeared in the 4th century BC, with groups of circular, conical-roofed houses within the enclosure. The main entrances through the inner rampart were furnished with massive timber gates.

modest hillfort to cover the whole of the hilltop in the 4th century BC. There followed a continuous process of enhancement and repair. The inner chalk rampart of the extended fort was first heightened by a turf breastwork, then a chalk mound, before a more ambitious enlargement engulfed these earlier structures in a rampart not of chalk but of clay. The clay was dug from quarry pits along the inside edge of the rampart.

In these later phases, both inner and outer faces of the inner rampart were faced with chalk or limestone blocks. In its final state, a palisade of massive timber uprights was erected along the crest of the inner rampart, which now merged directly with the V-shaped ditch in front to present a single steeply sloping incline 14 m (46 ft) high. Beyond this inner rampart were the outer circuits, two on the north and three on the south, providing an unforgettable image as they descend the crest of the hill. This defence in depth (up to 130 m (425 ft) deep on the south) may have been intended to counter enemy slingstones – many caches of slingstones were found during excavations – or alternatively it may simply have been designed to impress.

It is not known how many people were engaged in building Maiden Castle, nor how they were organized. We may perhaps envisage piecemeal building, repairs and reconstruction on an almost annual basis, over a period of 300 years or more. Within the fort were traces of streets and circular houses. The massive quantities of grain stored in pits and raised granaries at Maiden Castle, however, may well have been levied in large part from dependent communities and used to feed the labour force working at certain times of year on the defences. In this way the building of the hillfort provided a mechanism for binding together the communities of the surrounding area, both through co-operative labour and contributions of food. The result is a truly spectacular monument, designed as much for show as to defend whoever sought refuge within it.

The Circuit Walls of Syracuse

Time: 402–397 BC
Location: Sicily

Wanting the walls to be constructed as speedily as possible, he [Dionysius I] compelled agricultural labourers to assemble, 60,000 in all, and distributed them along the sector to be built.... The activity of so many men, who applied themselves with enthusiasm to their task, presented an extraordinary sight.... As a result the [section of the] wall was completed, beyond all expectations, in 20 days. It was 30 stades [5.3 km] long.

DIODORUS SICULUS, *c.* 40 BC

WHEN DIONYSIUS I became tyrant of Syracuse in 405 BC, he lost little time in fortifying his great city with a massive girdle of walls, incorporating sophisticated defensive devices, the like of which the ancient world had never seen before. Direct experience of the recently concluded conflict with Athens (415–413 BC), when the enemy had been able to camp with impunity on the flat plateau of Epipolae immediately overlooking the city, convinced Dionysius that the defensive impregnability of Syracuse could be guaranteed by nothing short of fortifying the whole plateau, together with the heartland of Ortygia island where his palace lay. That he was able to achieve this in the remarkably short period of barely six years (402–397 BC) speaks volumes about the vision and energy of the man, as well as the tremendous resources of manpower, materials and money he was able to summon. The ancient sources talk of one stretch 5.3 km (3.3 miles) long being built in just 20 days (see above). With an astonishing total length of 27 km (17 miles), the Syracuse walls were to remain the longest defensive circuit known in the ancient Greek world, hugging the natural defensive ridge that the plateau of Epipolae occupies.

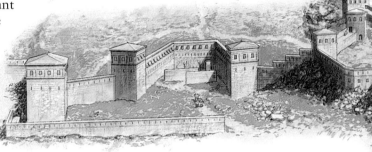

Top **Map showing the extent of the surviving fortifications.**
Centre **Artist's reconstruction of the Euryalos fortress (right) and the partially blocked west gate to Epipolae (above).**

Innovations in defence

It is not the sheer length of his walls alone that earns Dionysius a special place in the history of warfare. Another recent conflict, the siege of the western Greek city of Selinus by the Carthaginians in 409 BC, had also alerted Dionysius to the fact that the modernization of defensive circuits had to be a top priority. He set up 'war laboratories' in Syracuse and offered cash incentives for those who came up with bright ideas. Building techniques, for example, were changed to make stone defences stronger – the two large-block inner and outer faces of the defensive walls were now provided for the first time with cross-linking stretcher blocks spanning the interior, to compartmentalize the earth fill within and provide much greater stability, not least against the battering ram. Towers were also provided at strategic intervals along the circuit to protect vulnerable points like gateways and changes in direction of the wall. We do not know how tall most of the circuit was because it rarely survives above 2.5 m (8.2 ft);

FACTFILE

Length	27 km
Time taken to build	5 years
Width at base normally	10 Doric ft (3.3 m)
	up to 16.25 Doric ft (5.35 m)
Number of known towers on circuit	14 (including Euryalos)
Largest tower	26 Doric ft square (8.5 × 8.5 m)
Deepest ditch (at Euryalos fortress)	27 Doric ft (9 m)

but presumably it was high enough to thwart potential Carthaginian siege towers.

The limestone used for building the walls was quarried wherever possible from the immediate environs of the defences – several small-scale workings just below the walls are still visible; but the main Syracusan quarries on the northern outskirts of the built-up area doubtless supplied the bulk of the building material needed.

At the west end of the Epipolae plateau is the imposing fortress of Euryalos, protecting the main west gate to Epipolae immediately to the north. The latter is set at the back of an open court which gets narrower as the attacker approaches the gate itself – a deliberate ploy to 'crowd' the enemy. Later one of the openings of what was originally a double gate was blocked, and short walls were built obliquely in the court to make access to the opening more tortuous for the enemy. This almost certainly happened after Dionysius' day, and the Euryalos fort

Detail of the Euryalos fortress showing one of the defensive ditches with openings to the rock-cut galleries.

itself in its visible form is also later, having been enlarged and strengthened by Agathocles (317–289 BC) and also again later in the 3rd century BC. Nevertheless it stands as witness to the legacy of Dionysius' brilliant ideas in both offensive and defensive warfare.

The five massive platforms which dominate the site today were designed to take enormous catapult machines to out-gun the enemy. They were probably built under Agathocles or else at the time of the first Punic War (264–241 BC), although precise dating for all these works remains problematical. Outside was a large ditch, V-shaped in plan. A complex series of galleries (another legacy of Carthaginian siege warfare), which connect the inside of the fort to the ditch system, was designed for the secret transfer of troops, and for removing any earth thrown into the ditches by the enemy. A huge five-sided advance work, and a new outer ditch, both never finished, surely belong immediately before the Roman siege of Syracuse in 213 BC, and can therefore perhaps be linked with name of the great Syracusan mathematician and scientist, Archimedes, who helped design new defensive devices to keep the Romans at bay. The great man, however, perished during the Roman assault, despite the commander Marcellus' instructions to capture him alive.

The Great Wall of China

Time: 221 BC–AD1644
Location: China

If the other parts [of the wall] be similar to those which I have seen, it is certainly the most stupendous work of human hands, for I imagine that if the outline of all the masonry of all the forts and fortified places in the whole world besides were to be calculated, it would fall considerably short of that of the Great Wall of China.

LORD MACARTNEY, 1793

LEGENDS ABOUT the 'wall of ten thousand li', as the Chinese call the Great Wall, are legion. Said (incorrectly) to be the only man-made object visible from the moon, it conjures the idea of China as a vast, mysterious and closed land. The scale is unmatched in world history. It stretches some 2700 km (1678 miles) in a straight line from Shanhaiguan on the eastern coast in Hebei to Jiayuguan in Gansu in the west, but its actual length, including double, triple and even quadruple sections and loops at passes and other strategic points is at least double that. If earlier sections of the wall are included, the total length is nearly 10,000 km (6214 miles), more than 20 per cent of the world's circumference. Some 20,000 wall towers and 10,000 separate watch- or beacon-towers have survived and with all the wall's stones and bricks you could build a wall 1 m (3.25 ft) thick and 5 m (16 ft) high ten times round the globe.

In reality, however, the Great Wall is a general term for many long walls, built at different periods in Chinese history. From the outset, the wall was more than a defence: it marked the limits of civilization. The Chinese character for wall is the same as that for city; a wall marked an administrative unit, separating the organized, agricultural Chinese world from the disorganized barbarism of the steppe nomads. To pass 'within the wall' was thus to enter the known civilized world.

History

When the First Emperor unified China in 221 BC, he ordered general Meng Jian to join and extend a series of earlier walls, built by the states he had conquered, to make a continuous barrier against marauding tribes on the north and northwest frontiers. The hardship and loss of life involved in building this first Great Wall are commemorated in numerous legends and poetry. Over 300,000 men were conscripted including soldiers, peasants, disgraced officials, prisoners and scholars who disobeyed the order to burn the classics. Working in mountainous or desert regions, in extreme cold or heat, without adequate food or lodging, it is said that one man died for each metre built. Since then, the state of the wall has reflected China's strength and her attitude towards her nomadic neighbours. In times of peaceful co-existence, the wall was neglected and fell into disrepair; when China's neighbours were strong and hostile the wall was rebuilt as a defence against the swift horse-riding peoples of the steppes. The Han dynasty (221 BC–AD 220), extended the wall to its longest ever, building a loop westwards towards Lop Nor to protect the Hexi corridor in Gansu, gateway to the Silk Roads across Central Asia. Many later walls were built by non-Chinese peoples who occupied northern China and wished to protect themselves against new waves of invaders.

FACTFILE

Width at base	6 m
Width at top	4.5 m
Height	between 6 and 8.7 m
Height of battlements	2 m
Height of parapet	1 m

The Great Wall in fact consists of many different stretches of walls built at different periods; most of what survives today dates to the Ming dynasty. The builders of the wall made good use of the natural terrain for defence, enhanced by the massive square towers and gates that punctuate the wall along its length.

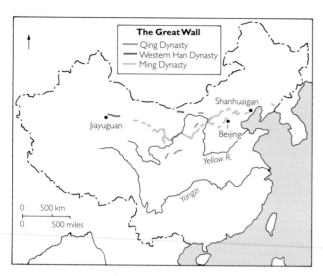

Map showing remaining sections of the Great Wall. Later dynasties added to and adapted sections of the earliest wall.

The Ming Wall

Most of the wall we see today was built by the Ming dynasty (AD 1368–1644). Winding along the crests of mountains, it is 6 m (20 ft) wide at the base and between 6 and 8.7 m (20 and 28.5 ft) high. The way along the ramparts, paved with four layers of brick and flanked by high battlements on the outer side and a parapet on the inner, is wide enough for five horses to ride abreast. At passes and in valleys extra walls provided additional defences. Watchtowers, every 70 m (230 ft), are reached by stone staircases and there are regular ramps leading up the wall for horses. An additional 10,000 beacon towers were built for rapid communication along the wall: in daylight messages were sent with smoke signals; at night, by fire. In the 7th century the standard requirement was that signals could travel 1064 km (661 miles) in 24 hours, the size of the attacking force indicated by the size of the signal.

Construction

The early walls were built from local materials with the rammed earth techniques used in all Chinese buildings. Planks are erected on both sides of the wall and layers of earth are then poured in the enclosed area and tightly pounded. Planks averaged 4 m (13 ft) long, and enclosed 80 cu. m (2825 cu. ft) of soil producing layers 8–10 cm (3–4 in) thick; layers have been found, however, from 3 to 20 cm (1.2–8 in) thick. Sometimes thin layers of reeds were sand-

wiched between earth layers to hasten the drying-out process.

In the Gobi desert and steppe regions, the wall was made from local plants, with 15-cm (6-in) layers of red palm fronds or reeds interspersed with thinner layers of pebbles and local soil. In the Tarim Basin, tower walls were made from large brushwood bundles and wild poplar trunks alternating with layers of tamped clay. The essential feature of all these constructions was that each thin layer was pounded hard before the next was added.

The durability of such constructions is shown by the survival of wall sections dating back to 656 BC. Sections of the 3rd-century BC Qin wall, still 3 m (10 ft) high, 4.2 m (13.7 ft) wide at the base and 2.5 m (8.2 ft) at the top, in northeast China consist of layers of yellow clay mixed with a small amount of rubble pounded by small tampers. Han walls up to 4 m (13 ft) high have survived in Gansu, including a large fortress at Yumenguan, Dunhuang. Here, rammed earth and small pebble layers are interspersed every 15 cm (5.9 in) with layers of reeds, laid criss-cross and still in good condition. The fortress walls connect alternately at the corners, and the tops of the squarely based gates taper to a point to prevent the walls from collapsing. Over 100 beacon towers of rammed earth or large, flat adobe – sun-dried bricks, $38 \times 25 \times 9$ cm ($15 \times 9.8 \times 3.5$ in) – have survived in this area. Built close to the wall on both sides, at intervals of 1.6–2.5 km (1–1.6 miles), the towers, 17 m (55 ft) square at the base and 25 m (82 ft) tall, are markedly tapered, and their walls bear traces of scaffolding.

The last great wall builders, the Ming, introduced new methods. While the western half of their Great Wall was built in the traditional way, the eastern half, protecting the capital, Beijing, from Mongol and Manchu attacks, was built with stone and brick over a rammed earth or rubble filling. Fortresses, such as that at Shanhaiguan, where the wall meets the sea, were like small towns with bunkers for shelter and concealment in war, a drawbridge, platforms for training soldiers and military storehouses as well as an outer enclosure for grain and animals.

Such constructions were time-consuming and expensive. Whereas one man with a wooden spade, a bamboo basket for carrying soil, and reusable

'The Strongest Fortress under Heaven' – this fortress at Yumenguan, Dunhuang, Gansu, marks the western end of the Great Wall and was rebuilt on Han foundations during the Ming dynasty.

planks and pounders, could build 5.5 m (18 ft) of earth walling in a month, it took 100 to achieve the same length in stone or brick and the workforce now had to include craftsmen skilled in brick, wood and stonework. Stone had to be hewn, with iron or steel hammers and chisels, and transported from quarries, often up precipitous cliffs, before being placed in the wall. River beds and gullies were paved to provide working sites and the stone slabs, up to 2 m (6.5 ft) long and weighing a ton, were lifted with pulleys or windlasses. Where possible, earthen ramps were used to raise blocks on to the upper levels of the wall, but in places the terrain was too steep and the workers relied on pulleys and hoisting bars in the form of wooden levers, or blocks were hauled by hundreds of men. The same system was used for the monumental granite slabs, 50 m (164 ft) long and 10 m (33 ft) wide, which form the base of the wall at Shanhaiguan where it meets the sea.

Brick facings were seven or eight layers thick. The bricks were baked in small kilns along the wall site; an intact kiln, excavated in 1991, produced bricks 41 × 20 × 10 cm (16 × 8 × 4 in) and it is reckoned that 22 such kilns would have been needed for each metre of the wall. There was strict quality control: records from the 5th century state that if the supervisor could drill his awl 2.5 cm (1 in) deep into a brick, the worker was killed and buried in the wall. A Ming stone inscription at Jiayuguan giving the date (1540) and the name of the supervisor of the workteam shows that the reconstruction works there, doubling the height of the walls to 9 m (29.5 ft) with new courses of bricks placed on top of the original rammed earth, took 100 years to complete.

The better-preserved sections of the wall retain the broad paved walk on the top, with high battlements on the outer side and a parapet on the inner.

Masada

Time: 1st century BC–1st century AD
Location: Es-Sebbeh, Israel

It was a stupendous illustration of the Roman perseverance, that subdued the world, which could sit down so deliberately, in such a desert, and commence a siege with such a work; and, I may add, which could scale such a fortress.

S.W. WOLCOTT, 1843

ES-SEBBEH, ancient Masada, is a high flat-topped outcrop of rock in the wilderness overlooking the western shores of the Dead Sea. This spectacular natural fortress had a strange and troubled history. Herod the Great (37–4 BC) turned it into an almost impregnable refuge sheltering a luxurious palace, a project surpassed only by the massive Roman ramp and extensive siege works needed to recapture Masada around a century later. It provides one of the finest surviving examples of defence and attack to survive from antiquity.

The fortress of Herod the Great

Herod had many reasons to feel insecure. There were rival claimants to his throne, and early in his reign he was threatened by Cleopatra, queen of Egypt, who had designs on his territory and enjoyed a powerful Roman admirer in Mark Antony.

Herod needed an impregnable fortress to which he or his family could retreat in times of crisis, and the rock of Masada was admirably suited to this purpose. It had already been fortified in the past, but Herod surrounded it with a fine casemate wall.

The fortress of Masada from the north, with Herod's palace visible at the front of the rock and the Roman siege-ramp on the right.

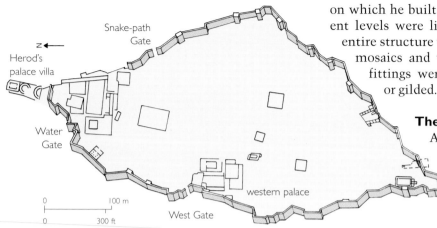

Snake-path
Gate

Herod's
palace villa

Water
Gate

western palace

0   100 m

0   300 ft

West Gate

on which he built a three-tiered palace. The different levels were linked by 120 hidden stairs. The entire structure was finally lavishly adorned with mosaics and wall-paintings; the architectural fittings were finished with plaster, painted or gilded.

The siege

After Herod's death Judaea became a Roman province, and in AD 66 it rebelled. Masada was occupied by a group of extreme nationalists, and by AD 72

There were ample stores and buildings inside, but water-supply was a problem. Always an ambitious builder, Herod acted with characteristic energy.

It was a straightforward if labour-intensive operation. Dams were built across two seasonal streams in the hills behind Masada and canals were gouged out of the cliffs beside them. Aqueducts bridged the gap between the hills and the fortress, carrying water into a series of rock-cut cisterns with a total capacity approaching 5000 cu. m (176,572 cu. ft). Only a few hours of rain could fill these cisterns, and there were others to which the surplus could be transferred. If an enemy cut the aqueducts, there was still enough drinking water for a very long time.

A palace clinging to the cliff

Far more of a challenge, but equally essential, was the creation of a palace where the king could live in the style to which he was accustomed. Only one position offered privacy, some degree of extra security, and a relatively cool and shaded environment combined with a magnificent view. This was at the precipitous northern tip of the rock, and here Herod, partly by cutting into the rock and partly by the construction of massive revetments resting on projections in the cliff below, created a series of terraces

Above **Plan of structures occupying the top of the rock of Masada.** *Right* **Reconstruction showing the walls of Masada from the west in AD 73. In the foreground Roman soldiers are starting work on the siege-ramp.**

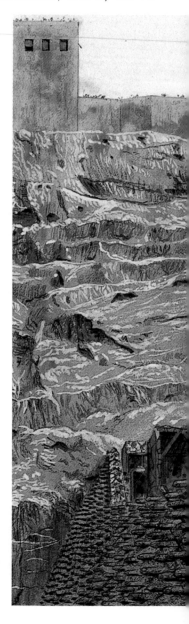

FACTFILE

Length	c. 650 m
Width	250 m
Fortified	c. 150–50 BC
Extensively improved by Herod the Great	c. 35 BC
Occupied by Roman garrison	c. AD 6–66
Occupied by Jewish nationalists	AD 66–73
Recaptured by Romans	AD 73
Occupied by Christian monks	c. AD 400–600

it was the last stronghold of the rebellion. The Romans surrounded Masada with a wall 3.5 km (2.2 miles) long to prevent any escape, but they had no wish for a prolonged siege. The next year they assaulted it by means of a ramp.

Starting from the closest suitable point outside the walls, and founded on a natural outcrop, the ramp was 200 m (656 ft) long and climbed to a height of 100 m (328 ft); in its eroded state, it now reaches a width of 200 m (656 ft). The earth was held in place by a timber framework. On top of it a stone platform was erected, another 25 m (82 ft) high, on which was positioned a 30-m (98-ft) high iron-clad tower. All

this was achieved under a continuous rain of missiles from the defenders. The historian Josephus ascribes the work to Roman soldiers, but the Romans had thousands of prisoners with them, and we may imagine that many of these were forced to work on the ramp and may lie buried beneath it.

When at last the works were high enough, Roman arrows and catapults cleared the defenders from the wall of Masada, and a battering-ram demolished it. That night the defenders avoided capture by killing their families and themselves. While the stone platform has disappeared, the earthwork remains as one of the great monuments of Roman pertinacity.

The Temple-Fortress of Sacsawaman

Time: late 15th–early 16th centuries AD
Location: Cuzco, Peru

The greatest and most splendid building erected to show the power and majesty of the Incas was the fortress of Cuzco ... those who have seen it ... imagine, and even believe, that it was made by enchantment, the handiwork of demons, rather than of men.

GARCILASO DE LA VEGA, 1609

AMONG THE most impressive of all the pre-Columbian monuments of South America is Sacsawaman, the temple-fortress poised on a hill overlooking Cuzco, the former Inca capital in the southern Andes of Peru. The first Europeans who saw it in 1533 compared it with the monuments of Spain, where 'neither the bridge of Segovia nor other constructions of Hercules or the Romans are as magnificent as this', and even suggested that Sacsawaman be included among 'the constructions known as the seven wonders of the world'.

The most notable feature of Sacsawaman today are its three massive retaining walls that flank one side of the hill on which the structure was built. They stretch for some 400 m (1312 ft), punctuated by around 50 zigzagging angles. The lowest wall contains the megalithic, perfectly fitted stones that so astounded the Spaniards: 'No one who sees them would say that they have been placed there by the hand of man. They are as big as pieces of mountains or crags....' One of these blocks is estimated to weigh around 128 tonnes and some of the monoliths measure 5 m (16.4 ft) in height and the same in width.

To the Spaniards the walls resembled those of a fortress, which is what Sacsawaman is often called by modern writers. There is no evidence, however, that it ever functioned as a fortress except during the siege of Cuzco in 1536, when the Inca rose against the Spanish invaders. One chronicler called it a 'house of the sun', which suggests that Sacsawaman played a religious role in the Inca solar cult. Its military purpose may have been symbolic, and the wide plaza or esplanade that lies between the ramparts and a large, carved stone outcrop opposite, known as the Rodadero, may have functioned as a

FACTFILE

Length of longest rampart	400 m
Size of largest limestone monolith	5 × 5 m
Estimated weight of largest monolith	128 tonnes

setting for ritual battles like the ones the chroniclers say took place in the city square below. Today this esplanade serves as the stage for a modern re-enactment of the Inca winter solstice festival that draws thousands of tourists every year.

Sacsawaman also functioned as a huge depository for goods, stored in small, square structures known as *qolqas* that overlooked Cuzco. They contained 'arms, clubs, lances, bows, arrows, axes, heavy jackets of quilted cotton, and other weapons of different types. And there was clothing for soldiers ... there was cloth and much tin and lead and other metals, and much silver and some gold.'

On the summit of the temple-fortress were two towers, one round and the other rectangular, whose foundations were uncovered in the 1930s (Garcilaso described a third tower, but its foundations are now difficult to discern). Beyond Rodadero hill lies an area called Suchuna, replete with aqueducts, cisterns, tunnels, terraces, patios, stairs and buildings as well as a large reservoir that once supplied water to the city of Cuzco.

Moving stones

What baffled 16th-century Spaniards and still puzzles modern scholars is 'how the stones were conveyed to the site ... since they had no oxen and could not make wagons; nor would oxen have sufficed to carry them.' Some early eyewitnesses attributed the feat to demons or to enchantment.

The answer, however, is quite simple: the Inca used their highly organized work crews to drag the stones, using ropes. The stones, remarked one chronicler, 'were in fact heaved by main force with the aid of thick cables. The roads by which they were brought were not flat, but rough mountain-sides with steep slopes, up and down which the rocks were dragged by human effort alone.' Indeed, the Spaniards saw native labourers move large stones during the construction of Cuzco's cathedral, using 'much human labour and great ropes of vine and hemp' as 'thick as a leg'. Like so much of Inca technology, quarrying, transporting and fitting stones was based on well-honed human skills, strength and organization, not on any special tools.

Aerial view of the ramparts of Sacsawaman, poised above Cuzco, the Inca capital. The foundations of the round and rectangular towers are visible on the summit.

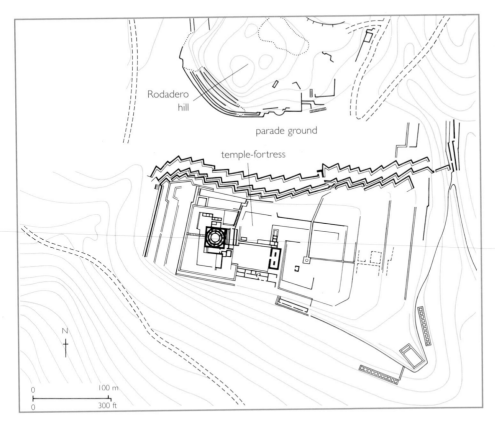

Rodadero
hill

parade ground

temple-fortress

N

0   100 m

0   300 ft

**Plan of Sacsawaman,
showing the foundations
the towers, the three sets of
zigzagging ramparts, as well
as the remains of store-
houses, bottom right.**

Some credit Pachakuti, the fabled 15th-century Inca king and alleged architect of imperial Cuzco, as the builder of Sacsawaman. 'He [Pachakuti] ordered twenty thousand men sent in from the provinces.... Four thousand of them quarried and cut the stones; six thousand hauled them with great cables of leather and hemp; others dug the ditch and laid the foundations, while still others cut poles and beams for the timbers ....' Others noted that Sacsawaman's construction was such an undertaking that it took 50 years to build, or that it was still under construction on the eve of the Spanish invasion.

Achieving the Inca fit

But how did Inca stone masons lower the stones into position and achieve the remarkable fit between the stones? The most plausible theories are based on evidence from the chronicles, archaeology and studies of Inca stone-working technology.

Professor of architecture Jean-Pierre Protzen, for instance, has demonstrated convincingly that Inca masons used hammerstones to shape blocks. He believes that the masons shaped and reshaped the blocks many times until they reached the desired fit. Earthen embankments were built to raise the

building blocks into position. None the less, Protzen acknowledges that this method, while adequate for smaller stones, is not an entirely satisfactory answer to the huge blocks of Sacsawaman.

Architect Vincent Lee offers an alternative explanation. Noting the sequences in which Sacsawaman's blocks were lowered into place and the curious indentations and bosses found at the bases of some of them, Lee developed a theory inspired by the way in which builders of traditional log cabins notch the trunks to each other using a sort of draftsman's compass. He suggests that the Inca used a method called scribing and coping and postulates that the Inca scribe or compass was made of string, wood and a stone plumb bob. This enabled the masons to transfer the precut shape of an upper stone to the stone already in place below it by moving the upper end of the stick along the precut surface of the upper stone. With the plumb bob centered in its hole, the lower end of the stick would precisely duplicate the profile of the upper stone. The intended seat for the stone was then pounded out with hammerstones.

Before this could take place, however, all the stones had to be transported to the work site and to a platform above the highest wall under construction. Lee proposes that this was accomplished by levelling off a portion of the hillside behind and above the retaining wall as a staging area and backfilling against the rear of the wall as its height increased. The Inca masons dragged the stones up low-angle ramps to the staging area.

Once cut to match, Lee postulates, the megaliths could have been lowered into place by using stacks of wood packed beneath the stone to be lowered. To remove the supporting logs from the indentations carved into the lower part of the rock, the masons tipped the stone from side to side, shifting the weight to the wood stacked beneath the stone. Continued shifting to remove the remaining logs allowed the stone to be lowered into its seat. But because chroniclers do not describe such a compass-like device nor have archaeologists found similar tools, Lee concedes that his theory is not entirely adequate. And both Protzen and Lee agree that there is room for alternative explanations.

Sources of stone

The great boulders that formed Sacsawaman's zigzagging ramparts are of limestone, quarried at the building site itself and from the many outcrops dotting the surrounding hills. Other stones, such as the smaller andesite blocks used to construct Sacsawaman's towers and the adjacent Suchuna sector, came from Rumiqolqa, a quarry 35 km (22 miles) southeast of Cuzco. After 1540, Cuzco's Spanish settlers regarded Sacsawaman itself as a convenient quarry and only the sheer size of its megalithic blocks saved the ramparts from being completely dismantled. 'And to save themselves the expense, effort and delay with which the Indians worked the stone,' lamented Garcilaso, the Spaniards removed the smaller stones to build their mansions and churches in the city below. 'In this way the majesty of the fortress was brought to the ground, a monument worthy of being spared such devastation which will cause everlasting regret to those who ponder on what it was.'

Llamas and alpacas lend scale to the enormous limestone blocks in the lowest tier of the retaining walls of Sacsawaman.

Harbours, Hydraulics & Roads

HARNESSING THE FORCES of nature can involve building roads, aqueducts and bridges, digging canals and creating harbours, sometimes on a truly massive scale. The irrigation systems of Meso-potamia go back to modest origins in the simple canals cut to bring water to the fields some 7000 or 8000 years ago. With the rise of cities, states and empires, these undertakings took on a new dimension. The Hanging Gardens of Babylon are a good example (if partly legendary) of what could be achieved: an artificial terraced garden rising high above the flat river floodplain of Mesopotamia, fed from the Euphrates by a system of canals and pumps which raised the water to the 'top of the edifice, whence it flowed downwards through channels and cascades. In the hot Mesopotamian summer this must indeed have been a wondrous site: a verdant garden in a dry level plain.

Water, however, is as much a ritual as a practical commodity. In South Asia, it was water for rituals (perhaps for spiritual purification) which inspired the Great Bath of Mohenjo-daro; a tank of 160 cu. m (5650 cu. ft) lined with bitumen, standing on a 'citadel' mound high above the Indus plain. Ingenuity and skill combine here to overcome formidable engineering problems, though filling the structure in the absence of lifts or pumps must also have presented enormous difficulties. One of the greatest wonders of the Hanging Gardens was the use of screw pumps (sometimes called 'Archimedean screws') to raise water on to the terraces.

The Roman aqueduct of Los Milagros, built during the 2nd century AD to bring water to the city of Emerita Augusta (modern Mérida) in southern Spain.

No less impressive was hydraulic technology applied to dams and aqueducts. The Roman aqueducts of Nîmes and Segovia, of Carthage and Rome, still stride confidently across their respective landscapes. Equally spectacular is the site of the ancient world's greatest dam, at Marib in southern Arabia: spectacular not only for its size, and for the massive stone sluice buildings at either end, but also for the immense depth of silt which has built up against its face, and for its ravaged and weathered appearance, cut through by torrents when the dam finally failed.

Canals to irrigate the fields double easily as waterways for ships or barges. Bulky goods can be shipped by water at a fraction of the cost involved in overland transport. The great Chinese canals were built for this purpose, as well as for irrigation and flood control. Greatest of all was the 7th-century Grand Canal, measuring 2700 km (1700 miles) in length, an achievement to rival the Great Wall. Large cities also grew up around natural waterways along coasts and rivers. In the busy shipping lanes of the Roman Mediterranean, the invention of concrete which could set under water was a vital ingredient in the construction of artificial harbours. One such was Portus near Rome, but perhaps the most spectacular is the harbour built at Caesarea on the Levantine coast. Such massive projects provided sheltered anchorages, but the conquest of nature was often only temporary, and silting has since filled up the channels and basins.

Roads, like harbours, have to do with transport and communication. Like them, they tied together states and empires, overcoming natural obstacles to provide rapid transit for orders, information and armies. Most of the great world empires had elements of a road system, usually equipped with posting stations for relays of horses or runners. Romans and Inca built immense stretches of all-weather road surface along the major routes within their empires. In engineering terms, however, it is where these roadways cross natural obstacles such as rivers and gorges that they become most impressive. The Roman network incorporated stone and timber bridges, sometimes of considerable length. The Inca network is famous above all for its suspension bridges, carried on ropes high above rivers and defiles in mountainous Andean terrain. They still provide a memorable crossing for those who use them today. Yet roads are never purely utilitarian. They may facilitate the journeys of merchants and messengers but they are also visible symbols of the communities who built them. The Chaco road system of the southwestern USA took symbolism a stage further, not only connecting outlying Great Houses but serving as spiritual conduits, linking the world of the living with the land of the dead.

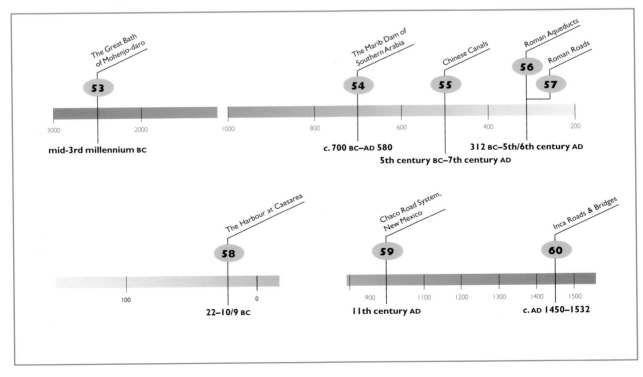

The Great Bath
of Mohenjo-daro

Time: mid-3rd millennium BC
Location: Sindh, Pakistan

In no city of antiquity was so much attention paid to this matter of bathing as in Mohenjo-daro; and we can hardly believe that the practice would have been so ubiquitous and firmly rooted there, had it not been regarded in the light of a religious duty.

SIR JOHN MARSHALL, 1931

THE GREAT BATH of Mohenjo-daro is one of the most striking monuments left by the famous Indus or Harappan civilization. Located within the semi-arid wastelands of Sindh province in Pakistan, it represents a unique feat of planning and hydraulic engineering dating from the 3rd millennium BC.

The Indus civilization once covered over 1,000,000 sq. km (386,000 sq. miles) and was the world's largest Bronze Age civilization. Its cities flourished between 2500 and 2000 BC and had trade contacts with Mesopotamian cities to the west. Mohenjo-daro, or 'the mound of the dead', was the largest Indus city and was located close enough to the great river to benefit from the annual inundation and the proximity of river transport, but far enough away to avoid the dangers of flooding.

Mohenjo-daro today consists of two mounds, the lower town and the citadel. The lower town forms the residential core, with houses divided into sectors by a grid of roads. The monumental structures, including the Great Bath, are clustered on the citadel mound to the west.

Close to the centre of the citadel mound is a large mud-brick complex. On the southern side of the building two doorways give access to a narrow antechamber which opens in turn on to a rectangular colonnaded courtyard, within which lay the

A view of the Great Bath and its surrounding colonnade from the west. In the background, on the summit of the citadel, is a Buddhist stupa dating from the 2nd or 3rd century AD.

FACTFILE

Overall		Citadel	
Area	200 ha	Area	10 ha
Number of wells	over 700	Height	12 m
		Volume	1,152,000 cu. m
Great Bath			
Size	12 × 7 m	**Lower town**	
Depth	2.4 m	Area	190 ha
Volume	160 cu. m	Height	9 m
		Number of inhabitants	c. 40,000

Great Bath. On its eastern side, the colonnade was flanked by eight brick-floored cells, some of them equipped with drains; on the north, openings led into a further colonnaded courtyard. In one corner of the complex, a staircase leading upwards suggests there was originally an upper storey. The whole arrangement has a ritual or ceremonial air.

The waterproofed Great Bath or tank itself measured 12 × 7 m (39 × 23 ft). Filling it would have been a laborious task, for water had to be drawn from the large well in one of the eastern cells; it could be

emptied through a corbelled drain, high enough for a person to walk through. The presence of such a tank, with a capacity of 160 cu. m (5650 cu. ft), on the top of a 12-m (39-ft) high mud-brick podium in the midst of an arid wasteland, makes the Great Bath of Mohenjo-daro a truly wondrous structure.

Building the Great Bath

Stone and timber are scarce if not absent from the flood plain of the Indus river. As a result the Great Bath was built almost entirely of brick and its rooms are never more than 4 m (13 ft) across – the maximum length of the available timber. The Bath's waterproofing consisted of three layers, and was extremely skilful. The outermost layer, a brick wall, was strengthened with buttresses to withstand the pressure of the water. It was insulated from the inner brick shell by a 3-cm (1.2-in) layer of waterproof bitumen. Broad flights of steps leading down

Left **The Great Bath from the south; steps lead down into the bath at either end and it is surrounded on all sides by a colonnade.** *Below* **Artist's reconstruction of the mud-brick complex containing the Great Bath. The twin entrances to the complex are visible at the left, and the great corbelled drain is in the foreground.**

into the bath at either end had treads of timber set into bitumen. The well which supplied it was cylindrical in shape and constructed of wedge-shaped bricks allowing the shaft to withstand the pressures of a 15-m (49-ft) depth. The drain too was built of brick, with a brick corbelled vault.

Bathing and purification

The Indus script, first identified in 1922, remains undeciphered and little is known of Indus social organization or religious beliefs. Until it is deciphered the function of the Mohenjo-daro citadel, and the monuments on its summit, are likely to remain unknown. The exceptional nature of the Great Bath, however, and the presence of such a body of water on the summit of a high podium, highlight its crucial importance. Add to this the bathing compartments in almost every house in the lower town, the provision of over 700 wells and the complex drainage systems, and we may conclude that this is more than mere civic pride. Indeed, the significance of water at Mohenjo-daro is highly reminiscent of its role within major religious traditions in the region today. Water is both valuable and purifying – a force critical for both life and afterlife.

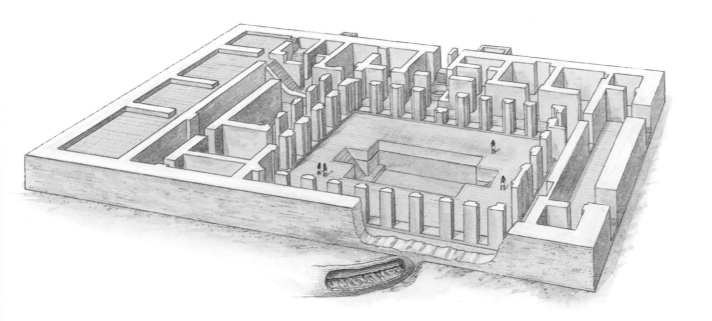

The Marib Dam of Southern Arabia

Time: c. 700 BC–AD 580
Location: Yemen

There was a marvel for the people of Sab'a in their home – two gardens, to north and south....
But they went astray, and we sent the storm flood against them, and changed their gardens into
gardens of bitter fruit.

QURAN (SURAH 34.14–15)

RAIN IS UNUSUAL in the mountains of southern Arabia, but when it comes it can be torrential. The water scours the bare slopes, eroding rock and soil, and finally pours out into the plains as a sudden short-lived flood. Then it is lost, sometimes reaching the sea, sometimes evaporating or sinking into the desert sand. For thousands of years the people of the region have tried to conserve this water, for use in fields and orchards. Perhaps the most elaborate of all the methods they devised, certainly the one that has left the most magnificent remains, is the Marib dam in central Yemen. It developed over many centuries, and its eventual huge size was not so much part of the original design as the unavoidable – even undesirable – consequence of earlier work.

Harnessing the spate

At Marib the Wadi Dhana, fed by a few weeks of rain twice a year, emerges through a narrow gap in the hills. The spate can reach 1000 cu. m (35,315 cu. ft) of water per second. Long before 2000 BC, people began to build simple earth dams, probably renewed each year, at various points along the river as it crossed the plain. These diverted water into a network of small canals, but silt was deposited in both canals and fields. To keep the water flowing, the silt had to be dug out of the canal-beds, and this created embankments which reduced the area of the fields. As they were levelled, the entire ground-level of the oasis gradually rose, at an average rate of 1.1 cm (0.4 in) per year according to one calculation. In places the sediments are now over 30 m (98 ft) high.

It was therefore necessary to build new dams, as high upstream as possible, and what is visible today is the last of a series of such structures. Each had to have elaborate sluices at either end, to control the

FACTFILE

Earliest dams	c. 3000–2500 BC
Construction, maintenance and enlargement of great dams	
	c. 700 BC–AD 580
Final breach and abandonment	c. AD 610
Length	620 m
Minimum height	16 m
Width at base	c. 30 m
Volume of final structure	c. 150,000 cu. m

water being diverted to the fields, and had its own network of canals. The basic problem was to create structures that were waterproof and strong enough, while ensuring a sufficient flow to avoid salinity.

From stone to concrete

Between 1000 and 500 BC, as the cities of South Arabia grew, the engineers of Marib developed or adopted stone masonry techniques comparable with those of their trading partners in Egypt and Palestine. A dense limestone was chosen for the dam, and blocks weighing one or two tonnes were manoeuvred into position on earth ramps. The blocks were fitted flush together without mortar: each one had to be individually dressed. The work was accelerated by building the wall in sections, from the corner of each section towards the centre, at which point a smaller, perfectly fitted wedge-shaped block was inserted from above in every course. These walls enclosed an unconsolidated rubble core.

From the later centuries BC onwards, however, the builders of the dam adopted a technique that was both more efficient and more economical. The critical innovation was the use of plaster and cement which incorporated volcanic stone; this stone is abundant in the locality, and the cement is highly resistant to water. The core effectively became concrete, held together by cross-walls and bonded to the facing walls by headers projecting outwards. The projecting heads, larger than the shafts behind, functioned as bolts to secure the face to the core. It did not greatly matter if inferior stone was used for the face of the dam and the sluices, and the stones themselves no longer needed such careful workmanship, though joints were frequently reinforced with iron clamps.

Unsustainable development

What the dam achieved was the intensive irrigation of almost 100 sq. km (38.6 sq. miles), supporting a population of up to 50,000 people, but it always required maintenance. In the early centuries AD Marib gradually lost political power, and it became more difficult to collect the labour to repair major breaches. At the same time the dam was reaching a crazy height, and there are several records of its breaking between AD 500 and 600. The last great flood occurred in Muhammad's lifetime, c. AD 610, and was commemorated in the Quran. It was a breach too far.

Below left **The structure of the southern sluice, with the tower of the principal off-take on the right. Here the dam itself has disappeared, and the Wadi Dhana below flows unrestricted.**
Below **A detail of the stonework of the dam.**

Chinese Canals

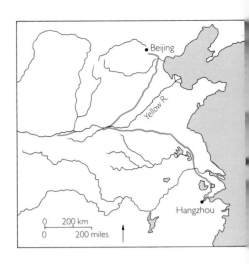

Time: 5th century BC–7th century AD
Location: China

Dig channels deep, keep dykes low.
    CHINESE MAXIM ON WATERWORKS, 3RD CENTURY BC

W HEN THE SUI emperor inaugurated the Grand Canal in AD 605, the imperial procession stretched for 96 km (60 miles). The canal, 40 m (131 ft) wide and 2700 km (1678 miles) long, as far as from Greece to Greenwich, linked the capital cities Chang'an (Xi'an) and Luoyang with the Beijing area in the north and Hangzhou in the south. Along its embankments ran an imperial highway with regular staging posts, repair workshops and gigantic warehouses for storing grain. In conjunction with connecting rivers and lakes, it created a water transport system unique in world history, providing 50,000 km (31,069 miles) of navigable waterways used by the largest collection of boats the world has ever seen. Over a million workers were conscripted for its construction and the expense and burden of the project contributed to the fall of the Sui dynasty 12 years later.

The Grand Canal was, however, only the most spectacular of a system of canals which began in the 5th century BC and is still in use today. Much of the Sui canal was built on the route of a 2nd-century BC network of canals nearly 2000 km (1243 miles) long. In the 13th century, the Mongols cut a direct route north to Beijing, shortening the Sui canal by 1000 km (621 miles).

Construction and hydraulic planning

The Chinese term for hydraulic engineering can be translated as 'water-benefit' and the canals were part of the overall system of water control designed to prevent floods and relieve drought. Locks to harmonize water levels were accompanied by sluices and weirs (submerged embankments aslant the main river course), combined with side canals by which flood water could be siphoned off or extra water provided from storage ponds. (In spate, the Yellow River carries 20,000 cu. m (706,290 cu. ft) per second, enough to reverse the current in the Grand Canal.) Where the canal entered another water system, it was often necessary to canalize part of the lake or river or build diversion dykes mid-stream to reduce the current and ensure a smooth passage for boats. To prevent silting up (the Yellow River carries *c.* 1,000,000,000 tonnes of silt p.a.), saw-teeth jetties were built on the inner side of curves which slowed the current, forcing the stream to scour the shoal on the far side.

Early canals relied on simple stop- or flash-locks with portcullis-like gates of logs slotted into stone grooves in the canal banks which were raised and dropped by windlasses or pulleys. Upstream traffic was hauled through the open sluice with winches; downstream the boats were carried by the 'flash' of water released when the gates were lifted. Around the 11th century, pound locks were introduced, similar to Western locks, in which boats enter an enclosure in which the water level can be raised or

---

FACTFILE

Sui dynasty Grand Canal

Length	2700 km
Width	40 m
Average depth	3.05–3.96 m
Highest point above the Yangzi River	42.08 m
Total length of navigable waterways	c. 50,000 km

Maximum weights for various means of transport

I pack horse	0.125 tonne
I horse and wagon on rough road	0.625 tonne
I horse and wagon on paved road	2 tonnes
I pack horse pulling river barge	30 tonnes
I pack horse pulling canal barge	50 tonnes

lowered, but the gates were still lifted, rather than swung open in Western style.

All canal, dyke and irrigation work was done by conscripted workers and soldiers with tools – long-handled wooden spades with iron caps and bamboo baskets for removing soil – which have remained unchanged for over 2000 years. Embankments were made with walls of rammed earth faced with stone slabs. To dam or deflect flowing water, huge bamboo net baskets (gabions) filled with stones, and enormous bundles of Kaoliang stalks were lowered with ropes from the banks. Each layer was then covered

Opposite **Map of the Grand Canal; it provided the main route from south to north.** *Below* **A canal barge can transport 50 tonnes, and water transport thus became the basis of all commerce and trade. Convoys several kilometres long were a common sight. This is a stretch of canal at Suzhou.**

with a layer of bamboo matting. Some idea of scale is given by a Western observer in 1904 who watched 20,000 men manoeuvring a Kaoliang bundle into a breached dyke. The method was cheap and effective. The porous bundles, able to withstand sudden surges of water, were flexible and could be used on light soils without deep foundations. Once in place, they quickly absorbed silt, becoming part of the river bed. The whole process depended on the use of bamboo ropes made from plaited bamboo strips. Lighter, more flexible and three times as strong as hemp ropes which lose 20 per cent of their strength in water, bamboo ropes gain strength when wet. A wet bamboo cable, 3.8 cm (1.5 in) in diameter can bear 6 tonnes, and cables from three twisted cords have a tension of 7362 lb per sq. in, roughly the same as steel wires.

Roman
Aqueducts

Time: 312 BC–5th century AD
Location: the Roman empire

If we take into account the abundant supplies of water in public buildings, baths, swimming pools, open channels, private houses, gardens and country estates near the city; if we consider the distances traversed by the water before it arrives, the raising of arches, the tunnelling of mountains and the building of level routes across deep valleys, we shall readily admit that there has never been anything more remarkable in the whole world.

PLINY THE ELDER, 1ST CENTURY AD

THERE IS PROBABLY no monument to the hydraulic engineering of the ancient world to compare with Roman aqueducts. Water is an essential commodity for life, and the need is particularly acute in the Mediterranean with its long, hot and dry summers. When settlements were relatively small, and the demands on water supply restricted to the essentials, local springs, wells and underground cisterns usually sufficed. The growth of urban centres put increasing demands on water supply, and at least from the 5th century BC some major Greek cities were served by water brought from distant springs by aqueducts. Rome's earliest aqueduct dates to 312 BC, and may have been inspired by the major public works of contemporary Hellenistic rulers.

The arches of the Aqua Claudia running across the countryside east of Rome, and carrying the channel of the Anio Novus on top.

FACTFILE

Aqueducts of Rome	Date built	Estimated capacity (cu. m per second)	Estimated total length (km)	Estimated length on arches (km)
Appia	312 BC	75,000	16	0.1
Anio Vetus	272–269 BC	180,000	81	–
Marcia	14?–140 BC	190,000	91	10
Tepula	125–125 BC	17,800	18	9
Julia	33 BC	48,000	22	10
Virgo	22–19 BC	100,000	21	1.2
Alsietina	2 BC	16,000	33	0.5
Claudia	AD 38–52	185,000	69	14
Anio Novus	AD 38–52	190,000	87	11
Traiana	AD 109	?	35–60	–
Alexandriana	AD 226	?	22	2.4

By the middle of the 1st century AD Rome had nine aqueducts, which were the subject of a detailed treatise written by the distinguished Roman senator and consul Sextus Julius Frontinus in his capacity as *curator aquarum* (head of the water board). Only two aqueducts were added in the later empire, bringing the total length to over 450 km (280 miles). It is Frontinus who gives us much of the statistical data usually cited on the aqueducts of Rome, although some of his figures are questionable.

Altogether it has been estimated that the city of Rome in antiquity had a greater per capita supply of water than the present city, although this figure has been disputed and it is clear that the aqueducts were

not built just to supply drinking water for the population of Rome, but had many other uses as well. Some of the water went on irrigation of the market gardens outside the city, and for industrial purposes like fulling, but increasingly large quantities of water were needed for the lavish public baths. Since individuals had to pay for the right to be connected to the public supply and had to obtain permission from the Roman Senate, piped water in the home was a luxury and the display of water in fountains and pools a matter of conspicuous consumption. In other parts of the empire, aqueducts were prestige items, often built by wealthy benefactors, sometimes in conjunction with the construction of a new set of baths. They were frequently embellished with spectacular fountains at the point where the aqueduct entered the town, as a way of advertising the munificence and social standing of the benefactors.

Aqueduct technology
Nearly all ancient aqueducts were simple gravity systems. By ensuring that the source was higher than the city it was to serve, and by plotting a course for the aqueduct which maintained a uniform downward gradient, the water would flow from one to the other purely by gravity. Until the water reached the city, it generally ran in a rectangular channel lined with waterproof cement made of lime and ground terracotta. The channel was covered to keep the water pure, but it was not sealed under pressure like modern water mains. The gradient had to be kept as low as possible to prevent the water scouring the floor of the channel, but high enough to maintain the flow. Ancient authors suggest minimum gradients between 1 in 5000 and 1 in 200, while actual examples range from 1 in 40 over the first 6 km (3.7 miles) of the Carthage aqueduct down

Below **Diagram showing the operation of an inverted siphon using a closed system of pipes to cross a deep valley.**

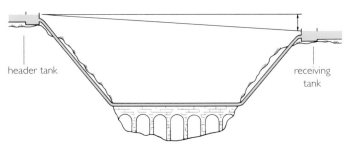

header tank   receiving tank

to one in 14,000 for a 10-km (6-mile) stretch of the Nîmes aqueduct. Where possible the aqueduct channel was cut into the ground, but could be raised on solid substructures of masonry to maintain an even gradient over small valleys or hollows. Occasionally short vertical sections like waterfalls were introduced to accommodate steeper gradients.

The use of a gravity system meant that at no point could the channel be allowed to climb higher than its source; the aqueduct had either to go round obstacles like mountains or tunnel through them. The difficulties which this might entail are vividly revealed in a long inscription from Algeria honouring the work of a Roman military engineer and surveyor called Nonius Datus. Datus had been responsible for laying out the line of an aqueduct for the town of Saldae in Mauretania Caesariensis. Unfortunately, during the building of a major tunnel nearly half a kilometre in length something went drastically wrong, since, as the inscription tells us, the two teams digging the tunnel from each end had both completed more than half the total length without meeting. Datus was recalled, resurveyed the line, and brought the enterprise to a successful conclusion. Tunnelling must always have been one of the most difficult parts of aqueduct construction. Studies of the Sernhac tunnel forming part of the aqueduct serving the Roman town of Nemausus (Nîmes) have shown that six teams, spaced out along 60 m (197 ft), worked for two months to complete this section.

Problems also arose if the aqueduct channel had to cross steep valleys. Where possible, the Romans preferred to go around the head of the valley, as this was presumably the simplest solution technically and the cheapest as well. The main alternative was to build an aqueduct bridge like the Pont du Gard which carries the 50-km (31-mile) Roman aqueduct over the River Gardon to Nîmes. At nearly 49 m high (165 Roman ft) and with a central span of 24.5 m (83 Roman ft), it is perhaps the most impressive of all Roman aqueduct bridges but was by no means unique. Equally spectacular are the remains of the long arcaded substructures, such as those of the aqueducts serving the city of Rome, still visible crossing the plains of the Campagna. The arches served to reduce the amount of construction and to

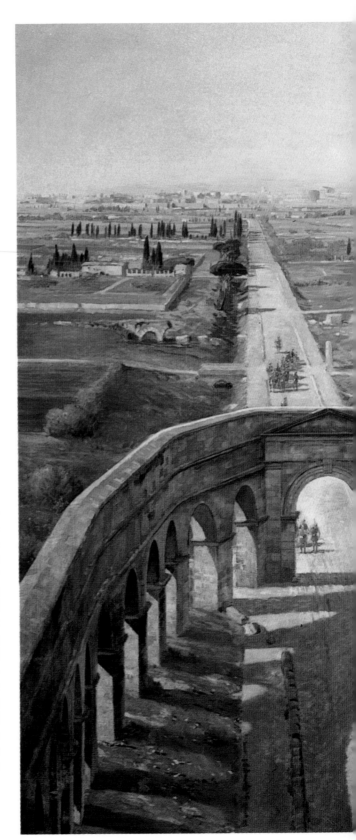

Artist's reconstruction showing the arches of the Aqua Claudia/Anio Novus cutting across a loop of the older and lower Aqua Marcia/Tepula/Julia at Tor Fiscale, just before the fourth milestone of the Via Latina leading out of Rome.

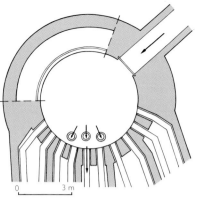

Far left & left **The *castellum aquae* at Nîmes, view and plan. The central basin was open and its surrounds were highly decorated. Ten pipes, 40 cm (16 in) in diameter, lead off the basin carrying water to different parts of the city.**

0   3 m

maintain easy communications where the aqueduct crossed fields or residential areas. It was quite common for aqueducts to be carried on arches in their final stretches, since many ancient cities were built on hills and the water channels had to be carried high enough for the head of water to be maintained. The result is impressive structures such as the three-tier Segovia aqueduct in Spain.

The other way of crossing valleys, used when the valley was too deep to be crossed by a bridge, was by means of a closed pressure system in the form of an inverted siphon. Here the water was carried in a battery of lead pipes between a holding tank on the higher side, down across the valley on a low bridge, and up under its own pressure to a slightly lower tank on the other side, after which the normal functioning of the aqueduct was resumed. There are impressive siphons at Aspendos in modern Turkey and Lyon in France. Lead pipes up to 0.3 m (1 Roman ft) in diameter have been recorded, and the whole system could cope with differences in level of over 100 m (300 Roman ft).

Where the aqueduct entered the city there was a distribution tank (*castellum aquae*) which divided the water between a number of main water pipes, with sluices to control the water supply, so that parts could be closed down for repair. The pipes, often of lead but also of terracotta or, especially in the northwestern provinces, of wood, were laid under the streets or pavements and carried the water under pressure in a closed system. In Pompeii, the water was further distributed to tanks on top of towers which prevented too great a build-up of pressure in the system. It is possible that, as the Roman architectural writer Vitruvius suggests, the smaller distribution pipes were arranged so that in times of shortage private supplies of water could be cut off first, followed by baths and public buildings, leaving the public fountains with whatever water was available; no household in Pompeii was more than 50 m (164 ft) from a street fountain, so that the whole urban population had access to clean water.

Taken separately, each element of aqueduct construction impresses. But it is the sheer scale of organization, and the practical genius and problem-solving capacity of Roman water engineers, demonstrated by the aqueducts as systems, which are really remarkable – making it easy to agree with ancient writers like Pliny the Elder and Frontinus that the aqueducts were indeed one of the greatest wonders of the ancient world.

The towering Pont du Gard carries the Nîmes aqueduct over the deep valley of the River Gardon.

Roman Roads

Time: 312 BC–6th century AD
Location: the Roman empire

After much laborious smoothing, the slabs were cut into polygonal shapes and he then laid them together without lime or anything else. And they were fitted together with such care and the gaps so well-filled that to the onlooker they appeared to be the work not of man but of nature.

PROCOPIUS, 6TH CENTURY AD

WHEN PROCOPIUS wrote this description of the Via Appia in the middle of the 6th century AD, it had already been in existence for over eight centuries. The first of Rome's great consular roads, it linked the city with the major Campanian centre of Capua, and was later extended south to Brundisium (modern Brindisi) where ships set sail for the eastern Mediterranean. By the end of the Republic the whole of Italy was connected by a web of major roads radiating out from Rome; 50 years later it was possible to travel from the Pillars of Hercules at the Atlantic mouth of the Mediterranean to the Bosphorus and beyond on well-built Roman roads.

As the primary function of the roads was strategic, it is not surprising to find that the network expanded with the empire, nor to find extensive road systems at the frontiers of the Roman world, from northern Britain to the Euphrates. Recent estimates suggest that there were 15,000–20,000 km (9000–12,500 miles) of roads in North Africa alone, not counting any purely military communication routes or caravan trails. While their military function was never entirely lost, the roads also served administrative needs by providing rapid communications for individuals and for the imperial post. Other travellers, including pilgrims both pagan and Christian, also benefited, as must have commerce,

FACTFILE

The Via Appia
Date
Rome to Capua	312 BC
Capua to Benevento	268 BC
Benevento to Brindisi, after	268 BC

Length
Rome to Capua	196 km (132 Roman miles)
Capua to Benevento	48 km (33 Roman miles)
Benevento to Brindisi	286 km (141 Roman miles)
Rome to Brindisi	530 km (365 Roman miles)
Normal travel time Rome to Brindisi	13–14 days
Shortest known travel time Brindisi to Rome	5 days (191 BC)

Aver. width of paved road	4.14 m (14 Roman ft)
Width of pavements	2.96 m (10 Roman ft)
Width of causeway across Pomptine marshes	15.8 m (50 Roman ft)

Major works
Viaduct at Ariccia	230 × 13 × 8.2 m (780 Roman ft long × 22 high × 8.5 wide)
Cutting at Terracina	36 m (120 Roman ft)

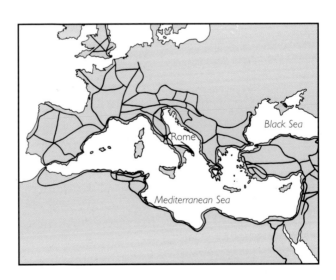

Top **A long straight stretch of Watling Street, one of the major roads of Roman Britain, between Wroxeter and Wall.**
Above **Simplified map of the major (consular) roads of the Roman empire.**

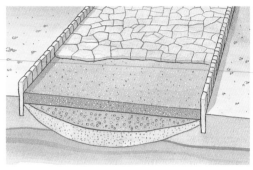

Above **The construction of Roman roads over marshy (top) and solid (bottom) terrain. In marshy areas tree trunks were laid across a timber framework; a layer of limestone flags was then covered with gravel and pebbles. On dry ground the layers consisted of rubble followed by gravel or hardcore, sand and finally the paving stones.** *Right* **The Via Appia just outside Rome, paved with large polygonal blocks of basalt.**

especially of low-bulk, high-value goods. Roman itineraries and maps, such as the late 3rd-century AD Antonine Itinerary, give a flavour of travel on the great routes of the empire, and their continuing use into the Middle Ages reminds us of the long-lasting impact that the Roman road system had on the landscape of Europe and the Mediterranean.

Constructing the roads

Like the aqueducts, but on a far grander scale, Roman roads vied with nature and set an indelible seal on the landscape. While the construction of the roads varied with their function and the nature of the local terrain, the great consular roads such as the Via Appia involved major engineering works. Some of these followed in part well-established trackways, which were straightened, levelled and paved in order to make permanent roads. Once the line of the road had been set out with a pair of furrows, 40 Roman ft (*c.* 12 m) apart, marking the outer edges of the road, a ditch was cut down between them to solid rock or clay; on unstable land, piles were used to form a solid base. It was then gradually filled, first with a layer of rubble bound with mortar or clay, then with hardcore or gravel followed by a layer of coarse sand on which were laid the closely fitted paving stones that so impressed Procopius.

Over time, the roads were improved by the creation of shortcuts to overcome natural obstacles. The emperor Trajan was probably responsible for cutting away a whole hillside to a depth of 120 Roman ft (*c.* 36 m) to allow the Via Appia to pass along the coast just south of Terracina instead of climbing steeply over the promontory. Further south, Domitian created an alternative route to Naples which involved laying many kilometres of

road on piles across marshy land; the contemporary description of this by the poet Statius (*Silvae* IV, 3, v) gives us an excellent idea of the logistical problems involved, amid its high-blown praise of the emperor.

Such causeways and cuttings, together with the many bridges and the few tunnels to survive, show a willingness to conquer nature where necessary to create an efficient route. The same impression is given by the overall layout of the roads, creating those long straight stretches of country roads which are still such a feature of European landscapes.

The skill of the Roman surveyors, often working in little-known territory, is extraordinary. The surveyors were well trained in complex geometry, and able, for example, to calculate the distance between two inaccessible points. They had at their disposal early forms of most of our common surveying instruments, including a type of theodolite (but without the optics) called a *dioptra,* and a long water-level called a *chorobates*. In addition they made use of the *groma* for siting lines and setting out right angles. Nevertheless, while each and every Roman road has its impressive features which reflect the skills of the men who made it, it is the vastness of the whole system which really portrays the power of Rome.

The Harbour at Caesarea

Time: 22–10/9 BC
Location: Caesarea, Israel

Along the coast Herod discovered a city named Strato's Tower, which, although in decay, was capable of benefiting from his generosity because of its favourable location. This he rebuilt entirely in marble and ornamented with the most splendid palaces. In this project he displayed his genius for grand designs, because the entire sea coast from Dor to Joppa ... had lacked a harbour.... Thus, by lavish expenditure and sustained by his ambition, the king conquered nature herself, constructing a harbour larger than the Piraeus...

JOSEPHUS, AD 75–79

THE VAST ARTIFICIAL harbour of Caesarea was one of the boldest engineering achievements the ancient world had ever seen. The city was founded by Herod the Great, king of Judaea from 37 to 4 BC, ostensibly in honour of his patron, the Roman emperor Augustus to whom he owed his power. But he must have had at least half an eye on the economic advantages of creating a new harbour linked with important east–west trade routes, and on the political advantages in his often turbulent country of a Greco-Roman city which owed its founder personal loyalty without any unfortunate associations with a strongly Jewish past. The shrewdness of Herod's move was demonstrated after his death when the Romans made Caesarea the capital of the new province of Judaea.

The harbour

The outer harbour, around 20 ha (almost 50 acres) in area, was formed by two huge artificial breakwaters, originally about 70 m (200 Roman ft) wide. The entrance was towards the north, with the longer, curved breakwater on the south and west taking the brunt of the weather. Within this was a second basin

FACTFILE

Area of outer basin	c. 200,000 sq. m
Area of inner basin	c. 105,000 sq. m
Length of northern breakwater	c. 200 m
Length of southern breakwater	over 500 m
Maximum width of southern breakwater	70m (c. 200 Roman ft)
Largest concrete block	11.5 × 15 × 2.4 m (39 × 51 × 8 Roman ft)
Largest stone blocks	5.5 × 1.25 × 1.25 m (58 × 4 × 4.25 Roman ft)

of a similar size, originally part of the earlier settlement of Strato's Tower. According to Josephus there were towers at intervals along the new breakwater, and on each side of the harbour mouth were three colossal statues set up on tall columns, resting in turn on giant substructures. A lighthouse would have been needed to guide ships into the harbour mouth. Josephus makes no mention of such a lighthouse, but the Drusion tower is a likely candidate (taking its name from Drusus, a popular member of Augustus' family), since it is described as the tallest and most magnificent in the whole complex.

Herod was clearly inspired by the great harbours of the Mediterranean, like Alexandria and Carthage, but the technology seems to have been imported from Rome. Josephus tells us that stone blocks 50 ft long by 10 ft wide and 9 ft high (roughly $15 \times 3 \times 2.5$ m) were used in the construction. The astonishing truth behind this unlikely statement was revealed by underwater excavations by the Caesarea Ancient Harbour Excavation project in the 1980s. As they discovered, the blocks of local stone used in the harbour works were actually rather small and the larger blocks proved to be not of stone, but concrete. These included the massive pierhead of the northern breakwater which measures $11.5 \times 15 \times 2.4$ m, or nearly $39 \times 51 \times 8$ Roman ft.

Because of the wet conditions, some of the wooden formwork used to shape the blocks has also been preserved, allowing the construction process to be established. The formwork was a major achievement in its own right, involving elaborate mortise

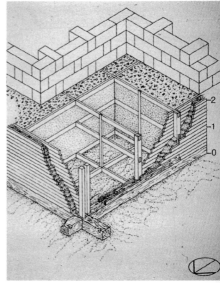

Above **Large blocks of stone would have been difficult to manouevre and position at sea, so complex wooden formworks were filled with hydraulic cement and towed into place.** *Left* **Artist's reconstruction of Herod's harbour at Caesarea.**

and lap joints. Many of the major timbers were from imported European species such as pine and fir which are not found locally. On a base of heavy beams, a narrow double skin of planks was erected, and the interior of the giant box strengthened with cross-beams. Analysis of the concrete has revealed a highly sophisticated technology. The mortar contains a type of volcanic sand known as pozzolana, which gives the concrete hydraulic properties that allow it to set under water. The pozzolana in the outer shell of each block was more finely ground than that in the centre, promoting rapid hardening. When dry, the resulting concrete was so light that it would float in water for a short time. Thus the outer skin of the formwork could have been filled on the shore or just in the water, which would have been much easier than filling it at sea, and the whole structure could have been towed out into place. As the concrete set and absorbed water, it became heavy enough to sink into place, creating a permanent form on the sea bed which was then filled with more concrete to create the giant blocks.

The pozzolana used in the concrete is certainly imported, and most likely came from Pozzuoli on the Bay of Naples, from which the material gets its name. The proportion of lime to pozzolana was roughly 1:2, as recommended by the Roman architect Vitruvius, who was writing in *c.* 27 BC, just before the harbour was built. The concrete harbour technology had been developed in central Italy over the previous two centuries, and relied on local materials such as the pozzolana. Herod, it appears, owed more to Rome than just political will in creating a harbour which 'conquered nature herself'.

Left **An aerial view of the remains of the harbour at Caesarea today.** *Above* **A team of underwater archaeologists led by Avner Raban has uncovered much of the ancient harbour.**

The Chaco Road System, New Mexico

Time: 11th century AD
Location: New Mexico, USA

Think beyond the magnificent ruins, the compelling architecture, the striking scenery, and the beautiful artwork. Think, too of the experiment in political and economic development that took place here.

DOUGLAS SCHWARTZ, 1984

EW ANCIENT North American people capture the imagination more powerfully than the Anasazi of the Southwest. The word Anasazi means 'The Early People' in Navajo and celebrates a pueblo culture that achieved great elaboration in the 11th and 12th centuries AD, then dispersed and vanished in the following century, having constructed a widespread and mysterious road system.

Between AD 850 and 1150, Chaco Canyon, New Mexico, was a major centre of Anasazi society, where at least five Great Houses, large pueblos like Pueblo Bonito, acted as ritual and trade centres. In its heyday in the 11th century Pueblo Bonito had at least 600 rooms in use and could house about 1000 people, the largest apartment-style building in North America until the New York apartment blocks of the 1880s. The multistorey Great Houses were agglomerations of households organized along kin lines. Each kin group used smaller kivas in the heart of the room blocks as workshops and as places for educating children, storytelling and family ceremonies. In the Great Kivas people gathered for more formal ceremonies and to make decisions about the governing of the community as a whole.

Above **Reconstruction of Pueblo Bonito by H.H. Nichols, 1881. The height of the cliffs is exaggerated.** *Right* **A view of Pueblo Bonito today, from the escarpment above the site. The circular Great Kivas can be seen within the semicircle.**

FACTFILE

Estimated length	650 km
Max. straight, continuous length	63 km
Width up to	9 m
Depth up to	1.5 m

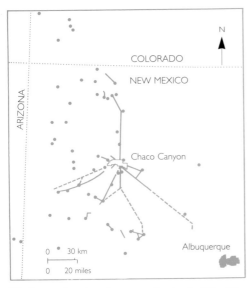

Simplified map showing the general extent of the Chaco road system.

The road system

By AD 1050 the 'Chaco Phenomenon' – a number of dispersed communities that interacted constantly with one another over considerable distances during a period of good rainfall – was in full swing. By 1115, at least 70 communities were dispersed over more than 65,000 sq. km (25,000 sq. miles) of northwestern New Mexico. These outlying sites, many of them settled from Chaco, share some common architectural features with the canyon pueblos. The canyon itself lay at the centre of an immense and

complex road system identified first in early aerial photographs of the 1930s, but not plotted on any scale until sidescan radar achieved more accurate pictures in the 1970s and 1980s.

An estimated 650 km (400 miles) of unpaved roadways links Chaco with over 30 outlying settlements. The shallow trackways are up to 12 m (40 ft) wide, usually cut a few inches into the underlying soil, and are demarcated by low banks or stone walls. Each highway runs for long distances, in one case as far as 96 km (60 miles). The trackways approach the canyon in straight lines, then descend stone-cut steps in the cliffs. Inside the canyon, the tracks merge in the narrow defiles and split, each leading to a different Great House. At three locations where they merge, a groove in the centre of the road clearly demarcates one side from the other.

The meaning of the Chaco road system defies easy explanation. For some years, archaeologists believed the roads formed a network that brought hundreds or even thousands of traders and pilgrims to the canyon for major rituals at the solstices and other times. They stayed in the Great Houses, whose store-rooms provided food for the visitors. This ingenious theory stumbles, however, because more thorough mapping shows many of the major Chaco roads go nowhere, although they are linked to a Great House or kiva. In the modern world roads are thought of as leading from A to B, which means that we have tended to join incomplete segments of Chacoan roads with straight lines. But they may not have actually been joined. Major north and south tracks radiated from Chaco, but only about 250 km (155 miles) have been verified on the ground.

A more likely explanation lies in Pueblo cosmology. The so-called 'Great North Road' travels 63 km (39 miles) north from Chaco before it disappears abruptly in Kutz Canyon. North is the primary direction among Keresan-speaking peoples, who may have ancestry among the Chaco people. North led to the origin, the place where the spirits of the dead travelled. Perhaps the Great North Road was an umbilical cord to the underworld and a conduit of spiritual power. The Keresan also believe in a Middle Place, a point where the four cardinal directions converge. Pueblo Bonito is laid out according to these directions and may have served as Chaco's Middle Place.

Thus, Chaco and its trackways may have formed a sacred landscape which gave order to the world and linked outlying communities with a powerful

Middle Place through spiritual ties that persisted even as many households moved away from the canyon.

Abandonment

In AD 1130, 50 years of intense drought settled over the Colorado Plateau. Soon the outlying communities ceased to trade and share food with the Great Houses, which forced the canyon towns to rely on their own already overstressed environment. Eventually, the Anasazi dispersed to other areas. Within a few generations, the Great Pueblos were largely empty as well over half Chaco's population dispersed into villages, hamlets and pueblos far from the great arroyo. The canyon and its roads were finally abandoned by the early 1200s.

The Chaco roads entered the canyon down rock-cut stairways, like this one carved into the sandstone mesa behind Casa Rinconada. Symbolic paths or actual highways which covered an enormous area, the Chaco roads are an unsolved enigma of pueblo history.

Inca Roads
& Bridges

Time: c. AD 1450–1532
Location: Inca empire

Oh, can anything comparable be said of Alexander, or of any of the mighty kings who ruled the world, that they built such a road...

PEDRO DE CIEZA DE LEÓN, 1553

THE INCA ROAD network was one of the greatest engineering feats ever undertaken in the New World, rivalling the Roman road system in the Old World. The 25,000-km (15,500-mile) network linked Cuzco, the Inca capital high in Peru's southern Andes, to the empire's far-flung domains. 'In the memory of people', wrote Pedro de Cieza de León, a young Spanish soldier who travelled over the principal highland road in the 1540s, 'I doubt there is record of another highway comparable to this, running through deep valleys and over high mountains, through piles of snow, quagmires, living rock, along turbulent rivers....'

Two roads formed the system's backbone: the *Qhapaq Ñan* ('opulent way') that ran between Cuzco and Quito (today in Ecuador), and a parallel coastal road. Scores of lateral roads connected these two, and spurs extended as far south as Santiago, in Chile, and east into northwestern Argentina. The highland road reached north to what is today the Colombia–Ecuador border and a so-called conquest road ran from the administrative centre of Huánuco Pampa in north-central Peru to Chachapoyas, on the

A villager walks across a newly completed rope bridge spanning the upper reaches of the Apurimac River.

FACTFILE

Overall length of system	25,000 km
Maximum width of highland road	16 m
Length of Apurimac suspension bridge (in 1870s)	45 m
Height of bridge at lowest point above river	35 m

Above **Map of the Inca road system, which covered some 25,000 km (15,500 miles).**
Right **The Inca road in Huánaco, north-central Peru, was built on a raised roadbed and measures some 10 m (33 ft) in width.**

forested slopes of the eastern Andes. Some roads, among the highest ever built, led to mountaintop sanctuaries, towering more than 5000 m (16,000 ft) above sea level.

The *Qhapaq Ñan* most impressed early Spanish travellers. No other road featured more Inca centres, or boasted longer stretches of formal construction, embellished with stone paving, culverts, drainage canals and causeways that raised the roadbed above swampy ground. Local quarries or outcrops near the road itself served as sources of building stone. Steep sections of road were negotiated with flights of steps, built of fieldstone or dressed stone. (Because Andean peoples did not have the wheel, steps were an easy solution to especially steep slopes.) The width of the road varied according to the terrain. South of Huánuco Pampa, for instance, researchers recorded a 20-km (12-mile) long section of paved road, 16 m (53 ft) wide, running through the bleak, uninhabited *puna*, or high plain.

In the high jungle or cloud forest, the Incas built daring, cobbled roads that clung to the sides of cliffs, with steps often cut into the living rock. There, the steep and rugged terrain forced engineers to design narrow roads that ranged from 1 to 3 m (3 to 10 ft) in width. On the desert coast, where it seldom rains, the road was never paved, and in general it was a less formal construction than its highland counterpart. Some sections of coastal road, however, were engi-

neered with flights of steps as the road made its way across low-lying hills. Widths varied from 3 to 10 m (10 to 33 ft), and as the road ran through the desert only stones or wooden posts served as markers. When the road reached irrigated valleys, however, walls of adobe or *tapia* (tamped earth) prevented people and llama caravans from leaving the road and trampling adjacent fields.

Spanning rivers

The Incas never invented the arch. Instead, they devised ingenious suspension bridges for crossing

wide spans. Constructed of braided ropes that sagged in the middle and pulled at stone abutments, these terrified the Spaniards. Original construction of a suspension bridge must have been an enormous undertaking; in 1534 Pedro Sancho, conquistador Francisco Pizarro's secretary, observed that it took Inca troops 20 days to rebuild a bridge under the direction of a *chaka-kamayoq*, or bridge master.

A few Inca-style bridges are still maintained today. At Huinchiri southwest of Cuzco, some 500 people from four scattered communities spend three days each year rebuilding a suspension bridge. Before the bridge is rebuilt, each household makes its share of rope, called *k'eswa*, from the dry flower stalks of the *q'oya* grass, which gives the bridge its name: K'eswa Chaka, or bridge of rope. Women spin-ply the stalks between the palms of their hands to produce a two-ply rope about as thick as a finger and 50 m (165 ft) long. On the first day, villagers assemble with their ropes on either side of the river. Groups of men from each community stretch the ropes out along the road in three groups of 24, and twist the strands tightly into cables that are then braided together. The finished rope-braids are about 20 cm (8 in) in diameter; it takes eight strong men to carry each one down to the bridge site.

Men from one village specialize in stretching the cables tightly across the canyon. The braided cables are sent across the canyon tied to a lead rope and are anchored to the beams behind the abutments. Then the men divide into two crews, and amid much heaving and shouting pull the ropes, wrapping the slack around stone beams on either side. At the end of the second day, the base of the bridge has been established: four heavy braids stretched tightly across the chasm; two smaller braided cables will serve as handrails. On the third and final day, the *chaka-kamayoq*, or master bridge builder, straddles all four braided cables, reaching out as far as he can and lashing a wooden spreader across the bottom of the bridge to establish spacing, then lashing them together. He works his way across the bridge, while a second man follows, lashing the handrail cable to the floor with a simple stitch. They then lay a floor of mats over the base, and the bridge is complete.

In Inca times, the bridge at Huinchiri was a minor, out-of-the-way crossing on the upper reaches of the Apurimac, small compared to the great Inca suspension bridges. None the less, the villagers use technology and principles of labour organization similar to those of their Inca forebears, and untainted by European influence.

Downstream from Huinchiri lies the site of the most famed suspension bridge of all. It crossed the gorge of the Apurimac, west of Cuzco, and was maintained well into the 19th century. The bridge measured 45 m (148 ft) in length, and at its lowest point loomed 35 m (118 ft) above the roaring river. It was built of five, 10-cm (4-in) thick cables of braided *cabuya*, an agave-like plant, and had a floor of small sticks and canes fastened with rawhide strings. The braided ropes were anchored to stone abutments.

The Incas also built less intimidating bridges of stone and wood and on occasion used ferries to cross rivers. But it is the suspension bridges and their close relative the *oroyas* – a basket suspended from a cable connected to both banks of the river – that leave the most vivid impression of Inca bridge-building technology.

Building a bridge. *Opposite left* **Villagers gather ropes to twist into braids.** *Centre* **Laying the ropes out along the road before twisting into braids.** *Below* **The completed bridge swinging high above the Apurimac River.**

Colossal Statues & Monoliths

IN SEEKING TO IMPRESS, whether it be their subjects, their enemies, or their heirs, individuals and societies down the ages have had recourse to size, raising statues and other monuments whose sheer scale has often given rise to legends of superhuman feats involving divine or magical powers. Size is especially effective where it is deployed on that most powerful of symbols, the human face or form. Heads, or whole bodies, at dimensions more than human convey a spectacular and evocative message. Here the modern example of Mount Rushmore in North America joins hands with the Bamiyan Buddha in Afghanistan or the Great Sphinx at Giza, the Colossi of Memnon in Egypt or the Olmec heads in Mexico: colossal carvings of individuals real or fictitious, represented at such a scale as to dominate their surroundings, conveying a deep impression of power and mystery.

The strength of the image lay partly in its being visible from afar, which was a consequence of both size and location. The Colossi of Memnon, like the Buddha of Bamiyan, furnished a landmark to royal or religious power which was visible throughout the countryside around. Elsewhere, advantage might be taken of the terrain to site a monument on a hilltop, to enhance its visibility still further. The colonnaded monument of La Turbie (a victory memorial) was one such, placed on a hilltop overlooking the Mediterranean, the better to proclaim the message of the might and invincibility of Roman arms, and the power of the emperor Augustus.

A row of monolithic Easter Island statues standing on a ritual platform. Originally furnished with inlaid eyes, these statues demonstrate the evocative power of the human form and may have commemorated dead ancestors.

Size and visibility may sometimes be joined with another cause for surprise; for many of these works are not only large, but monolithic. The impression of superhuman power is reinforced by the difficulty of conceiving how such an immense block of stone or such a huge casting in metal could have been shaped and positioned. The Colossus of Rhodes, one of the original Seven Wonders, is an excellent example; ancient writers show that the 'wonder' lay in the incredible technological feat which this statue represented, cast *in situ*, section upon section.

Similar responses are evoked even today by the very greatest monolithic structures erected in ancient times: the Grand Menhir Brisé in Brittany, weighing around 280 tonnes; or the huge stelae of Aksum in Ethiopia, the largest weighing over 500 tonnes; but even these would have been dwarfed by the amazing granite obelisk lying unfinished in the quarries of Aswan, in southern Egypt, which would have weighed an incredible 1150 tonnes. Stela 1 at Aksum is probably the largest monolith which people have ever attempted to erect, the Aswan obelisk the largest monolith which people have ever begun to carve.

In each case the technology had to be capable not only of freeing the monolith from the parent rock, but also of dragging it (or shipping it) over some-

times substantial distances to the place where it was to be raised into position. So large are these stones that they have puzzled modern experts who have sought to discover how they could be created without the aid of 20th-century technology. All the more must they have impressed contemporaries, carrying a message once again of immense knowledge, and power, coupled with the mystery of their creation. It was costly but effective propaganda.

Yet the power of colossal images is frequently associated with the sacred, and many of them were acts of piety as well as power. The Bamiyan Buddha, the Rhodes Colossus and the Great Sphinx at Giza, all had a religious meaning. The Easter Island statues, too, had a sacred identity: representations of the ancestors whose intercession was believed to be so crucial to the well-being of their descendants. Sacred, too, were the images formed by the famous Nazca lines scratched into the surface of the South Peruvian desert. The Nazca lines do indeed give a particular meaning to the view from afar. For while some simply defined processional ways, to be walked on the ground, others took the form of birds, fish or monkeys which would have made sense only when viewed from far above the desert surface. It seems they were made to be seen by gods or shamans, not ordinary humans.

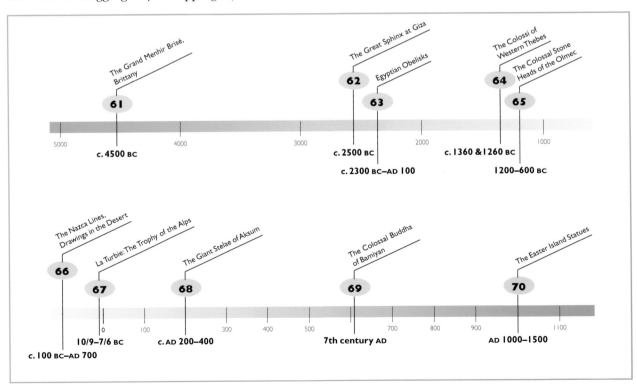

The Grand Menhir Brisé, Brittany

Time: c. 4500 BC
Location: Brittany, France

We should recollect that the erection of the obelisk of Locmariaker was the work of a rude age, ignorant, probably, of the mechanical powers, and mainly effected by human strength.

JOHN BATHURST DEANE, 1834

ON THE SOUTH COAST of Brittany, near Locmariaquer, four enormous broken blocks of stone lie spread across the ground. These are the remains of the Grand Menhir Brisé (literally 'Great Broken Standing Stone'), the largest monolith ever erected in Europe in prehistoric times. When intact, it would have stood 20 m (66 ft) tall and the four fragments together weigh an estimated 280 tonnes. One might imagine that only a society with many centuries of expertise in the cutting, moving and raising of large blocks of stone would have been capable of such a feat. But in fact recent evidence suggests that the Grand Menhir belongs to the earliest phase of the Neolithic of Brittany, around 4500 BC.

Transporting and finishing the stone

The stone of the Grand Menhir is a coarse-grained granite, the most likely source of which is the outcrop in the estuary of the Auray River, 12 km (7.5 miles) to the north. Transport by water may have played a part in the journey but incredible ingenuity coupled with a considerable labour force would have been required to drag this block even a few metres. We should not forget that it is seven times as heavy as the largest of the stones of Stonehenge, and over twice as long.

At first sight, the Grand Menhir Brisé may appear relatively unshaped, but closer inspection reveals traces of the intense process of pounding and hammering employed to smooth the surface of the stone. The finishing was carried out after the stone had been raised upright, since the base of the menhir, buried in the ground, was left unworked.

As part of its final finishing a carving was added about half way up the upright menhir. This now survives in very eroded form near the broken end of the second largest fragment and is usually thought to represent a stone axe in a wooden haft, though

Figures perched on the stump of the Grand Menhir Brisé illustrate the enormous dimensions of the stone. The careful shaping is also evident, with narrow rounded edges and bulbous broader faces.

the axe blade is short and curiously rounded. Years of exposure have taken their toll, and the carving is difficult to make out except in oblique evening sunlight. Originally it would have stood out more clearly, and may even have been painted.

Erection and destruction

The Grand Menhir is so large that for many years there was doubt as to whether it had ever successfully been raised upright. Local tradition holds that it was erected but was toppled by earthquake or lightning within the last 2000 years. Close examination of the breaks between the fragments, however, led French archaeologist Jean L'Helgouach to conclude that the menhir was felled by human agency, and in two distinct stages. First, while it was still erect, a ring of wedges was driven into the stone, eventually splitting off the upper two-thirds which fell to the east and broke into three. The marks of the wedges can still be seen in a tooth-like pattern around the rim of the lowest fragment. This left a massive stump still standing firmly in the ground, but in a second operation it was dragged from its socket and overturned, this time towards the west. Thus it is that the top and bottom of the Grand Menhir today lie fallen in opposite directions.

Above **The relief carving on the Grand Menhir Brisé probably represents a stone axe in an elaborate wooden haft.**
Opposite **The fallen fragments of the Grand Menhir Brisé, with the reconstructed passage grave of La Table des Marchand behind.**

Sockets discovered near the Grand Menhir show that it did not stand alone, but was the last in a line of menhirs, stretching in a roughly straight row some 55 m (180 ft) towards the north. The sockets of the other stones diminish in size as they move away from the Grand Menhir; but of the monoliths themselves only tiny fragments remain.

What happened to the stones that once stood in these holes? The answer is given by the passage graves of La Table des Marchand, a few metres from the Grand Menhir, and Gavrinis, on an island 4 km (2.5 miles) to the east. The hafted axe and long-horned cattle carved on the underside of the capstone of La Table des Marchand had long been known; but in 1984 excavations exposed the upper side of the Gavrinis capstone, and showed that it was a continuation of the same stone. The two capstones had evidently been part of a single massive standing stone, which had been toppled and broken up. Whereas the Grand Menhir Brisé was left where it fell, the parts of this second menhir were hauled away and reused in Neolithic monuments nearby. Thus the destruction must have happened during the Neolithic period, when the sacred stones of one generation were violently overthrown to be incorporated into the burial monuments of their descendants.

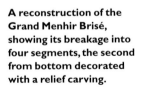

A reconstruction of the Grand Menhir Brisé, showing its breakage into four segments, the second from bottom decorated with a relief carving.

The Great Sphinx at Giza

Time: c. 2500 BC
Location: Giza, Egypt

In front of the pyramids is the Sphinx, which is perhaps even more to be admired than they. It impresses one by its stillness and silence, and is the local divinity of the inhabitants of the surrounding district.

PLINY THE ELDER, 1ST CENTURY AD

THE GREAT SPHINX at Giza remains one of Egypt's most extraordinary monuments. Though dwarfed by the adjacent pyramids, it still stands to its original height of around 20 m (66 ft) and is over 72 m (236 ft) long. The Egyptian sphinx combined the head, and therefore the intelligence, of the ruling king with the powerful body of the lion which was also associated with solar symbolism. Although sphinxes are a common feature of later Egyptian art, the Great Sphinx is one of the earliest and is by far the largest of its kind. The original significance of the Great Sphinx is uncertain but the later Egyptians considered it a manifestation of the sun god Horemakhet, 'Horus-of-the-horizon', who was also associated with primeval kingship.

The Sphinx was carved from the rock of the Giza plateau, probably in the reign of the Old Kingdom king Khafre (Chephren) (*c.* 2520–2494 BC) as it lies adjacent to the causeway and valley temple of his pyramid. Although it has recently been proposed that the weathering on the Sphinx suggests that it was carved several millennia before the pyramids were built, the archaeological context shows that it is very unlikely that the carving of the Sphinx predates the Khafre complex.

Construction

It is difficult to assess the topography of the site prior to the construction of the Sphinx as it had been extensively quarried to provide core blocks for the pyramids. However, the Sphinx's head seems to have been carved from a natural nodule of rock left standing above the level of the plateau; a similar but unworked natural outcrop of stone can still be seen nearby. This lump of rock must have been deliberately left *in situ* when the surrounding stone was quarried for use in the pyramids as the head and upper body of the Sphinx stand above the surrounding ground level.

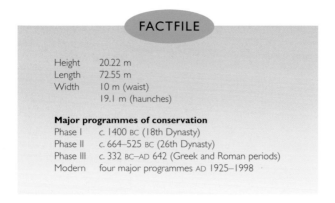

FACTFILE

Height	20.22 m
Length	72.55 m
Width	10 m (waist)
	19.1 m (haunches)

Major programmes of conservation

Phase I	*c.* 1400 BC (18th Dynasty)
Phase II	*c.* 664–525 BC (26th Dynasty)
Phase III	*c.* 332 BC–AD 642 (Greek and Roman periods)
Modern	four major programmes AD 1925–1998

The lower parts of the Sphinx were carved below the level of the plateau, and to achieve this a U-shaped trench was dug around the rock core which was to form the body. Like the pyramids and adjacent temples, the Sphinx is oriented precisely towards the east, but the ditch cut around it is actually trapezoidal as to the south it follows the line of the Khafre causeway. By the time of the Sphinx's construction the Egyptians were adept at quarrying and transporting very large blocks of stone and excavating this trench would not have posed a problem for the workforce.

When the rock could be approached from above, the Egyptians quarried blocks by sinking a grid of narrow trenches into the surface of the stone. The workmen excavated the trenches with hard stone pounding tools and picks of stone and probably also copper. The trenches were cut to a little below the intended depth of a block which was then slightly undercut, split from its bed using wooden levers and dragged out from the front. In the case of the trench around the Sphinx, many of the massive blocks seem to have been dragged only a short distance to the Sphinx Temple where they were used as core blocks: the strata in these blocks correspond very closely to the strata seen in the sides of the trench and on the body of the Sphinx.

When all the excess stone had been removed from around the Sphinx it was shaped and carefully dressed with copper chisels and wooden mallets.

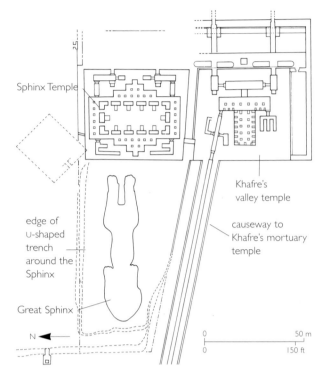

Sphinx Temple

edge of
U-shaped
trench
around the
Sphinx

Great Sphinx

N

Khafre's
valley temple

causeway to
Khafre's mortuary
temple

0   50 m
0   150 ft

Above **Plan of the Sphinx showing the U-shaped trench excavated around the statue and the adjacent temples.**
Left **Combining the body of a lion with the head of Khafre, the Sphinx stands in front of the king's pyramid. The remains of the Sphinx Temple are visible in the foreground.**

Stylistically, the carving of the features of the head relates well to royal statuary of Khafre, as does the royal regalia such as the folded *nemes* headdress and the cobra on the king's brow. Traces of red paint can still be seen on the face of the Sphinx: this colour dates back at least as far as Pliny's visit in the 1st century AD and most probably well before it. Pliny ascribes a cultic significance to the colour and this is likely to be correct as the Egyptians associated red with the cult of the sun.

The Sphinx is, in fact, not particularly well proportioned: the body is too long and the head too small. The ancient sculptors may have been constrained by their material: the size of the head will have been limited by the size of the natural rock nodule from which it was carved, and the body may have been lengthened following the discovery of a vertical fault, now running just in front of the back legs. However, the strange proportions also testify to the inexperience of the sculptors. As far as we know, this was the first piece of statuary carved on such a colossal scale in Egypt and the ancient artists may not have been comfortable working on so large a piece. Odd proportions in some life-size statuary of the period show that the Egyptians had not yet developed the grid-proportioning systems used so successfully in later sculpture and the workmen may also have had difficulties in carving into an uneven lump of rock. Egyptian sculptors preferred to work from a rectangular block on which they could draw their subject and position elements correctly in two dimensions.

The soft stone of the body is now badly weathered but the head of this 4500-year-old sculpture is relatively well preserved. This variation in preservation is caused by the different geological strata through which it is carved. Mark Lehner has identified three different types of limestone: the hard, good-quality

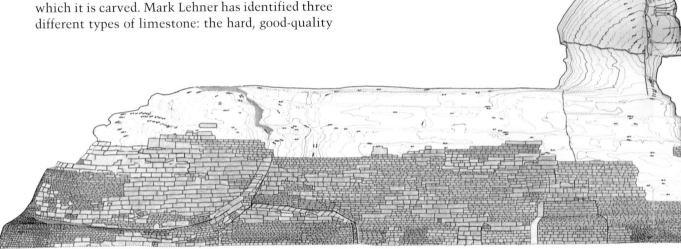

Above **The Sphinx from the southeast. The weathering on the upper body and the various phases of restoration are clearly visible.** Below **Photogrammetric elevation of the Sphinx from the south showing the different phases of restoration covering the lower body.**

Phase I c. 1400 BC	Phase III, c. 332 BC–AD 642	Egyptian Antiquities Service, 1960s–70s	
Phase II c. 664–525 BC	E. Baraize 1925–26	missing stone	
Phase I, recut for Phase II, fallen away	Egyptian Antiquities Service, 1940s	natural rock	

stone of the head; the soft, banded layers of the upper body; and the brittle, fossil-rich base layer. The erosion has been caused by wind-blown sand eating away the softer parts of the stone, leaving the harder areas exposed as sloping ridges. However, not all the damage to the Sphinx has been the result of natural forces: the nose was lost sometime around the 8th century AD when its face was defaced by a Sufi who considered the statue a blasphemous idol, and the cobra's head missing from the brow and the fragments of beard found in the sand below may also be the result of deliberate damage.

Restoration and excavation
Conservation and restoration of the Great Sphinx has been an on-going project since ancient times, probably beginning in the mid-2nd millennium BC

Above **A statue of Khafre from the valley temple of his pyramid at Giza. The *nemes* headdress, cobra and beard are similar to those of the Sphinx.** *Left* **The head and upper body of the Sphinx: the variation in the erosion of the head and body is caused by the different strata of limestone. The stela of Tuthmosis IV (c. 1401–1391 BC) can be seen; it shows the king making an offering to the Sphinx.**

lower half of the body is now almost entirely faced with masonry blocks of varying sizes dating to a number of different periods: there seem to have been at least three major campaigns of ancient restoration (Lehner's Phases I–III), and four major modern campaigns, the most recent of which was completed in 1998.

Descriptions and drawings by the many visitors to the site over the last two millennia show that for much of its history the Sphinx was buried by wind-blown sand with only its head visible. From the mid-19th century, attempts were made to clear the site, unfortunately destroying much valuable archaeological information in the process. The remaining sand was finally cleared by Selim Hassan in the 1930s, and he also undertook a careful and extensive study of the archaeological evidence. Although the area immediately surrounding the Sphinx has been cleared down to bedrock, study of its construction and significance continue: in the words of Gaston Maspero, Director General of Egypt's Antiquities Service in the 1880s, 'the Sphinx has not yet told us all its secrets'.

when the cult of the Sphinx was revived. New temples were built to the northeast of the Sphinx and a chapel was created between its paws. The focus of this chapel was a stela showing the pharaoh Tuthmosis IV (c. 1401–1391 BC) making an offering to the Sphinx. The text describes how the Sphinx had appeared to the young prince in a dream and offered him the throne of Egypt in return for clearing away the surrounding sand and repairing its body. The

Egyptian Obelisks

Time: c. 2300 BC–AD 100
Location: Luxor, Egypt

She [Hatshepsut] made as her monument for her father Amun … two great obelisks of enduring granite from the south, their upper parts of electrum … Their rays flood the two lands when the sun-disc rises between them at its appearance on the horizon of heaven.

INSCRIPTION ON OBELISK OF HATSHEPSUT, KARNAK, C. 1458 BC

OBELISKS ARE AMONG the most recognizable of all Egyptian monuments. They are massive monoliths, square in section and tapering slightly to a pyramidal summit which was often gilded to reflect the rays of the sun. Solar temples with massive masonry constructions in the form of squat obelisks are known from the 5th Dynasty (*c.* 2465–2323 BC) and the first monolithic obelisks of classical proportions were probably carved soon afterwards. The earliest complete royal obelisk dates to the 12th Dynasty (*c.* 1950 BC), but the largest and most impressive obelisks date to the mid-18th Dynasty (c. 1504–1425 BC). Obelisks were sacred to the sun god Re and are found at sites associated with the worship of solar gods. They were usually erected in pairs flanking the pylon gateways of Egyptian temples, although single obelisks are also known.

The obelisks of Tuthmosis I and Hatshepsut at Karnak, showing the polished surfaces and finely carved hieroglyphs. The tips were originally sheathed in electrum.

FACTFILE

Largest obelisk: The Unfinished Obelisk

Date	c. 1430 BC
Planned length	41.75 m
Planned weight	1150 tonnes

Largest standing obelisk in Egypt: Hatshepsut's obelisk, Karnak

Date	c. 1458 BC
Distance transported	c. 220 km
Height	29.56 m
Weight	c. 320 tonnes
Time taken for quarrying, transportation and erection of 2 obelisks	7 months
Number of quarrymen	c. 500
Number of men required to move each obelisk overland	c. 1000

Largest standing obelisk: Tuthmosis III

Date	c. 1430 BC
Present location	Piazza S. Giovanni in Laterano, Rome
Original location	Karnak
Height	32.18 m
Weight	c. 450 tonnes

Moved by Constantine and Constantius to the Circus Maximus, Rome, inaugurated AD 357; moved to present location by Pope Sixtus V 1588

Quarrying

Obelisks were carved from very hard stones which were strong enough to be cut to the slender proportions of the finished object without cracking and to withstand transportation. Aswan granite was by far the most popular stone for obelisks and the preference for pink and red granites may reflect the solar associations of these colours. A particularly useful source of information on granite quarrying and the production of obelisks is an unfinished obelisk preserved in a quarry at Aswan. This obelisk is thought to date to the reign of Tuthmosis III (1479–1425 BC) and, had it been completed, it would have been the largest obelisk in Egypt, standing 41.75 m (137 ft) high and weighing around 1150 tonnes. Unfortunately the monolith cracked during quarrying and was abandoned, preserving clear evidence of the methods used to carve it.

Granite is a very hard stone and cannot be cut with the relatively soft metal tools that were available to the Egyptians and so stone tools were used. Ball-shaped dolerite pounders were used to crush the quartz grains to powder which could then be brushed away. The outline of the obelisk was marked on to the rock surface and the rock around it was pounded out. A trench was cut just wide enough to allow a man to work in the gap, and deep enough to be able to undercut the obelisk. Around 150 men could have worked simultaneously pounding stone in this trench. The obelisk was split from its base with levers and was jacked up above the level of the surrounding stone using wooden struts. It was then manoeuvred on to a wooden sledge for transport.

Transport

Obelisks quarried at Aswan had to be transported substantial distances to their final destinations. For example Karnak, where Hatshepsut's two obelisks were erected, is around 220 km (137 miles) north of Aswan. An embankment was constructed from the quarries to the river to provide a level surface for dragging the sledges loaded with the massive obelisks. Assuming that a man could pull approximately a third of a tonne over level ground (p. 269), a team of around 1000 men would have been needed to move each of Hatshepsut's 320-tonne obelisks. Had the unfinished obelisk been completed, a team of around 3500 men would have been required.

When the obelisk had been dragged to the river bank it was loaded on to a barge for its journey

downstream. This must have been a tricky operation. Pliny, writing in the 1st century AD, described a method of loading obelisks on to barges which may have been a traditional Egyptian practice. According to him, the barge was moved into a canal near the quarry site and weighted down with blocks heavier than the obelisk. The obelisk was dragged into position across the canal and the barge unloaded until it took the weight of the obelisk at its centre. The obelisk could then be rotated until it lay along the centre-line of the barge.

A relief at the Temple of Hatshepsut at Deir el-Bahri shows a pair of obelisks being transported to Karnak. Both obelisks are loaded on to one barge and are positioned end-to-end with their bases touching. This would ensure that the weight was fairly evenly distributed with heaviest parts of the obelisks in the centre. If the representation is reasonably accurate, the barge was over 100 m (328 ft) in length and it must also have been broad to provide stability. Such a large boat would have been unwieldy: it has four rudders at the stern, each controlled by a helmsman, and it is towed by a whole series of rowing boats

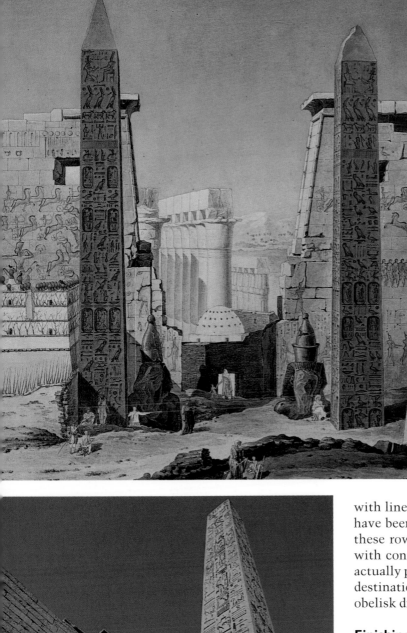

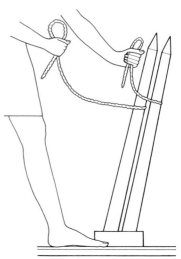

Above **A symbolic representation of an Egyptian king raising a pair of obelisks with ropes.** *Left* **An early 19th-century lithograph by François-Michel Cecile showing Ramesses II's obelisks in front of Luxor temple. The one on the right now stands in Paris.** *Below* **The sole remaining obelisk of Ramesses II at Luxor.**

with lines attached. The barge's momentum would have been provided by the current of the river, and these rowing boats were probably more concerned with controlling and directing the barge than with actually pulling it along. When the barge reached its destination it was docked and unloaded and the obelisk dragged to its intended location.

Finishing

The Egyptians preferred to put the finishing touches to their monuments once they were installed. However, an obelisk of Tuthmosis III at Karnak had been decorated but not erected, suggesting that this was not always the case. The obelisk was polished to a high shine using stone grinders and a fine quartz powder, and then the decoration was drawn on to the surface by a draftsman and carved by a skilled sculptor using stone tools. Finally a cap of sheet metal was placed over the tip of the obelisk and hammered into the grooves of the relief decoration. This silver-gold capping would make the obelisk shine with reflected sunlight which could be seen from afar.

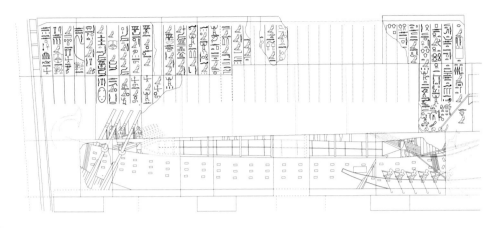

Drawing of a relief from the Temple of Hatshepsut at Deir el-Bahri, showing a barge transporting a pair of obelisks to Karnak. The obelisks are placed end to end and are still strapped to the sledges used to move them over land. One of the many rowing boats towing the barge can be seen near the bow.

Erection

We have no pictorial or written evidence to show how the Egyptians managed to erect their obelisks, apart from a small symbolic representation of a king erecting a tiny obelisk by pulling a rope looped around it. There are two broad theories as to the Egyptian methods. One is that the obelisk was dragged base first up a sloping ramp and then tipped over the end until it rested at an angle and could be pulled upright with ropes. A sand fill could have been used to control the descent of the base of the obelisk. The second theory suggests that the obelisk was manoeuvred on the ground until its foot rested in a groove in the plinth and that the top end was then jacked up with levers and wooden struts until the angle was great enough for the obelisk to be pulled upright with ropes. Although this second method sounds extremely dangerous and difficult, both the grooves in preserved obelisk plinths and the slight mispositioning of some obelisks on their bases suggest that this is more likely to have been the method used by the Egyptians.

Later history

The problems of transport and erection of Egyptian obelisks did not end with the Egyptian civilization which made them. Their distinctive shape and ancient symbolic associations made them very popular with Roman emperors. Augustus transported the first obelisks to Rome around 10 BC, and later rulers added many others to Rome's growing collection. Several of these were later recovered from the ruins of ancient Rome and were re-erected by Popes of the 16th to 18th centuries as part of their programmes of urban renewal. In the 19th century three more obelisks were removed from Egypt and erected in Paris, London and New York. Today there are 13 standing Egyptian obelisks in Rome compared with only four in Egypt itself.

Different solutions, many employing scaffolds, pulleys and pivots, were found to the problems of transport and erection each time an obelisk was removed from Egypt. However, none of these complex engineering methods can compare with the achievement of the Egyptians in creating these extraordinarily refined monuments with nothing but stone tools, and in transporting and erecting them without the help of modern machinery.

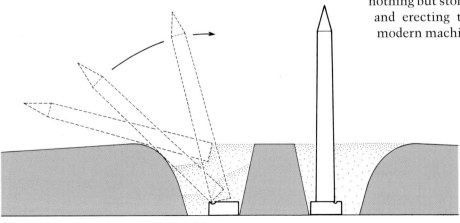

Diagram showing one possible method of erecting an obelisk. The obelisk is lowered from a ramp using a sand fill and ropes to control its movement.

The Colossi of Western Thebes

Time: c. 1360 and 1260 BC
Location: Luxor, Egypt

I met a traveller from an antique land
Who said: Two vast and trunkless legs of stone
Stand in the desert. Near them on the sand,
Half sunk, a shattered visage lies …

P.B. SHELLEY, 1817

SHELLEY'S FAMOUS LINES were inspired by the torso of Ramesses II (*c.* 1290–1224 BC) in the British Museum and by descriptions of the fallen red granite colossus of the same pharaoh in his mortuary temple on the West Bank at Thebes. Although it is broken and the upper part of the statue lies on its side, its massive scale and the quality of its workmanship never fail to impress. This statue, which represented Ramesses as a god, was nearly 19 m (62 ft) tall and weighed around 1000 tonnes. It was the largest seated colossus in Western Thebes.

The sheer size and power of these massive Egyptian statues is best conveyed by the Colossi of Memnon which, although slightly smaller than the Ramesseum colossus, are much better preserved. They represent Amenhotep III (*c.* 1391–1353 BC) and originally flanked the entrance to his mortuary temple at Western Thebes; only its foundations survive and the statues are now surrounded by fields. Each colossus was carved from a single block of yellow quartzite, chosen because of the solar associations of its golden colour. The colossi are now around 15.6 m (51 ft) high, but have lost their tall crowns which would have increased their height to

The Colossi of Memnon, which represent the pharaoh Amenhotep III, originally flanked the entrance to his mortuary temple, of which only the foundations now survive.

Quarrying and transporting the stone

The blocks of quartzite used for the Colossi of Memnon were quarried at Gebel el-Ahmar, about 700 km (435 miles) from Thebes. Quartzite is a hard stone and cannot have been worked with the metal tools available. However, the marks left on the quarry walls are very different from those produced by pounding at Aswan and suggest that some sort of chiselling tool was used, perhaps a heavy stone pick. As with obelisks (p. 263), the blocks for the colossi will have been quarried by cutting separation trenches around and underneath the block. The blocks were probably cut from a vertical rock-face to simplify the problem of removing them from the quarry.

The Egyptians carved their statuary from carefully proportioned rectangular blocks. On to each face of the block a grid of squares was drawn, and this was used to draft the correct proportions of the statue. Next, the excess stone was cut away until the statue was roughly in its final form. Master sculptors were then brought in to finish the statue and to carve any texts or reliefs. Depending on the material, statues were often polished or painted. Egyptian statuary and architectural elements were usually finished once they had been installed as the excess stone on a block would protect it from chipping and damage during transport and erection.

about 18 m (59 ft). Each sits on a pedestal 2.3 m (7.5 ft) high cut from a separate block of stone.

Although the Colossi of Memnon and the Ramesseum Colossus are enormous, they are not the largest sculptures made by the ancient Egyptians – both the Great Sphinx (p. 258) and the colossi on the façade of the Great Temple at Abu Simbel (p. 105) are larger. However, these latter examples were carved *in situ* and did not have to be moved. One of the most amazing features of the Memnon and Ramesseum colossi is that they were carved from single blocks which were dragged from distant quarries. But even they are not the largest monolithic colossi transported by the Egyptians: at Tanis in northern Egypt, fragments of four granite colossi of Ramesses II have been found which are thought to have been 21–28 m (69–92 ft) high.

Opposite **The fallen colossus of Ramesses II at the Ramesseum.**
Below **In 1816 Belzoni removed the 'Young Memnon' statue of Ramesses II from the Ramesseum.**

However, with colossal statuary and other very large blocks of stone much of the carving was probably done at the quarry to reduce the weight as much as possible before it was moved.

The blocks Amenhotep III and Ramesses II used for their colossi are the largest objects ever moved by the Egyptians. The Colossi of Memnon weighed around 700 tonnes each, while the Ramesses II statues were around 1000 tonnes; they are thought to have been moved overland. Although there are no records relating to the journey of these particular blocks, a representation of the Middle Kingdom (c. 1850 BC) shows the transport of a smaller colossal statue of a man called Djehutyhotep. This is estimated to have weighed around 58 tonnes and is shown mounted upright on a wooden sledge to which four ropes are attached. Each rope is pulled by a team of 43 men. A man is shown standing on the sledge and pouring water in front of its tracks to lubricate its passage.

Experimental work with a loaded sledge has shown that about three men are required per tonne of load over level ground. This suggests that about 2100 men were required to pull each of the Memnon colossi, and about 3000 men for each of the Ramesses II statues. This figure would increase dramatically if the ground was not level: about three times this number of men would be needed to drag the colossus up a 1 in 10 slope. More men would be needed to construct a solid and level slipway to ease

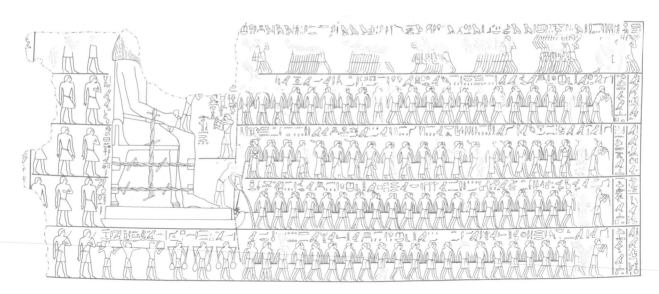

Drawing of a wall relief showing the transport of the colossal statue of Djehutyhotep. The statue is mounted upright on a sledge, pulled by 172 men. A man in front of the statue pours water to lubricate the passage of the sledge.

the passage of the statue and to prevent it sinking into soft ground. It has been suggested that wooden rollers could have been used beneath the sledge to reduce friction but this would have made the statue difficult to control even over level ground, and extremely dangerous on sloping ground. As in the Djehutyhotep representation, water will almost certainly have been used to lubricate the runners of the sledge to reduce friction.

The overall size of the expedition, including quarrymen, guards and skilled labour, is likely to have been considerably larger than the minimum number of men required to move each block. Around three times this number would allow for these additional men and would ensure that the manpower was present to move the statue over difficult ground if required. Thus figures of 9000 men for the Ramesses II colossus, and possibly up to around 12,000 men for the two Memnon colossi are reached.

The colossi had to be moved over great distances: the blocks for the Colossi of Memnon were brought from quarries around 700 km (435 miles) downstream from Thebes. It is generally agreed that these blocks were too heavy to be transported by boat against the Nile current and were probably moved overland. Nevertheless, it should be noted that it was necessary to move the blocks across the river to the west bank at some point in their journey, when they must have been loaded on to boats. It therefore seems possible that the statues could have been towed along canals (where the current would have been weaker) for at least part of their journey.

When the statues finally arrived at their destinations after months or years in transit they had to be placed upright on their pedestals. Although the Djehutyhotep representation shows the statue being transported in an upright position, colossi would almost certainly have been transported on their sides in order to spread the load over a larger area and to reduce the possibility of the statue falling in transit. The method of erecting colossi was probably very similar to that used for obelisks (p. 266). Once they were in position on their pedestals, wooden scaffolding will have been put up around the statues to allow skilled sculptors to put the finishing touches to the figures and to carve the relief scenes on the sides of the thrones.

The Colossi of Memnon still stand, long after the temple they were erected in front of was destroyed. They were a popular tourist attraction in Greek and Roman times and became even more famous when they were damaged in an earthquake in 27 BC. The northern colossus was particularly badly affected and is reported to have emitted an eerie noise when the sun rose. This is thought to have been caused by moisture in the cracked figure warming and expanding in the morning sun. Classical travellers called the statue 'vocal Memnon' – hence the modern name – after the Homeric character Memnon who sang to his mother Eos, the goddess of the dawn. Unfortunately, the 'singing' ceased when the statue was restored as an act of piety by the Roman emperor Septimius Severus.

The Colossal Stone Heads of the Olmec

Time: 1200–600 BC
Location: Gulf Coast of Mexico

If something of the Olmecs has endured that allows us to speak of a civilization, it is their extraordinary sculpture, which in many aspects has not been surpassed by any other Mesoamerican people.

IGNACIO BERNAL, 1969

THE GREATEST MONUMENTAL sculptors in ancient Mesoamerica were the Olmec, whose distinctive culture dominated the Gulf Coast of Mexico between approximately 1200 and 400 BC. Superb and prolific stoneworkers, the Olmec carved countless objects ranging from tiny jade figures to immense basalt heads, stelae and thrones. A characteristic feature of Olmec art is that even the small-est carvings can project an impression of monumental solidity and mass. Portable Olmec stone and ceramic sculptures were widely disseminated throughout Mesoamerica, and many Olmec-like objects were made in other regions. The ubiquity of these sculptural forms and their detailed symbolism are one hallmark of the first pan-Mesoamerican cultural horizon. Some archaeologists believe that

Matthew Stirling, a principal discoverer of the Olmec civilization, next to a newly excavated colossal head (Monument 4) from La Venta, Tabasco, Mexico.

FACTFILE

Smallest stone head		Largest stone head	
Height	1.47 m	Height	3.4 m
Approx. weight	4.8 tonnes	Approx. weight	50 tonnes

cap that ties under the chin, and several have ear flares or plugs, symbols of elite status in ancient Mesoamerica. None appears to have been painted. Despite the obvious conventionalization, there is considerable variation in overall shape, specific facial features and especially details of the headgear. While much of this variation might reflect the nature of the raw material, local iconographic conventions and/or the differential skill of particular artisans, many archaeologists are convinced that the heads are actual portraits.

the Gulf Coast Olmec were the 'mother culture' of Preclassic Mesoamerica, while others prefer to regard them as only one of many independent, precocious, regional cultures that were emerging at this time. All agree, however, that the Olmec created earthen buildings and stone monuments on an unprecedented scale.

The colossal heads

Approximately 300 Olmec monumental sculptures are known. By far the most distinctive are colossal, freestanding effigies of human heads. The first was discovered near the site of Tres Zapotes in 1862, and 16 others have since been found. They occur only in or near large Gulf Coast sites – specifically La Venta (4), San Lorenzo (10) and Tres Zapotes (3) – and are the single most characteristic product of Olmec culture. Each depicts a formulaic Olmec visage: a young to middle-aged male individual with a fleshy, rather forbidding face, a wide, flat nose, full lips and slightly crossed eyes with suggestions of epicanthic folds. Each wears a kind of close-fitting, helmet-like

Seen from the front the heads typically appear spherical in shape, but in fact they are generally flattened from front to back, with the rear portions often unfinished. Most of the great stone heads range in height from about 1.47 m (4.82 ft) to 2.85 m (9.35 ft), although one is as high as 3.4 m (11.15 ft). Most weigh in the range of 8 to 13 tonnes, but the Olmec are known to have moved much larger stones of up to 25 to 50 tonnes, and the largest colossal head approaches this upper limit. Basalt, the most common raw material, was not found in the immediate environs of the Olmec centres where the heads were displayed. The nearest source is the Tuxtla Mountains, a small volcanic range on the northern fringes of the Olmec heartland. Here – and particularly around Cerro Cintepec in the southern Tuxtlas – the Olmec found basalt boulders along the lower slopes of the hills.

Altar 4 from La Venta. In reality, such 'altars' probably served as outdoor thrones. Thrones were the largest Olmec monumental sculptures, and were sometimes recarved as colossal heads.

Above **A colossal head from San Lorenzo shows a typically forbidding visage.** *Right* **At 2.85 m tall, San Lorenzo Monument 1 is one of the largest and best preserved colossal Olmec heads.**

Transport and construction

The Olmec lacked wheeled vehicles, draft animals or block-and-tackle devices, and moved these heavy objects using only raw human muscle. Cerro Cintepec is 60 km (37.3 miles) from San Lorenzo, where the largest number of stone heads has been recovered, and even further – about 100 km (62 miles) – from La Venta. In all likelihood the stones were dragged to a nearby river, then rafted down streams or along the coast to within short distances of their final destinations. Water transport, for example, would have brought them to a point about 2.5 km (1.6 miles) from the ridge-top site of San Lorenzo. From there they would have been dragged, perhaps along a specially prepared roadway, to the southern, ramp-like slopes of the ridge, and eventually hauled to the top, a vertical distance of over 50 m (164 ft).

Although archaeologists have experimentally shifted large Olmec monuments with 25 to 50 people, long-distance movement would have required hundreds. Labour would have been most available in the dry season, but it probably made more sense to procure the stones during the wettest months when river levels were high and the ground was naturally lubricated. It is uncertain whether the monuments were moved as finished objects or as unmodified boulders. The risk of loss in water transport suggests the latter, as do the large blanks at San Lorenzo. Small Olmec stone carvings depict what seem to be plain rectangular blocks of stone elaborately bound with thick cords with human figures sitting on top of them. These effigies might well show blocks in the process of transport, as observed more recently in other parts of the world.

Wherever it was done, shaping the basalt (or more rarely andesite) raw blocks was extremely laborious and time consuming. The Olmec had no metal tools, nor were they well provided with stone tools harder than the basalt they had to carve. Most of the shaping was thus accomplished by percussion and grinding. Basalt workshops located near what appear to be elite residences have been found on the summit of the San Lorenzo plateau, and it is clear that the Olmec recycled large stone objects into smaller ones, such as grinding stones for food preparation. Some of the great stone heads appear to have been made from recycled thrones. Thrones are in fact the largest, and among the earliest monumental stone objects made by the Olmec, predating many of the heads. One of the most impressive thrones, San Lorenzo Monument 14, measures 1.8 m (5.9 ft) high, 3.98 m (13.05 ft) long, and 1.52 m (4.99 ft) wide, and could easily have been cut down into a stone head.

Use and meanings of the colossal heads

A few Olmec stelae have glyph-like symbols, but these have not been deciphered, and so the Olmec are from our perspective prehistoric. However, some conclusions about how their sculptures were used and what they mean can be drawn from the content and contexts of the monuments, and later traditions of historically more well-documented Mesoamerican peoples. Matthew Stirling, one of the early excavators of Olmec centres, believed that the great stone heads were portraits of prominent individuals. Some think that the heads represent warriors or ballplayers, but today a consensus has emerged that they are portraits of chiefs or rulers. According to this view the distinctive adornments of the headgear of each stone head, which include animal pelts, tassels, feathers, claws, cords and mirrors, served to distinguish either individual rulers or specific ruling lines. Public depictions of rulers were common elsewhere in later Mesoamerican complex societies, most notably the Classic Maya, whose cultural roots extend back into Olmec times, although the tradition of colossal stone head carvings is confined to the Gulf Coast Olmec.

Some monuments have been found in what appear to be their original positions: colossal heads, thrones and stelae were set up in public spaces in or near ritual buildings or palaces at La Venta. Others have obviously been moved, perhaps in the process of recycling, or have been displaced by erosion or slippage. The Olmec seem to have positioned sets of monumental sculptures in their landscapes in scenic displays that commemorated or re-enacted historical or mythical events. No doubt most of the great stone heads were parts of such displays.

In addition to the political message inherent in the portraits of chiefs or kings, many archaeologists and epigraphers agree that the colossal stone heads were part of a larger tradition that incorporated, codified and communicated shamanistic themes. In particular, stone images were conduits of animistic energies. Like other Mesoamerican peoples the Olmec probably had many metaphors that identified parts of the body with elements of the cosmos. Much attention was paid to detailing and finishing the heads of sculptures, which as body parts might have symbolized centrality and have been identified with the sky or celestial domains. But whatever their exact uses or meanings, the colossal stone heads of the Olmec are certainly among the most impressive megalithic sculpture produced anywhere in the world.

Three colossal heads from San Lorenzo. Note the varied depiction of facial features and headgear.

The Nazca Lines, Drawings in the Desert

Time: c. 100 BC–AD 700
Location: southern Peru

The variety of [Nazca] markings … challenges our imagination, and means there will always be room for alternative theories. It seems unlikely that the mystery will ever be fully exhausted, and it would surely be a pity if it was.

EVAN HADINGHAM, 1987

THE NAZCA LINES – large-scale drawings etched on the desert of southern Peru – are both very famous and highly enigmatic. Their renown in part reflects the mystery surrounding their significance: were they created by ancient sky-watchers to mark astronomical events? Did they form part of irrigation schemes, giant textile work-shops, racetracks, or serve as landing strips for visitors from other worlds? Were they observed from above by gods or flown over by hallucinating shamans? Did they point to water sources in a parched landscape, or were they ceremonial pathways, linked to ancient rites for bringing forth water?

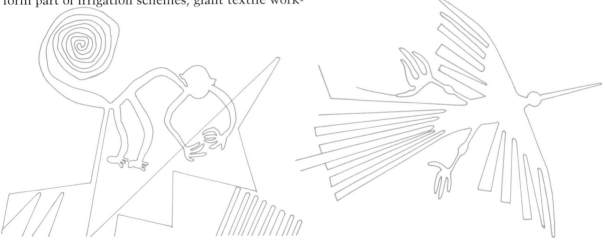

Aerial view of a giant monkey etched on the plain of Nazca. Both the monkey and the bird (above) are composed of a single, unbroken line. The monkey is over 100 m (328 ft) wide and measures 78 m (256 ft) from head to tail, while the bird measures over 135 m (443 ft) from beak to tail.

The markings, or geoglyphs, are concentrated on the Pampa, or plain, of Nazca, a 220-sq. km (85-sq. mile) alluvial fan sandwiched between the region's three largest rivers, bordered to the east by the Andean foothills. The markings include geometric shapes such as trapezoids, rectangles, straight lines, spirals, zigzags and concentric ray systems. The largest trapezoids are over a kilometre long, while straight lines often extend for many kilometres. Human, animal and plant forms – birds, killer whales, a monkey, a spider, a flower – are also found on the Pampa. These are much smaller than the geometric shapes and are found on a 10-sq. km (4-sq. mile) strip on the northern edge of the Pampa. The spider is over 50 m (180 ft) long and the monkey is more than 100 m (328 ft) wide. Both are made up of a single, unbroken line that never crosses itself.

Creating the markings

How were the markings created and who made them? Similarities between designs on Nazca-style pottery and textiles and the markings offer compelling evidence that ancient Nazca people, whose civilization flourished from c.100 BC to AD 700, made most of the animal and plant figures on the Pampa. Indeed, researchers have found Nazca pottery sherds, probably left as offerings, scattered across the Pampa. While other markings, such as straight lines and trapezoids (a few of which cut across animal figures or even obliterate them) may also have been made by Nazca peoples, some have been dated to after AD 700.

The technology used to create the lines was quite simple: the darker surface layer of the Pampa was removed to reveal the lighter-coloured soil beneath. (Over the millennia, manganese and iron oxides deposited on the Pampa by aerobic micro-organisms have left a thin patina on the surface, known as desert varnish.) The outlines of the markings were enhanced by laying the cleared stones along the edge. Yet how did they keep the lines straight? Again, the technology was probably quite simple. In an experiment carried out in Nazca, it took 12 people just over an hour to clear an area, creating a

The Pan-American highway slices through the plain at the edge of the Nazca valley, cutting across a large trapezoid.

line 12 m (40 ft) long that ended in a spiral 25 m (83 ft) long. They used only string and poles to delimit the border of the line, with the string serving as an arc, like a compass, to create the spiral.

Despite their age – some of the markings are more than 2000 years old – the geoglyphs have survived because of scant rainfall in the region. Most of the damage to the markings dates from the construction of the Pan-American highway and from vehicle and foot traffic on the fragile Pampa itself, which have not only left tracks but erased markings.

In fact, in a region often beset by drought, it was probably the ancient preoccupation with water which led to the creation of certain Pampa geoglyphs. Recent geological and hydrological studies have identified fault lines and aquifers and suggest that the lines and trapezoids form a giant map of the area's subterranean water system. Researchers have also identified 62 so-called ray centres – lines converging on a specific area. These ray centres occur on natural rises overlooking stream beds and along bases of mountains. Perhaps delineating the flow of water across the Pampa, the ray centres may have been linked to some sort of ritual for summoning up water, not surprising in a region where it rarely rains and where rivers depend on rainfall in the Andes to the east. Because clouds gather on mountaintops, people believed that mountains controlled weather and worshipped them as the dwellings of mountain gods. Some markings – for instance, the spider, the monkey, birds and spirals – have been associated with age-old Andean fertility symbols connected with water.

Perhaps the most widely accepted popular view is that the markings formed part of a giant astronomical calendar that signalled the onset of the rainy season in the highlands and marked celestial events in the Nazca skies. Yet, efforts to link certain markings to constellations, or to connect lines with solstices, have been inconclusive.

While most researchers concur that there is no single solution to the mystery of the Nazca Lines, they agree that the most compelling explanations are based on rituals connected to mountain worship, water and fertility.

La Turbie: The Trophy of the Alps

Time: 10/9–7/6 BC
Location: southern France

…the inscription from the Trophy of the Alps … is as follows: To the emperor Augustus, son of the deified Julius Caesar, chief priest, supreme commander for the 13th time, holding tribunician power for the 17th, the Senate and the People of Rome [dedicated this] because under his command and under his auspices all the peoples of the Alps which run from the Adriatic to the Mediterranean were brought under the power of the Roman people…

PLINY THE ELDER, 1ST CENTURY AD

THE SPECTACULAR monument at La Turbie, perched high above the Mediterranean, provides eloquent and impressive testimony to the power of the Roman empire. Even after Julius Caesar's conquest of Gaul, Rome was cut off from its western empire by the Alps. In a series of campaigns from 25 to 14 BC, the emperor Augustus and his generals brought to heel 44 of the mountain tribes and made allies of several others. The conquest allowed the opening of a major strategic road over the southern edges of the Alps, the Via Julia Augusta, more familiar to us now as the Grande Corniche. Completed in 7–6 BC, the Trophy of the Alps was set up at the highest point of this road, 6 km (4 miles) from modern Monte Carlo, on the natural border between Italy and Gaul, as a monument to Augustus' achievement.

The monument

The Trophy of the Alps was a tripartite monument consisting of a square base, a circular drum surrounded by a portico of 24 Tuscan columns, and a stepped pyramidal cone topped by a colossal bronze statue of Augustus, set almost 45 m (150 Roman ft) above ground. The archetype of the design was the famous Mausoleum of Halicarnassus (p. 37) and there are many later tomb monuments of similar type

FACTFILE

Base
Square	32.5 m
Height	12.9 m
(110 × 44 Roman ft)	

Circular plinth
Diameter	27.1 m
Height	3.6 m
(92 × 12 Roman ft)	

Conical stepped pyramid
Base diameter	16.6 m
Top diameter (estimated)	3.2 m
Height (estimated)	7.2 m
(56 × 11 × 24 Roman ft)	

Total height to base of statue	c. 45 m (150 Roman ft)
Estimated height of statue	6 m (20 Roman ft)

Circular drum (including colonnade)
Diameter	10.4 m
Height	20.7 m
(35 × 70 Roman ft)	

Columns
Height	8.80 m (30 Roman ft)
Lower diameter	1.1 m (3.75 Roman ft)
Number	24

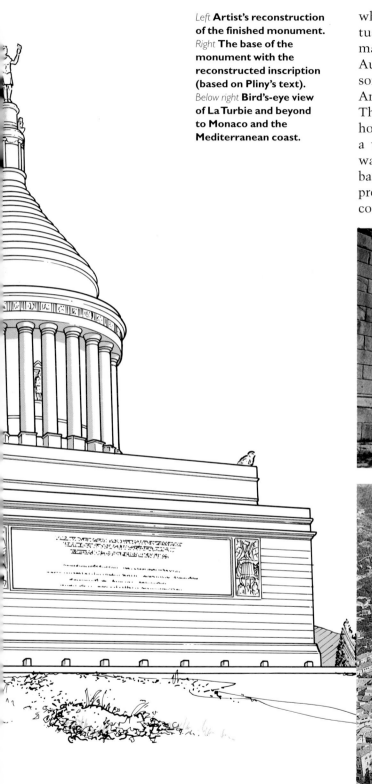

Left **Artist's reconstruction of the finished monument.**
Right **The base of the monument with the reconstructed inscription (based on Pliny's text).**
Below right **Bird's-eye view of La Turbie and beyond to Monaco and the Mediterranean coast.**

which followed this model, including that of Augustus himself begun in 28 BC. Indeed the monument may have been a kind of heroic shrine in honour of Augustus. The design of the Trophy may also owe something to another of the Seven Wonders of the Ancient World: the Pharos of Alexandria (p. 45). Though there is no evidence that it acted as a lighthouse, it would have been visible out to sea, forming a valuable landmark for ships in the treacherous waters of the Côte d'Azur. And stairs built into the base lead up to the level of the circular colonnade, providing spectacular views to the Mediterranean coast of Italy.

279

Although it has only been reconstructed to the base of the crowning pyramid, the Trophy still towers over the medieval and modern village.

Setting up a permanent trophy to immortalize major victories was by this time a well-established practice in the Roman world. Originally a trophy was a pile of weapons taken from a defeated enemy and dedicated at a temple to one of the major Roman divinities, after it had been displayed in the triumphal procession of the victorious general. In time, such piles of weapons came to symbolize the triumph itself, and they were often depicted on triumphal arches or as freestanding sculptures. The religious association, however, was never lost, as is seen in the fragments of an altar found at La Turbie.

Construction

The La Turbie monument would not have disgraced the city of Rome, and building such a sophisticated structure at the highest point of a new road through recently acquired territory was an ambitious undertaking. Before construction could start, a rocky outcrop had to be levelled, although the solid substratum meant that foundation work could be kept to a minimum. Most of the structure is made of local limestone, either cut into ashlar blocks (some weighing as much as 5 tonnes) for the facing, or used as rubble set in lime mortar for the core. Unused column drums and marks of ashlar blocks can still be seen in quarries at Mont des Justices, 700 m (2300 ft) east of the site, while the stepped cuttings for extracting the blocks are visible at a second quarry 750 m (2500 ft) to the north. In trying to imagine the logistics of such an undertaking, the opening of new quarries is a major factor to be taken into account.

While these quarries would have produced most of the 20,000 cu. m (215,000 cu. ft) of stone required for the monument, the blocks carrying the inscription, the sculptured reliefs of trophies and much of the architectural ornament were made of Cararra marble from Italy and hauled by road from Cap Martin, some 500 m (1640 ft) below the site. The replacement of one of the marble capitals with limestone suggests that they may have met problems in transit, or that what was damaged in the construction process could not easily be replaced. Though vandalized in the Middle Ages, the remains of La Turbie have been restored in recent times to give an impression of its former splendour.

The Giant Stelae of Aksum

Time: c. AD 200–400
Location: northern Ethiopia

The mania for the gigantic reflected the tastes of the Aksumite monarchy and the monuments were the concrete realization of its ideological purpose, which was to instil awe-inspiring admiration for the greatness and strength of the potentate.

YURI KOBISHCHANOV, 1979

THE GIANT STELAE OF AKSUM are among the largest monoliths ever erected by human agency, rivalling even the great obelisks of Egypt in their dimensions. Aksum itself, in the Tigray highlands of northern Ethiopia, was the capital of a major state which flourished during the first seven centuries AD, and had extensive trading contacts with the eastern Mediterranean, Arabia and India. Today, it is a local administrative and commercial centre but also, more importantly, a place of great significance to the Ethiopian Orthodox Church, Christianity having been adopted by the rulers of Aksum as early as the 4th century AD.

It is the huge, elaborately carved monolithic stelae, however, which are Aksum's main claim to fame. They feature prominently in Aksumite traditions concerning, among others, Menelik I, the son of Solomon and the Queen of Sheba. Excavations have shown that they are grave-markers, mostly dating from the 3rd and 4th centuries AD, although belonging to a tradition widespread in northeastern

Stela 3 is still standing at Aksum; it is 20.6 m high. The carved decoration represents a 10-storey building.

FACTFILE

Stela number	Storeys	Faces carved	Overall length	Section at ground level	Estimated weight
1	13	4	c. 33 m	3.84 × 2.35 m	520 tonnes
2	11	4	24.6 m	2.32 × 1.26 m	170 tonnes
3	10	3	20.6 m + c. 3 m	2.65 × 1.18 m	160 tonnes
4	6	4	18.2 m	1.56 × 0.76 m	56 tonnes
5	6	4	15.8 m	2.35 × 1 m	75 tonnes
6	4	3	15.3 m	1.47 × 0.78 m	43 tonnes

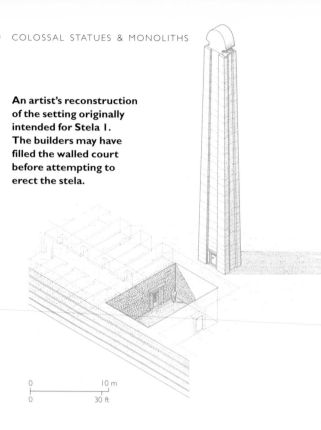

An artist's reconstruction of the setting originally intended for Stela 1. The builders may have filled the walled court before attempting to erect the stela.

Above **The largest of the Aksumite stelae (Stela 1), now fallen and broken, was originally 33 m long and weighed about 520 tonnes. It was probably never successfully erected.**
Right **Stela 4 at Aksum, showing the base-plate and details of the monument's construction.**

Africa for much of the past 5000 years. When Christianity was adopted, the production of monumental stelae seems to have been abandoned, and later tombs are of distinct although related types.

Size and decoration

Stelae occur at Aksum in great variety – from unworked stone slabs less than 1 m (3 ft) in length to the largest, Stela 1, a huge and elaborately carved example, now fallen and broken. Originally this would have weighed some 520 tonnes and, had it ever been erected, it would have stood about 30 m (97 ft) high. The differences between the stelae apparently relate to the wealth and status of the individuals whose graves they marked. The largest and most elaborate are grouped in a central area, built up as a huge terrace overlooking the town.

Stela 1, carved in an elaborate representation of a 13-storey building, exceeds in bulk if not in height even the largest ancient Egyptian obelisks and may be the largest monolith people have ever attempted to erect. It is the only one of the great Aksumite stelae whose original setting has been thoroughly investigated. It was intended to stand at the rear of a walled court, some 17 × 8 m (55 × 25 ft), immediately behind the front wall of the stelae terrace, with entrances to a complex monumental tomb set in each side. The original plan may well have been to erect the stela at a higher level, filling in the tomb area before the process was begun. Most likely the stela was never successfully erected, but fell and broke while this operation was in progress.

Six of the stelae at Aksum are carved in representation of multistorey buildings. Despite fanciful 19th-century comparisons with Indian pagodas, they are now recognized as depicting an exaggerated form of contemporary Aksumite architecture. Parallels can be found with surviving buildings of later date, such as the monastery-church at Debra Damo some 80 km (50 miles) to the east. Although

the stelae depict buildings of up to 13 storeys, there is no evidence that buildings at Aksum were ever more than two or, at the most, three storeys high. Taller buildings in a related style were, however, erected in South Arabia.

In cross-section the stelae are either simple rectangles or have central recesses on one, two or four sides, resembling the ground-plans of known Aksumite buildings. Carved recessed horizontal bands represent wooden beams. Above each of these are rows of round bosses, clearly imitating the projecting ends (popularly known as 'monkey heads') of beams set at right-angles to the line of the wall to strengthen it and also, in some cases, to support internal floors. At the foot of the stelae there is a false door on the front, and sometimes also on the back. This is carved in the likeness of a wooden doorway with square projections at the corners imitating the ends of beams. In some instances the false door boasts the representation of a lock or ring-handle. Above some of the false doors a horizontal band of vertical dentils represents in schematic form the vertical planks that were sometimes inserted in this position, as still preserved at Debra Damo.

Upper storeys are marked by rows of windows. On the largest of the stelae, the windows on three upper storeys depict complex tracery almost identical to wooden examples that survive at Debra Damo. At the rounded top of each stela are single or double concavities, with one or two recessed areas on the front which appear originally to have housed metal plaques held in place by pegs. Most of the stelae have horizontal base-plates, sometimes elaborately carved, and intended perhaps for the placement of offerings.

Production and erection

The granite-like stone (nepheline syenite) used for stelae and other large pieces was extracted from extensive quarries, the principal remains of which may be seen at Gobedra Hill some 4 km (3 miles) west of Aksum. Intended breaks were marked out by pecked lines, along which series of rectangular sockets were cut. Traces of these are still visible in areas where quarrying was abandoned. They can

also be seen on stelae which were taken to Aksum and erected without the marks being fully obliterated by subsequent dressing. The tools used have not yet been identified: it is likely that wooden wedges were inserted into the sockets and made to expand by percussion, by the insertion of metal wedges, or by the application of water, causing the rock to fracture.

At one of the quarries are the clear remains of a slipway down which stones may have been moved to the foot of the hill, from where a reasonably level route led into Aksum. It is possible that elephants were used, but even so, the transport of such huge objects indicates a plentiful and well-organized labour force.

Initial dressing, like some of the quarry work, seems to have been done with a series of blunt, square-sectioned iron punches. A finer finish was achieved through use of a toothed instrument. The presence of several unfinished stelae at Aksum itself suggests that final shaping and dressing were carried out there rather than at the quarries. The sequence of marking out and carving can be ascertained from unfinished monuments and also Stela 5, which broke while being carved and was redesigned on a smaller scale.

The largest stelae were set up on gently sloping ground, facing southwards towards the main urban centre. It is noteworthy that, in each case, the area immediately upslope is not obstructed by earlier features. This would have allowed space for construction ramps.

The second largest stela, Stela 2, fallen and broken, was taken to Rome in 1937–38, but its former position has been located and investigated. Its substructure, cut into the natural clay and measuring 6 m (19 ft) across, consisted of a layer of large boulders on a rubble foundation. To the north, and surviving to a height of over 4 m (13 ft), was a masonry podium on which rested stone slabs, apparently marking the base and south side of the pit in which the stela had originally stood. The associated pottery suggests that these features date from the 3rd or 4th centuries AD.

Stela 4, although fallen and broken, is particularly informative. It seems that vertical stone slabs were set in the ground to line a pit. The stela was raised to a near-vertical position by means of a ramp, and its foot toppled into the pit. Any subsequent adjustment would have been both difficult and dangerous, and may explain why the only storeyed stela still standing at Aksum is not perfectly vertical. The space between the stela foot and the pit lining was filled with stone packing to hold the stela in place. Finally, base-plates were installed at ground level, recessed to fit closely around the stela in front and back, covering over and hiding from view the slabs and stone packing in the pit which hold the monument upright.

There are indications that the stelae may have been intentionally destabilized many centuries ago. These echo traditions that some of the Aksum stelae were cast down by invaders around the 10th century.

The principal stelae at Aksum today, seen from the south.

The Colossal Buddha of Bamiyan

Time: 7th century AD
Location: Bamiyan, Afghanistan

To the northeast of the royal city there is a mountain, on … which is placed a stone figure of the Buddha, erect, in height 140 or 150 feet. Its golden hues sparkle on every side, and its precious ornaments dazzle the eyes with their brightness.

HIUEN TSIANG, AD 632

THE LARGEST BUDDHIST image of the ancient world stands in the Bamiyan valley, some 330 km (205 miles) northwest of Kabul, in the Hindu Kush mountain range. Gazing over the widest part of the valley, this 55-m (180-ft) high Buddha is flanked by a smaller, 38-m (125-ft) high, statue and a thousand chapels, all sculpted from a huge cliff. Carved in the 7th century AD, the Buddha stands on a pedestal within a trefoil niche. The torso, with representations of fabric folds, is well preserved, but the figure is missing both arms below the elbow, part of its left and right shin and, more strikingly, its face.

The image is also provided with two rock-cut ambulatories, one consisting of 11 chapels at ground level, and a second, level with the statue's head, illuminated by apertures cut into the niche itself. The niche and some of the ambulatory chapels were originally decorated with a series of paintings of Bodhisattvas (enlightened beings), demi-gods and royalty. The style of the painting and rock-cut architecture have long been held to be the result of a merging of cultural styles from southern, western, central and eastern Asia.

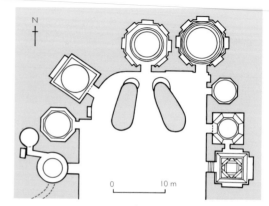

Plan of the lower ambulatory of chapels surrounding the Buddha's feet.

Located at the pivot of the Silk Road, Bamiyan was the capital of a small kingdom which was part of a loose confederation of local Turkic and Hephthalite princes led by the Yabghu of the Western Turks between AD 557 and the 9th century. Stretching from the borders of the Sasanian empire in the west to the Punjab in the south, the Khanate reached its zenith during the rule of the expansionist Yabghu T'ung Shih-hu (AD 618–630), an ardent exponent of Buddhism, before being nominally incorporated into the Chinese T'ang empire over the next century. It is apparently during T'ung Shih-hu's reign that the colossal Buddha was created by his subordinate ruler in Bamiyan.

Carving the Buddha

The Bamiyan Buddha was created by cutting a high-relief figure into the face of the soft conglomerate cliff. It is probable that the niche was carved out first, using scaffolding slotted into holes cut into the cliff, before the ambulatory galleries were carved;

FACTFILE

Standing Buddha

Height	55 m
Pedestal	
Height	2 m
Niche	
Height	58 m
Width at base	24 m
Width at summit	16 m

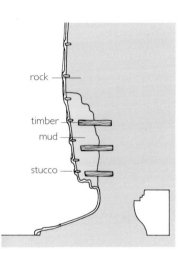

Above **Diagram showing the construction of the Buddha's right leg. The timber framework was coated with mud and finished with stucco-coated pegged ropes to create the impression of fabric folds.** *Right* **View of the 55-m tall Buddha and trefoil niche.**

rock

timber

mud

stucco

the scaffolding later being replaced by a series of permanent wooden ladders, landings and façades. The torso was roughly shaped and the detailing of the folds of the gown was built out by cutting lines of shallow holes for wooden pegs on which were hung ropes coated with thick stucco. A somewhat similar technique was used to construct the lower right leg. Arms and face were formed by timber superstructures or armatures covered with sheets of brass or gilded metal; massive metal earrings may have been attached in the deep grooves under the stucco ears.

Holes above the shoulders could have supported an external gallery which would have made it possible to hang and change huge vestments. Finally, the rough surfaces of the niche, galleries and chapels were thickly coated with clay mixed with vegetable fibres before a thin, white layer of burnt gypsum was applied, to which pigments, bound by animal glue, were then added. Most pigments seem to have been available locally, with the exception of copper silicate for green and ground lapis lazuli for blue.

Purpose and symbolism

The rock-cut façade of Bamiyan has often been interpreted as symbolizing the spiritual journey of the Gautama Buddha, projecting the message of the Lokottaravadin-Mahasamghika doctrine, that is the Buddha as the 'Lord of the World'. The Chinese pilgrim Hiuen Tsiang, who visited the valley in AD 632, recorded that the king of Bamiyan performed an annual ceremony in the presence of his people during which he offered all his wealth and power to the Buddha as confirmation of his devotion. The monks then returned it to him, confirming his position as rightful ruler and worthy protector of the lay and Buddhist community.

The Buddha may have been carved on the instruction of the princeling himself; the surrounding chapels, however, were created by hundreds of pilgrims, merchants and residents seeking safe passage and success for their expeditions. The Bamiyan colossus has been noted by travellers, pilgrims and soldiers for over a thousand years; so far defying the assaults of Genghis Khan, Aurangzeb and the Taliban, it continues to project the message of the Buddha.

View across the valley to the colossal Bamiyan Buddha surrounded by rock-cut caves.

The Easter Island Statues

Time: AD 1000–1500
Location: eastern Polynesia

We could hardly conceive how these islanders, wholly unacquainted with any mechanical power, could raise such stupendous figures, and afterwards place the large cylindric stones on their heads.

CAPTAIN JAMES COOK, 1774

DOTTED AROUND the coast of Easter Island, atop stone platforms set against the blue Pacific, rows of tall gaunt figures once stood, their rugged faces carved from hard volcanic tuff, with staring eyes inlaid in white and red. These are the enigmatic Easter Island statues – or so they were, before being toppled in a paroxysm of destruction. Not surprisingly, the question of how and why such massive monoliths were carved and erected has exercised the energies and imaginations of western travellers and archaeologists since the 18th century.

Easter Island, more properly known by the native name of Rapa Nui, is the remotest inhabited spot on the face of the earth. Triangular in shape, its longest side measures only 22 km (13.75 miles), and its breadth a mere 16 km (10 miles). It lies 2250 km (1400 miles) from the next nearest inhabited land, the tiny Pitcairn island, and 3747 km (2340 miles) from the coast of South America. So remote is it, that the wonder is it was discovered at all before modern navigation. Yet the intrepid Polynesian mariners who colonized the scattered islands of the

A giant statue on the outer slopes of the Rano Raraku quarry. The importance of the face is evident from the contrast between the prominent facial features and the truncated, flattened back of the head.

FACTFILE

Estimated number of statues	c. 1000
Statues abandoned in the Rano Raraku quarry	394
Largest statue: El Gigante	
length	20 m
weight	c. 270 tonnes
Number of ceremonial platforms	250–300
Platforms with statues	c. 125

Pacific reached Rapa Nui between AD 450 and 690, establishing a population which grew and prospered, in complete isolation, for over 1000 years.

The statues

The Easter Island statues or *moai* are instantly recognizable by their shape and style. They depict the head and upper body, to a point just below the waist; legs are not shown. Shoulders and arms are present, but forearms are merely shallow relief carvings across the front of the stomach, below the navel. Fingertips are extended and point towards an oval or rectangular feature which is interpreted as the fold of a loincloth. The back of the statue is sometimes carved in low relief, with straight, curved and spiralling lines which may represent tattoo designs indicating rank. This, and the fact that no two statues are alike, has suggested that they may portray individuals, perhaps tribal elders.

The most powerful carving is reserved for the head, which is characterized by projecting mouth, nose and chin, and jutting brow ridges. The back of the head is generally flat, but elongated ears stand out in relief at either side.

In terms of size, the Easter Island statues include some of the largest human images ever carved, ranging from 2 m to almost 10 m (6.5 to 32 ft) in height. Originally set up on ceremonial platforms, or *ahu*, around the coast of the island, the largest to have been successfully placed in position was 'Paro' which weighed 82 tonnes. The largest statue of all, the aptly named 'El Gigante', measured 20 m (66 ft) long and would have weighed around 270 tonnes; it was left abandoned in the Rano Raraku quarry.

The quarry

There are hundreds of ancient statues on the island, mainly carved from porous volcanic tuff from the Rano Raraku quarry, the crater of an extinct volcano. Rano Raraku stone proved the most suitable for the statues, though a few were made of basalt or of red scoria. The quarry site is still littered with abandoned, unfinished statues, and around them are thousands of basalt picks, the hard stone tools used to cut the statues from the rock and carve them into shape. Beneath the tough weathered surface the rock is relatively easy to carve, though it hardens on exposure to the elements. The basalt picks were effective tools, and applying water to the porous stone may have made it softer to cut. Without the benefit of metal implements, however, the carving

of statues must have been a gruelling undertaking. Cautious estimates suggest that the largest of the island's statues, such as the famous Paro, would have taken a team of 10 or 20 men up to 12 months to complete.

The process is illustrated by the 394 statues in the quarry in various stages of completion. They were carved face uppermost, and undercut, leaving only a keel of rock holding the statue to the bedrock beneath. The features of the face and head were finished *in situ* in the quarry, only the eyes being left for completion later.

Transporting the statues

Once the statues were complete they were detached from the rock and lowered by ropes down the sloping quarry face. The keel on the statue's back ran along a groove and helped to guide the descent. Ropes attached to the statue ran round a series of

The statues standing in the Rano Raraku quarry (left) **lack the finishing touches added when they were erected on their ceremonial stone platforms** (above)**, the eyes and topknot of white coral and red scoria.**

colossal timbers placed in sockets around the lip of the quarry; for though no large trees have grown on Rapa Nui in recent centuries, evidence of fossil nuts and root channels suggests that palm trees, including the huge Chilean wine palm, covered parts of the island before the settlers felled them.

Timber would have been essential for moving the statues from the quarry to the ceremonial platforms. That not all of them made it is demonstrated by the scatter of finished statues left abandoned en route, most of them having travelled only a short distance. A large statue such as Paro had to travel 6 km (3.75 miles) from the quarry to its destination. An experiment carried out in the USA using a concrete replica of a 4-tonne Easter Island statue showed that it could be moved by only 25 men if strapped in an upright position on a wooden sledge and pulled over a bed of small wooden rollers. The theory is supported by the fact that some of the statues abandoned in transit appear to have fallen and broken from an upright position. Alternatively the statues might have been moved on their backs, or even their fronts, in a timber cradle, and certainly some such system must have been used when they were being manoeuvred up or down steep slopes. It is also possible that statues were dragged from the quarry to the sea, loaded on to rafts and floated to their destinations.

The final stage

Most of the statues were intended for erection on the ceremonial stone platforms which ring the coast of Rapa Nui. Up to 150 m (492 ft) long and 3 m (10 ft) high, these drystone structures were built as close as possible to the sea; but the statues were erected facing inland, rather than out to sea. The platforms themselves are often wonders of construction, with rubble cores faced by massive, carefully shaped

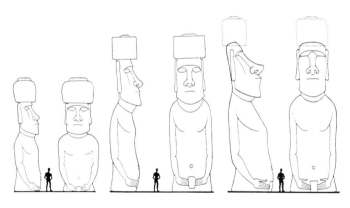

Above **Easter Island statues come in a range of shapes and sizes.** *Right* **El Gigante, the largest of them all, lies unfinished in the Rano Raraku quarry.**

blocks up to 3 m (9.8 ft) across. Ropes, ramps and timber levers were probably used to lift the statues into position. It was at this point that the eyes were added. Excavations beneath a fallen statue in 1978 discovered traces of white coral and red scoria that formed respectively the white of the eye and the pupil. It was eyes that gave the statues their spiritual power; and significantly when the statues were felled, most were toppled face forwards to conceal the eyes; on those that fell backwards the eye areas were obliterated by heavy pounding.

The final feature – for the latest of the statues – was the provision of a drum-like topknot or *pukao* of red scoria stone from a quarry at Puna Pau. The largest of these are over 2 m (6.5 ft) across and weigh more than 10 tonnes. They must have been added after the statues themselves were raised into position, once again with the aid of ropes and stout timbers.

The question remains as to what the statues represent. Some have argued they were gods, but the interpretation now generally accepted is that they were revered ancestors, deceased elders of the community. Some may have been carved during the individual's lifetime, but only completed and raised into position when the person died. The heavy demand for timber which the flurry of statue-raising created was no doubt one factor behind the collapse of the whole system. Deforestation, land exhaustion and over-population led to hunger and warfare, in which the statues of the ancestors were obvious targets for hostile groups.

The statues were still standing when the first Europeans visited the island in 1722; 50 years later, they had been toppled. Today, several of them have been restored, raised back into position on their *ahu* platforms, and provided with eyes and topknots. Set in lines looking over the land – gazing slightly upwards, so as not to unsettle the living – they provide a striking illustration of what can be achieved with relatively simple technology and a limited population where deep-seated beliefs and powerful rivalries provide the motivating force.

Overthrown in the 18th century, some of the Easter Island statues have now been re-erected on their platforms and once again gaze out across the island, their backs to the sea.

Further Reading

The Seven Wonders

1   The Pyramids of Giza
Arnold, D., *Building in Eygpt: Pharaonic Stone Masonry* (New York & Oxford, 1991)
Edwards, I.E.S., *The Pyramids of Egypt* (Harmondsworth, 1993)
Lehner, M., *The Complete Pyramids* (London & New York, 1997)

2   The Hanging Gardens of Babylon
Dalley, S., 'Nineveh, Babylon and the Hanging Gardens: cuneiform and classical sources reconciled', *Iraq* 56 (1994), 45–58
Koldewey, R., *The Excavations at Babylon* (London, 1914)
Koldewey, R., *Die Königsburgen von Babylon, II: die Hauptburg und die Sommerpalast Nebukadnezars im Hügel Babil*, edited by F. Wetzel (Osnabrück, 1932)
Reade. J.E., 'Alexander the Great and the Hanging Gardens of Babylon', *Iraq*, forthcoming
Stevenson, D.W.W., 'A proposal for the irrigation of the Hanging Gardens of Babylon', *Iraq* 54 (1992), 35–55
Wiseman, D.J., *Nebuchadrezzar and Babylon: The Schweich Lectures of the British Academy 1983* (Oxford, 1985)

3   The Temple of Artemis at Ephesus
Coulton, J., *Ancient Greek Architects at Work. Problems of Structure and Design* (New York, 1977)
Trell, B., 'The Temple of Artemis at Ephesos' in *The Seven Wonders of the Ancient World*, Clayton, P. & Price, M. (eds) (London, 1988), 78–99

4   The Statue of Zeus at Olympia
Lapatin, K., 'Pheidias "elejantourgos"', *American Journal of Archaeology* 101 (1997), 663–82
Price, M., 'The Statue of Zeus at Olympia' in *The Seven Wonders of the Ancient World*, Clayton, P. & Price, M. (eds) (London, 1988), 59–77

5   The Mausoleum of Halicarnassus
Jeppesen, K., 'Explorations at Halicarnassus', *Acta Archaeologica* 38 (1976), 29–58
Jeppesen, K. & Zahle, J., 'Investigations on the Site of the Mausoleum 1970/1973, *American Journal of Archaeology* 79 (1975), 67–79
Romer, J. & Romer, E., *The Seven Wonders of the World* (London, 1995), 77–106
Waywell, G.B., 'The Mausoleum at Halicarnassus' in *The Seven Wonders of the Ancient World*, Clayton, P. & Price, M. (eds) (London, 1988), 100–23

6   The Colossus of Rhodes
Higgins, R., 'The Colossus of Rhodes' in *The Seven Wonders of the Ancient World*. P. Clayton & M. Price (eds) (London, 1988), 124–37
Romer, J. & Romer, E., *The Seven Wonders of the World* (London, 1995), 25–47

7   The Pharos of Alexandria
Empereur, J.-Y., *Le Phare d'Alexandrie: La Merveille retrouvée* (Evreux, 1998)
Empereur, J.-Y., *Alexandria Rediscovered* (London, 1998)
Clayton, P., 'The Pharos at Alexandria;, in *The Seven Wonders of the Ancient World*, Clayton, P. & Price, M. (eds) (London, 1988), 138–57
Romer, J. & Romer, E., *The Seven Wonders of the World* (London, 1995), 48–76

Tombs & Cemeteries

8   The Megalithic Tomb of Newgrange
O'Kelly, M., *Newgrange. Archaeology, Art and Legend* (London & New York, 1982)
Powell, A.B., 'Newgrange – science or symbolism?' *Proceedings of the Prehistoric Society* 60 (1994), 85–96

9   The Treasury of Atreus at Mycenae
Cavanagh, W. G. & Laxton, R.R., 'Problem Solving and the Architecture of Tholos Tombs' in *Problems in Greek Prehistory*, French, E.B. & Wardle, K.A. (eds) (Bristol, 1988)
Taylour, W. D., *The Mycenaeans* (London & New York, 1983, rev. ed.)
Wace, A.J.B., *Mycenae. An Archaeological History and Guide* (Princeton, 1949)

10   The Valley of the Kings: the Tomb of Seti I
Bierbrier, M., *The Tomb-builders of the Pharaohs* (London, 1982)
Hornung, E., *The Valley of the Kings: Horizon of Eternity* (New York, 1990)
Hornung, E., *The Tomb of Pharaoh Seti I* (Zurich & Munich, 1991)
Reeves, N. & Wilkinson, R., *The Complete Valley of the Kings* (London & New York, 1996)

11   The Etruscan Cemetery of Cerveteri
Blanck, H. & Proietti, G., *La Tomba dei Rilievi di Cerveteri* (Rome, 1986)
Cristofani, M., Nardi, G. & Rizzo, M.A., *Caere I: Il parco archeologico* (Rome, 1988)
Proietti, G., *Cerveteri* (Rome, 1986)
Spivey, N.J., *Etruscan Art* (London & New York, 1997)

12   Mount Li: the Tomb of China's First Emperor
Cotterell, A., *The First Emperor of China* (New York, 1981)
Guisso, R. et al., *The First Emperor of China* (London, 1989)
Ledderose, L., *Der Erste Kaiser von China und seine Terrakotta -Armée* (Munich, 1990)
Wen Fong (ed.), *The Great Bronze Age of China* (New York, 1980)

13   The Nabataean Royal Tombs at Petra
Browning, I., *Petra* (London, 1974)
Glueck, N., *Deities and Dolphins: the Story of the Nabataeans* (London, 1965)
Hammond, P.C., *The Nabataeans – their History, Culture and Archaeology*. Studies in Mediterranean Archaeology, vol. XXXVII (Gothenburg, 1973)
Lawlor, J.I., *The Nabataeans in Historical Perspective* (Grand Rapids, Michigan, 1974)
McKenzie, J., *The Architecture of Petra*, British Academy Monographs in Archaeology no. 1 (Oxford, 1990)
Maqsood, R., *Petra, a Traveller's Guide* (Reading, 1994)
Taylor, J., *Petra* (London, 1993)

14   The Moche Pyramids
Bawden, G., *The Moche* (Oxford, 1996)
Benson, E., *The Mochica: A Culture of Peru* (London, 1972)
Hagen, A. von & Morris, C., *The Cities of the Ancient Andes* (London & New York, 1998)
Moseley, M.E., *The Incas and their Ancestors. The Archaeology of Peru* (London & New York, 1993)
Shimada, I., *Pampa Grande and the Mochica Culture* (Austin, 1994)

15 The Tomb of Emperor Nintoku, Japan

Barnes, G.L., *Protohistoric Yamoto* (Ann Arbor, University of Michigan Centre for Japanese Studies, 1988)

Brown, Delmer M., 'The Yamato Kingdom', in Brown, D.M., *The Cambridge History of Japan. Vol. 1. Ancient Japan* (Cambridge, 1993)

Kaya, K., 'Daisen kofun', in Kondo, Yoshiro (ed.) *Zenpo Koenfun Shusei Kinki [Corpus of Keyhole-Shaped Tombs. Kinki Region]* (Tokyo, 1992)

Miki, Fumio, *Haniwa* (New York & Tokyo, 1974)

Mori, Shoichi, *Osaka-fu Shi [History of Osaka Prefecture], Vol. 1. Kodai [Ancient Times]* (Osaka, 1978), 672–84

Nakai & Okuda, 'Dennintokuryo kofun koenbu maiso shisetsu ni tsuite' [On the burial facility in the rear circular mound of the tomb said to be the Nintoku Mausoleum] *Kokogaku Zahhi* 62.2, 164–76

Tsude, Hiroshi, 'The kofun period and state formation', *Acta Asiatica* 63 (1992), 64–86

16 The Tomb of Pakal, Palenque

Abrams, E., *How the Maya Built their World* (Austin, 1994)

de la Garza, M., *Palenque* (Mexico City, 1992)

Mathews, P. & Schele, L., *Lords of Palenque – The Glyphic Evidence* (Pebble Beach, 1974)

Ruz Lhuillier, A., *El Templo de las Inscripciones* (Mexico City, 1973)

Schele, L. & Mathews, P., *The Code of Kings* (New York, 1998)

Stephens, J.L., *Incidents of Travel in Central America, Chiapas, and Yucatan* (New Brunswick, 1949 [1842])

Webster, D. & Kirker, J., 'Too Many Maya, Too Few Buildings', *Journal of Anthropological Research* 51, 363–87

17 The Temple-Mausoleum of Angkor Wat

Jacques, C. & Freeman, M., *Angkor: Cities and Temples* (London, 1997)

Mabbett, I & Chandler, D., *The Khmers* (Oxford, 1995)

Nafilyan, G. et al., *Angkor Vat: description graphique du temple* (Paris, 1969)

Srivastava, K.M., *Angkor Wat* (Delhi, 1987)

Temples & Shrines

18 Ġgantia & the Maltese Temples

Bonanno, A. 'Technice costruttive dei templi megalitici Maltesi' in Fradkin, A. & Anati, E. (eds), *Missione a Malta* (Capo di Ponte, 1988) 110–11

Evans, J.D., *The Prehistoric Antiquities of the Maltese Islands* (London, 1971)

Trump, D., *Malta: An Archaeological Guide* (London, 1972)

19 Stonehenge

Chippindale, C. *Stonehenge Complete* (London & New York, 1994)

Cleal, R., Walker, K. & Montague, R., *Stonehenge in its Landscape* (London, 1995)

Cunliffe, B. & Renfrew, C. (eds), *Science and Stonehenge* (Oxford, 1997)

Souden, D., *Stonehenge* (London, 1997)

20 The Ziggurat of Ur

Lloyd, S., *The Archaeology of Mesopotamia* (London & New York, 1978)

Postgate, J.N., *Early Mesopotamia: Society and Economy at the Dawn of History* (London & New York, 1992)

Reade, J., *Mesopotamia* (London, 1991)

Woolley, L., *The Ziggurat and its Surroundings: Ur Excavations, vol. V* (London & Philadelphia, 1939)

Woolley, L. & Moorey, P.R.S., *Ur 'of the Chaldees'* (London, 1982)

21 The Temples of Karnak

Arnold, D., *Building in Egypt: Pharaonic Stone Masonry* (New York & Oxford, 1991)

Bourbon, F. & Attini, A., *Egypt: Yesterday and Today. Lithographs and Diaries by David Roberts, R.A.* (Shrewsbury, 1996), 138–51

Lauffray, J., *Karnak d'Égypte: Domain du divin* (Paris, 1979)

Schultz, R. & Seidel, M., *Egypt: the World of the Pharaohs* (Cologne, 1998), 153–74

22 The Great Temple of Abu Simbel

Badawy, A., *A History of Egyptian Architecture*, Vol. III: *The Empire* (Berkeley, 1968), 304–14

Baines, J. & Málek, J., *Atlas of Ancient Egypt* (Oxford, 1980), 184–5

MacQuitty, W., *Abu Simbel* (London, 1965)

23 The Cult Centre of Chavín de Huántar

Burger, R.L., *Chavín and the Origins of Andean Civilization* (London & New York, 1992)

Hagen, A. von & Morris, C., *The Cities of the Ancient Andes* (London & New York, 1998)

Moseley, M.E., *The Incas and their Ancestors. The Archaeology of Peru* (London & New York, 1993)

24 The Parthenon at Athens

Burford, A., 'The Builders of the Parthenon', *Greece and Rome* 10 (1963)

Carpenter, R., *The Architects of the Parthenon* (London, 1970)

Jenkins, I., *The Parthenon Frieze* (London, 1994)

Korres, M., *From Pentelicon to the Parthenon* (London, 1995)

Tournikiotis, P., *The Parthenon and its Impact in Modern Times* (Athens, 1994)

25 The Pyramid of the Sun at Teotihuacan

Berlo, J.C. (ed.), *Art, Ideology, and the City of Teotihuacan* (Washington DC, 1992)

Berrin, K. & Pasztory, E. (eds), *Teotihuacan: Art from the City of the Gods* (London & New York, 1993)

Heyden, D., 'Caves, gods, and myths: world-view and planning in Teotihuacan', in *Mesoamerican Sites and World-Views* (Washington DC, 1981), 1–35

Millon, R., Drewitt, B. & Cowgill, G., *Urbanization at Teotihuacan, Mexico: the Teotihuacan Map* (Austin, 1973)

Pasztory, E., *Teotihuacan: An Experiment in Living* (Norman, Oklahoma, 1997)

Sahagún, Fray B. de, *The Origin of the Gods.* Book 3 of the Florentine Codex (Santa Fe, New Mexico, 1978 [1959])

26 The Great Stupa of Sanchi

Brown, P., *Indian Architecture: Buddhist and Hindu* (Bombay, 1946)

Marshall, J.H. & Foucher, A., *The Monuments of Sanchi* (London, n.d.)

Mitra, D., *Buddhist Monuments* (Calcutta, 1971)

27 The Buddhist Caves of Ajanta

Behl, B.K., *Ajanta Caves: Ancient Paintings of Buddhist India* (London & New York, 1998)

Dehejia, V., *Early Buddhist Rock-cut Temples: A Chronological Study* (London, 1972)

Mitra, D., *Ajanta* (New Delhi, 1968)

Plaeschke, H. & Plaeschke, I., *Indische felsentemple und hohlenkloster: Ajanta und Elura* (Leipzig, 1982)

Weiner, S.L., *Ajanta: Its Place in Buddhist Art* (Berkeley, 1977)

28 The Pantheon at Rome

Davies, P., Hemsoll, D. & Wilson-Jones, M., 'The Pantheon: triumph of Rome or triumph of compromise' *Art History* 10 (1987) 133–53

de Fine Licht, K., *The Rotunda in Rome: A Study of Hadrian's Pantheon*, Jutland Archaeology Society, 8 (Copenhagen, 1968)

MacDonald, W.L., *The Architecture of the Roman Empire, I: An Introductory Study* (New Haven & London, 1965)

Mark, R. & Hutchinson, P., 'On the structure of the Roman Pantheon' *Art Bulletin* LXVIII, 1 (1986) 24–34

29 The Earthworks of Newark, Ohio

Brose, David S. & Greber N'omi (eds), *Hopewell Archaeology: The Chillicothe Conference* (Kent, OH, 1979)

Dancey, William & Pacheco, Paul J. (eds), *Ohio Hopewell Community Organization* (Kent, OH, 1997)

Hiveley, Ray & Horn, Robert, 'Geometry and Astronomy in Prehistoric Ohio' *Archeoastronomy* 4 (1982), 1–20

30 The Buddhist Monastery at Paharpur
Dikshit, R.B.K.N., *Excavations at Paharpur* (New Delhi, 1938)
Qadir, M.A.A., *Paharpur* (Dhaka, 1980)
Sanday, J., Frost, A., Smyth, J., Lohuizen de Leeuw & Antonio, R.,
    *Masterplan for the Conservation and Presentation of the Ruins of the
    Buddhist Vihara at Paharpur and the Historic Mosque-city of
    Bagerhat* (Paris, 1983)

31 The Buddhist Shrine of Borobudur
Dumarcay, J., *Historie architecturale du Borobudur* (Paris, 1977)
Dumarcay, J., *Borobudur* (Kuala Lumpur, 1978)
Soekmono, R. et al., *Borobudur, Prayer in Stone* (London, 1990)

32 Monk's Mound, Cahokia
Emerson, T.E., *Cahokia and the Archaeology of Power* (Tuscaloosa,
    1997)
Emerson, T.E. & Lewis, R.B. (eds), *Cahokia and the Hinterlands: Middle
    Mississippian Cultures of the Midwest* (Urbana, 1991)
Pauketat, T.R. & Emerson, T.E. (eds), *Cahokia: Domination and
    Ideology in the Mississippian World* (Lincoln, 1997)

33 The Mud Mosques of Timbuktu
Insoll, T., 'Archaeological Research in Timbuktu, Mali', *Antiquity* 72
    (1998), 413–17
Mauny, R., 'Notes d'Archéologie sur Tombouctou', *Bulletin de l'Institut
    Français d'Afrique Noire (B)* 14 (1952), 899–918
Miner, H., *The Primitive City of Timbuctoo* (Princeton, 1953)
Prussin, L., *Hatumere: Islamic Design in West Africa* (Los Angeles, 1986)
Prussin, L., 'Sub-Saharan West Africa' in Frishman, M. & Khan, H.-U.
    (eds), *The Mosque. History, Architectural Development and Regional
    Diversity* (London & New York, 1994)

34 The Great Temple of the Aztecs
Boone, E.H. (ed.), *The Aztec Templo Mayor* (Washington DC, 1987)
Broda, J., Carrasco, D. & Matos Moctezuma, E., *The Great Temple of
    Tenochtitlan: Center and Periphery in the Aztec World* (Berkeley,
    1987)
Graulich, M., 'Mexico City's "Templo Mayor" revisited', in Saunders,
    N.J. (ed.), *Ancient America: Contributions to New World
    Archaeology* (Oxford, 1992)
Heyden, D. & Villaseñor, L.F., *The Great Temple and the Aztec Gods*
    (Mexico, 1984)
López Lujan, L., *The Offerings of the Templo Mayor of Tenochtitlan*
    (Niwot, Colorado, 1994)
Matos Moctezuma, E., *The Great Temple of the Aztecs: Treasures of
    Tenochtitlan* (London & New York, 1994)

Palaces, Baths & Arenas

35 The Minoan Palace of Knossos
Evely, D., Hughes-Brock, H. & Momigliano, N., *Knossos. A Labyrinth of
    History* (Oxford, 1994)
Farnoux, A., *Knossos. Unearthing a Legend* (London & New York, 1996)
Graham, J.W., *The Palaces of Crete* (Princeton, 1969)

36 The Palace of Sennacherib at Nineveh
Barnett, R.D., et al., *Sculptures from the Southwest Palace at Nineveh*
    (London, 1998)
Layard, A.H., *Discoveries in the Ruins of Nineveh and Babylon* (London,
    1853)
Reade, J.E., *Assyrian Sculpture* (London, 1998, 2nd ed.)
Russell, J.M., *Sennacherib's Palace without Rival at Nineveh* (Chicago
    & London, 1991)

37 The Palace of Persepolis
Lecoq, P., *Les inscriptions de la Perse achéménide* (Paris, 1997)
Roaf, M., 'Sculptures and Sculptors at Persepolis', *Iran* 21 (1983)
Schmidt, E.F., *Persepolis*, vols I–III (Chicago, 1953–70)

Tilia, A.B., 'A study on the methods of working and restoring stone in
    Achaemenian architecture and sculpture', *East and West* 18 (1968),
    67–95
Tilia, A.B., *Studies and Restorations at Persepolis and other Sites in Fars*
    (Rome, 1972, 1978)
Wilber, D.N., *Persepolis* (London, 1969)

38 The Colosseum at Rome
Brightwell, R., 'The Colosseum' in Barnes, M., et al., *Secrets of Lost
    Empires* (London, 1996), 136–79
Cozzo, G., *Ingegneria Roma* (Rome, 1928), 195–253
Rea, R., 'Amphitheatrum' in Steinby, E.M. (ed.), *Lexicon Topographicum
    Urbis Romae*, Vol. 1, A–C (Rome, 1993), 30–5

39 Hadrian's Villa at Tivoli
Erlich, T.L., 'The waterworks of Hadrian's Villa', *Journal of Garden
    History* 9.4 (1989), 161–76
Giuliano, A., et al., *Villa Adriana* (Rome, 1988)
Jacobson, D.M., 'Hadrianic architecture and geometry' *American Journal
    of Archaeology* 90.1 (1986) 69–85
MacDonald, W.L. & Pinto, J.A., *Hadrian's Villa and Its Legacy* (New
    Haven & London, 1995)
Moneti, A., 'Nuovi sostegni all'ipotesi di una grande sala cupolata alla
    "Piazza d'Oro" di Villa Adriana' *Analecta romana Istituti Danici* 20
    (1992) 67–92

40 The Baths of Caracalla, Rome
Adam, J.-P., *Roman Building. Materials and Techniques* (London, 1994)
DeLaine, J., *The Baths of Caracalla in Rome: a study in the design,
    construction and economics of large-scale building projects in
    imperial Rome, Journal of Roman Archaeology* Supplement 25
    (Portsmouth, R.I., 1997)
DeLaine, J., 'The "cella solearis" of the Baths of Caracalla in Rome: a
    reappraisal', *Papers of the British School in Rome* 55 (1987), 147–56
DeLaine, J., 'An engineering approach to Roman building techniques: the
    Baths of Caracalla in Rome', *Papers in Italian Archaeology IV, Part iv:
    Classical and Medieval*, BAR IS 246 (Oxford, 1985), 195–206
Yegül, F.K., *Baths and Bathing in Classical Antiquity* (Cambridge, Mass.
    & London, 1992)

41 The Palace & Pleasure Gardens of Sigiriya
De Silva, R.H., *Sigiriya* (Colombo, 1976)
Ellepola, C., 'Conjectured hydraulics of Sigiriya', *Ancient Celyon* 11
    (1990), 168–227
Paranavitana, S., 'Sigiri – the abode of a god-king', *Journal of the Ceylon
    Branch of the Royal Asiatic Society* (ns) I (1950), 129–62
Paranavitana, S., *The Sigiri Graffiti*, 2 vols (Oxford, 1956)

42 The Arch of Ctesiphon
Bruno, A., 'The preservation and restoration of Taq-Kisra', *Mesopotamia*
    I (1966), 89–108.
Kurz, O., 'The date of the Taq i Kisra', *Journal of the Royal Asiatic
    Society* (1941), 37–41
Reuther, O., *Die Ausgrabungen der deutschen Ktesiphon-Expedition im
    Winter 1928–9* (Berlin, 1930)
Reuther, O., 'Sasanian architecture: a history', in Pope, A.U. (ed.), *A
    Survey of Persian Art* (London & New York, 1938), vol. V, 493–578

43 The Royal Compounds of Chan Chan
Hagen, A. von & Morris, C., *The Cities of the Ancient Andes* (London &
    New York, 1998)
Moseley, M.E., *The Incas and their Ancestors. The Archaeology of Peru*
    (London & New York, 1993)
Moseley, M.E. & Mackey, C.J., *Twenty-four Architectural Plans of Chan
    Chan, Peru* (Cambridge, Mass., 1974)
Moseley, M.E. & Day, K.C. (eds), *Chan Chan: Andean Desert City*
    (Albuquerque, 1982)
Moseley, M.E. & Cordy-Collins, A. (eds), *The Northern Dynasties:
    Kingship and Statecraft in Chimor* (Washington, 1990)

44 Great Zimbabwe

Beach, D., *The Shona and their Neighbours* (London, 1994)

Garlake, P.S., *Great Zimbabwe*, (London & New York, 1973)

Huffman, T.N., *Snakes and Crocodiles: Power and Symbolism in Ancient Zimbabwe* (Johannesburg, 1996)

Fortifications

45 Mycenae & Tiryns

Iakovidis, S., 'Cyclopean Walls', *Athens Annals of Archaeology* 3 (1969), 468–72

Iakovidis, S., *Late Helladic Citadels on Mainland Greece* (Leiden, 1983)

Loader, N.C., *Building in Cyclopean Masonry, with Special Reference to the Mycenaean Fortifications*, Studies in Mediterranean Archaeology Pocketbook Series (Gothenburg, 1998)

Mylonas, G., *Mycenae and the Mycenaean Age* (Princeton, 1966)

Wace, A.J.B., *Mycenae. An Archaeological History and Guide* (Princeton, 1949)

46 The Fortresses of Van

Belli, O., *The Capital of Urartu, Van, Eastern Anatolia* (Istanbul, 1988)

Burney, C. & Marshall Lang, D., *The Peoples of the Hills: Ancient Ararat and Caucasus* (London, 1971)

Forbes, T. B., *Urartian Architecture*. British Archaeological Reports, International Series 170 (Oxford, 1983)

Kleiss, W., 'Grössenvergleiche urartäischer Burgen und Siedlungen', in Boehmer, R.M. & Hauptmann, H. (eds), *Beiträge zur Altertumskunde Kleinasiens* (Mainz, 1983), 283–90

Loon, M.N. van, *Urartian Art* (Istanbul, 1966)

Wartke, R.-B., *Urartu das Reich am Ararat* (Mainz, 1993)

Zimansky, P.E., *Ecology and Empire: the Structure of the Urartian State* (Chicago, 1984)

47 The Walls of Babylon

Koldewey, R., *Das Ischtar-Tor in Babylon* (Leipzig, 1918)

Koldewey, R., *The Excavations at Babylon* (London, 1914)

Matson, F.R., 'The brickmakers of Babylon', in Kingery, W.D. (ed.), *Ceramics and Civilization*, vol. I: *Ancient Technology to Modern Science* (Columbus, OH, 1985), 61–75

Oates, J., *Babylon* (London & New York, 1979)

Wetzel, F., *Die Stadtmauern von Babylon* (Osnabrück, 1930)

48 Maiden Castle

Sharples, N., *Maiden Castle: Excavation and Field Survey 1985–6* (London, 1991)

Sharples, N., *Maiden Castle* (London, 1991)

Wheeler, R.E.M., *Maiden Castle, Dorset* (London, 1943)

49 The Circuit Walls of Syracuse

Karlsson, L., *Fortification Towers and Masonry Techniques in the Hegemony of Syracuse, 405–211 BC* (Stockholm, 1992), esp. 22–38, 106–16

Lawrence, A.W., *Greek Aims in Fortification* (Oxford, 1979)

Mertens, D., 'Die Befestigungen von Selnunt und Syrakus', *Akten des XIII. internationalen Kongresses für klassische Archäologie Berlin 1988* (Mainz, 1990), 474–8

Pugliese Carratelli, G. (ed.), *The Western Greeks* (London, 1996), 347–50

Winter, F.E., 'The chronology of the Euryalos fortress at Syracuse', *American Journal of Archaeology* 67 (1963), 363–87

Winter, F.E., *Greek Fortifications* (Toronto & London, 1971), esp. 313–17

50 The Great Wall of China

Fryer, J., *The Great Wall of China* (London, 1975)

Needham, J., *Science and Civilization in China* vol. 4, pt 3 sections 28–9 (Cambridge, 1997)

Schwartz, D., *The Great Wall of China* (London & New York, 1990)

Waldron, A., *The Great Wall of China – from History to Myth* (Cambridge, 1990)

Luo Zewen, et al., *The Great Wall of China* (New York, 1991)

51 Masada

Avi-Yonah, M., et al., *Masada: Survey and Excavations 1955–1956* (reprinted from *Israel Excavation Journal* 7, 1957), 1–60

Foerster, G., *Masada V: Art and Architecture* (Jerusalem, 1995)

Josephus, *The Jewish War*. English translation by H. St. J. Thackeray. Loeb edition (London & Cambridge, Mass., 1961)

Netzer, E., *Masada III: the Buildings: Stratigraphy and Architecture* (Jerusalem, 1991)

Yadin, Y., *Masada: Herod's Fortress and the Zealots' Last Stand* (London, 1966)

52 The Temple-Fortress of Sacsawaman

Hagen, A. von & Morris, C., *The Cities of the Ancient Andes* (London & New York, 1998)

Hemming, J., *The Conquest of the Incas* (Harmondsworth, 1983)

Hemming, J. & Ranney, E., *Monuments of the Incas* (Boston, 1982)

Hyslop, J., *Inka Settlement Planning* (Austin, 1990)

Gasparini, G. & Margolies, L., *Inca Architecture* (Bloomington, 1980)

Lee, V., *The Building of Sacsayhuaman* (Wilson, 1987)

Moseley, M.E., *The Incas and their Ancestors. The Archaeology of Peru* (London & New York, 1993)

Protzen, J.P., 'Inca Quarrying and Stonecutting', *Journal of the Society of Architectural Historians* XLIV/3 (1985), 161–82

Harbours, Hydraulics & Roads

53 The Great Bath of Mohenjo-daro

Jansen, M., Mulloy, M. & Urban, G., *Forgotten Cities on the Indus: Early Civilization in Pakistan from the 8th to the 2nd Millennium BC* (Mainz, 1991)

Kenoyer, J.M., *Ancient Cities of the Indus Valley Civilization* (Karachi, 1998)

Marshall, J.H., *Mohenjo-daro and the Indus Valley Civilization*, 3 vols (London, 1931)

Wheeler, R.E.M., *The Indus Civilization* (Cambridge, 1953)

54 The Marib Dam of Southern Arabia

Antonini, S., et al., *Yémen: au pays de la reine de Saba* (Paris, 1998)

Brunner, U., *Die Erforschung der antiken oase von Marib* (*Archäologische Berichte aus dem Yemen*, vol. II) (Mainz, 1983)

Doe, B., *Monuments of South Arabia* (Cambridge, 1983)

Schmidt, J., 'Baugeschichtliche Untersuchungen an den Bauanlagen des grossen Dammes von Marib' (*Archäologische Berichte aus dem Yemen*, vol. I (1982), 9–20.

Wright, G.R.H., 'Some preliminary observations on the masonry work at Marib', *Archäologische Berichte aus dem Yemen*, vol. IV (1988), 63–78

55 Chinese Canals

Deng Shulin, 'The Grand Canal – Still Grand', *China Reconstructs* (Beijing, 1983/9)

Needham, J., *Science and Civilisation in China*, vol. 4, pt 3, (Cambridge, 1954–)

Price, W., 'Grand Canal Panorama', *National Geographic Magazine*, 1937

56 Roman Aqueducts

Aicher, P.J., *Guide to the Aqueducts of Ancient Rome* (Wauconda, 1995)

Hodge, A.T., *Roman Aqueducts and Water Supply* (London, 1992)

Evans, H.B., *Water Distribution in Ancient Rome: The Evidence of Frontinus* (Baltimore, 1994); includes a translated text of Frontinus

Fabre, G., et al., *The Pont du Gard. Water and the Roman Town* (Paris, 1992)

57 Roman Roads
Adam, J.-P., *Roman Building. Materials and Techniques*, (London, 1994)
Chevallier, R., *Roman Roads* (London, 1989, rev. ed.)

58 The Harbour at Caesarea
Holum, K.G., Hohlfelder, R.L., Bull, R.J. & Raban, A., *King Herod's Dream: Caesarea on the Sea* (New York & London, 1988)
Oleson, J.P. & Branton, G., 'The technology of King Herod's harbour', in Vann, R.L. (ed.), *Caesarea Papers*, *Journal of Roman Archaeology* Supplement 5 (Ann Arbor, 1992)
Raban, A., et al., *The Harbours of Caesarea Maritima. Results of the Caesarea Ancient Harbour Excavation Project, 1980–1985*, British Archaeological Reports, International Series 491 (Oxford, 1989)

59 The Chaco Road System, New Mexico
Cordell, L., *The Prehistory of the Southwest*, 2nd ed. (Orlando, 1997)
Lekson, S., *Great Pueblo Architecture of Chaco Canyon, New Mexico* (Albuquerque, National Park Service Publications in Archaeology 18B: Chaco Canyon Studies, 1984)
Lekson, S.H., 'Rewriting Southwestern Prehistory', *Archaeology* 50(1) (1997), 52–5
Nabakov, P., *Native American Architecture* (New York, 1989)
Plog, S., *Ancient Peoples of the American Southwest* (London & New York, 1997)
Vivian, G., 'Chacoan Roads: Morphology', *The Kiva* 63(1) (1997), 7–34
Vivian, G., 'Chaco Roads: Function', *The Kiva* 63(1) (1997), 35–67

60 Inca Roads & Bridges
Gade, D., 'Bridge Types in the Central Andes', *Annals of the Association of American Geographers* 62/1 (1972), 94–109
Hagen, V. von, *Highways of the Sun* (New York, 1955)
Hagen, A. von & Morris, C., *The Cities of the Ancient Andes* (London & New York, 1998)
Hyslop, J., *The Inka Road System* (New York, 1984)
Moseley, M.E., *The Incas and their Ancestors. The Archaeology of Peru* (London & New York, 1993)

Colossal Statues & Monoliths

61 The Grand Menhir Brisé, Brittany
Bailloud, G., Boujot, C., Cassen, S. & Le Roux, C.-T., *Carnac. Les premières architectures de pierre* (Paris, 1995)
Burl, A., *Megalithic Britanny* (London, 1985)
Le Roux, C.-T., 'Et voguent les menhires…?' *Bulletin d'information de l'Association Manche-Atlantique pour la Recherche archéologique dans les Iles* 10 (1997), 5–18

62 The Great Sphinx at Giza
Arnold, D., *Building in Egypt: Pharaonic Stone Masonry* (New York & Oxford, 1991)
Hassan, S., *The Sphinx: Its History in the Light of Recent Excavations* (Cairo, 1949)
Jordan, P. & Ross, J.G., *Riddles of the Sphinx* (Phoenix Mill, 1998)
Lehner, M., *The Complete Pyramids* (London & New York, 1997)

63 Egyptian Obelisks
Arnold, D., *Building in Egypt: Pharaonic Stone Masonry* (New York & Oxford, 1991)
Barnes, M., 'The Obelisk', in Barnes, M., et al., *Secrets of Lost Empires* (London, 1996), 94–135
Clarke, S. & Engelbach, R., *Ancient Egyptian Masonry* (Oxford, 1930)

Engelbach, R., *The Problem of the Obelisks* (London, 1923)
Habachi, L., *The Obelisks of Egypt: Skyscrapers of the Past* (London, 1978)

64 The Colossi of Western Thebes
Arnold, D., *Building in Egypt: Pharaonic Stone Masonry* (New York & Oxford, 1991)
Bourbon, F. & Attini, A., *Egypt: Yesterday and Today. Lithographs by David Roberts, R.A.* (Shrewsbury, 1996), 170–9
Schultz, R. & Seidel, M., *Egypt: The World of the Pharaohs* (Cologne, 1998), 188–90, 192–5

65 The Colossal Stone Heads of the Olmec
Benson, E. & De La Fuente, B. (eds), *Olmec Art of Ancient Mexico* (Washington, DC ,1996)
Bernal, I., *The Olmec World* (Berkeley, 1969)
Coe, M. & Diehl, R., *In the Land of the Olmec* vol. 1 (Austin, 1980)
Sharer, R. & Grove, D. (eds), *Regional Perspectives on the Olmec* (Cambridge, 1989)
Various *The Olmec World: Ritual and Rulership* (New Haven, 1996)

66 The Nazca Lines: Drawings in the Desert
Aveni, A.F. (ed.), *The Lines of Nazca* (Philadelphia, 1990)
Hadingham, E., *Lines to the Mountain Gods: Nazca and the Mysteries of Peru* (New York, 1987)
Hagen, A. von & Morris, C., *The Cities of the Ancient Andes* (London & New York, 1998)
Morrison, T., *Pathways to the Gods* (New York, 1978)
Morrison, T., *The Mystery of the Nazca Lines* (Woodbridge, 1987)
Moseley, M.E., *The Incas and their Ancestors. The Archaeology of Peru* (London & New York, 1993)

67 La Turbie: the Trophy of the Alps
Formigé, J., *Le Trophé des Alpes (La Turbie)*, Supplément a Gallia, II (Paris, 1949)

68 The Giant Stelae of Aksum
Buxton, D., *The Abyssinians* (London & New York, 1970)
Munro-Hay, S.C., *Aksum: an African Civilization of Late Antiquity* (Edinburgh, 1991)
Munro-Hay, S.C., *Excavations at Aksum* (London, 1989)
Phillipson, D.W., *The Monuments of Aksum* (Addis Ababa & London, 1997)
Phillipson, D.W., *Ancient Ethiopia* (London, 1998)

69 The Colossal Buddha of Bamiyan
Baker, P.H.B & Allchin, F.R., *Shahr-i Zohak and the History of the Bamiyan Valley, Afghanistan* (Oxford, 1991)
Higuchi, T. (ed.), *Bamiyaan* (Kyoto, 1984)
Klimburg-Salter, D., *The Kingdom of Bamiyan: Buddhist Art and Culture of the Hindu Kush* (Naples, 1989)
Tarzi, Z., *L'architecture et le décor rupestre des grottes de Bamiyan* (Paris, 1977)

70 The Easter Island Statues
Bahn, P. & Flenley, J., *Easter Island, Earth Island* (London & New York, 1992)
Bellwood, P., *The Polynesians* (London & New York, 1987)
Orliac, C. & Orliac, M., *The Silent Gods: Mysteries of Easter Island* (London, 1995)
Van Tilburg, J., *Easter Island: Archaeology, Ecology and Culture* (London & New York, 1994)

Sources of Illustrations

a: above; t: top; b: bottom; c: centre; l: left; r: right.

The following abbreviations are used to identify sources and locate illustrations: AMNH – Courtesy Dept. of Library Services, American Museum of Natural History; AWS – Archivio White Star; WB – Warwick Ball; CB – Chris Brandon; BM – © British Museum; CMHS - Cahokia Mounds Historic Site; PC – Peter Connolly (illustrator); EH – English Heritage; SF – Sian Frances (illustrator); HG – Photo Heidi Grassley/© Thames & Hudson Ltd, London; RHPL – Robert Harding Picture Library; CS – Chris Scarre; AVH – Adriana von Hagen; TW – Tracy Wellman (illustrator); PW – Philip Winton (illustrator).

Half-title *after* Swaddling from Clayton and Price (eds), *The Seven Wonders of the Ancient World*, 1988; **frontispiece** Gavin Hellier/RHPL; **4** HG; **5l** Alberto Ruz, r Tim Insoll; **6l** CS, r AVH; **7l** A.F. Kersting, r Elizabeth Pendleton; **10–11** Mountain High Maps® Copyright 1993 Digital Wisdom Inc.; William Reade; **12** Robert Estall; **12–13t** AVH, b John G. Ross; **14** Adam Woolfitt/RHPL; **14–15** RHPL; **15t** Pat Aithie/Ffotograff, b Werner Forman Archive; **16** Jeremy Stafford-Deitsch; **16–17** Antonio Attini/AWS; **17** N.J. Saunders; **18–19** HG; **21** John G. Ross; **22–3** Guido Alberto Rossi/Image Bank; **23** HG; **24a** Mark Lehner, **24b** PW; **25t** PW; **25r** Audrain Samivel; **26l** Kate Spence, r George Taylor; **27** PW; **28b** PW *after* J.E. Reade; **28–9t** BM, b Stephanie Dalley; **29** BM; **30–1** SF; **32t** *after* Trell, 1988, r from Coulton, 1977, b N. Claire Loader; **33** HG; **34–5a** PW; **35l** PW; **35** Lesley & Roy Adkins Picture Library; **36** SF; **37** CS; **38–9** *after* G.B. Waywell; **39t** Byron Bell *after* K. Jeppesen; **39b** BM; **40** BM; **41** PW *after* Byron Bell; **42–3** from Fischer von Erlach, *Entwurf einer historischen Architektur*, 1721; **43b** Peter Clayton, t A.F. Kersting; **44** SF; **45** Stéphane Compoint/Sygma; **46** Jean-Claude Golvin/Éditions Errance; **47t** Peter Clayton, b TW; **48–9** Dúchas, The Heritage Service, Dublin; **51r** CS, b Annick Boothe *after* O'Kelly, 1982; **52** PW; **52–3** Adam Woolfitt/RHPL; **54** Peter Clayton; **54–5** from E.R. Dodwell, *Views and Descriptions of Cyclopian or, Pelasgic Remains in Greece and Italy*, 1834; **55** *after* Hood, 1978; **56–7** Christopher A. Klein/National Geographic Image Collection; **58t** Hirmer Fotoarchiv, b Fitzwilliam Museum, Cambridge; **58–9** TW; **59** Richard Wilkinson; **60** Alberto Siliotti; **61** Marcello Bellisario/ Autorizzazione SMA n1313 del 28/12/1987; **62** Nigel Spivey; **63t** TW, c RHPL, b PW; **64–5** Daniel Schwartz/Lookat, Zürich; **66** Shaanxi Provincial Museum, Xian; **66–67** Museum of Qin Shihuangdi's tomb, Mount Li, Shaanxi; **67** l&r Shaanxi Provincial Museum, Xian; **68–9** Mark Hannaford/Ffotograff; **70** WB; **71** Shippee-Johnson Expedition, AMNH; **72** Frank Spooner Pictures; **72–3** Frank Spooner Pictures; **74–5** Sakai, Osaka; **75t** Teruya Yamamoto, c PW; **76–7** PW; **78** Alberto Ruz; **79t** Merle Greene Robertson, b Alberto Ruz; **80** Michael D. Coe; **81** Michael Freeman; **82–3** Michael Freeman; **84–5** PW *after* Brown; **85** PW; **86–7** RHPL; **89** C.M. Dixon; **90** Adam Woolfitt/RHPL; **90–1** Robert Estall; **92** t PW, c PW; **93** l & c PW, tr TW by Souden, 1997; **94** PW *after* Cunliffe & Renfrew, 1997; **94–5** RHPL; **96c** PW *after* Souden, 1997, b BBC; **97** WB; **98** PW; **98–9** after L. Woolley; **100** TW; **100–1** Jean-Claude Golvin/Éditions Errance; **102–3** Jeremy Stafford-Deitsch; **103** TW *after* Arnold, 1991; **104** Kate Spence; **105** HG; **106** Kate Spence; **106–7** Jeremy Stafford-Deitsch; **108** PW *after* Richard L. Burger; **109l** Alejandro Balaguer, r Johan Reinhard; **110** t&c AVH; **111** Hirmer Fotoarchiv; **112–13** PW; **113b** BM, c Royal Ontario Museum, University of Toronto; **114** from A. Orlandos, *H'Architektonike tou Parthenos*, Athens, 1986; **115** Manolis Korres, Athens; **116–17** Antonio Attini/AWS; **118t** *after* G. Kubler, b Jeremy Sabloff; **119** bl PW *after* Morelos Garcia, 1993, tl PW *after* R. Millon, r Irmgard Groth-Kimball; **121** AKG, London; **122** PW; **123** India Office Library & Records; **124** PW after Brown; **125** Benoy K. Behl; **126** India Office Library & Records; **127t** AKG, London, b Paris, École nationale supérieure des Beaux-Arts; **128** AKG, London; **130–1** Marcello Bertinetti/AWS; **132–3** Ohio Historical Society; **133** from E.G. Squier & E.H. Davis, *Ancient Monuments of the Mississippi Valley*, 1848; **134** PW, *after* Dikshit 1938; **135** Robin Coningham; **136–7t** *after* Dumarcay, b Kon. Instituut v/d Tropen; **138tl** Jill Jones/Ffotograff, bl Pat Aithie/Ffotograff; **138–9** RHPL; **140–1** Lloyd K. Townsend/CMHS; **142t** & b CMHS; **143** Tim Insoll; **144** TW *after* Mauny, *Bulletin de l'Institut Français d'Afrique Noire (B)* 14 1952; **145** The Aga Khan Visual Archives, MIT/Labelle Prussin, 1983; **146t** *after* Mauny, 1952, r Tim Insoll; **147** Codex Tovar; **148** N.J. Saunders; **148–9** PW; **150** Gaynor Chapman *after* Marguina; **151t** & b Salvador Guilliem, courtesy Great Temple Project; **152–3** RHPL; **155** Peter Clayton; **156–7** AKG, London; **157** Lesley & Roy Adkins Picture Library; **158** PW; **159l** PW *after* J.E. Reade, r BM; **160–1** PW; **161** BM; **162** A.H, Layard; **163** courtesy the Oriental Institute, University of Chicago; **164** PW; **164–5t** RHPL, b WB; **166** courtesy the Oriental

Institute, University of Chicago; **167** Josephine Powell **168l** PW; **168–9** Marcello Bertinetti/AWS; **170** F. Sear, *Roman Architecture*, 1988; **171** Scala; **172–3** Marcello Bertinetti/AWS; **174** PW; **174–5** Dr E. Richter; **175** Janet DeLaine; **176** l CS,r TW *after* MacDonald & Pinto, 1995; **177** AWS; **178–9** Kevin Gould/Janet DeLaine; **180t** George Taylor; b Roger Wilson; **181** Roger Wilson; **182–3** Robin Coningham; **184l** PW *after* Brown, 1946, r Robin Coningham; **185** D. Collon; **186** from Reuther, *A Survey of Persian Art* ed. A.U. Pope, 1938, by permission of Oxford University Press; **187** D. Collon; **188–9** Neg No. 334881, AMNH,; **189t** AVH, br Michael Moseley; **190–1 & 191** David Coulson/Robert Estall; **192l** ML Design *after* Garlake, r Federal Information Dept., Zimbabwe; **193l** Barney Wayne, r R.D.K. Hadden, courtesy of FID; **194–5** Miao Wang/Image Bank; **197** Edwin Smith; **198–9** PC; **199** N. Claire Loader; **200** CS; **201** CS; **202–3** CS; **204** courtesy Oriental Institute, University of Chicago; **205t** Annick Petersen, b Staatliche Museen zu Berlin, © bpk; **206** George Taylor; **207** EH; **208** Peter Chèze-Brown; **209** Paul Birkbeck/EH; **210** TW; **210–11** PC; **211** Leonard von Matt; **213** RHPL; **214** PW; **214–15** Daniel Schwartz/Lookat, Zürich; **216** RHPL; **217** Zev Radovan; **218** George Taylor; **218–19** PC; **220–1** AVH; **222** TW *after* Hemming & Ranney, 1982; **223** AVH; **224–5** Antonio Attini/AWS; **227** WB; **228** RHPL; **229** PW; **230–1** CS; **231** CS; **232** PW; **233** Telegraph Colour Library; **234–5** Anderson, **235** TW; **236–7** Deutsches Museum, Munich; **238** al Lesley & Roy Adkins Picture Library, ar TW, b A.F. Kersting; **239a** Baker Collection, b Annick Boothe; **240** PW; **240–1** RHPL; **242–3** CB; **243** CB; **244–5** Zev Radovan; **245** CB; **246l** from Morgan, *Houses and House Life of the American Aborigines*, 1881; **246–7** Arizona State Museum, photo: Helga Teiweg; **247** TW; **248** Mick Sharp; **249** AVH; **250l** *after* Hyslop, b AVH; **250–1t** AMNH, photo: Hyslop, b AVH; **251** AVH; **252–3** RHPL; **255** CS; **256b** Serge Cassen *Carnac: Les premières Architectures de Pierre*, CNRS, tr CS; **257** Serge Cassen; **258–9** Peter Clayton **259** TW; **260–1** b Mark Lehner, t John G. Ross; **262l** Egyptian Museum, Cairo, r John G. Ross; **264–5** RMN – Chuzeville; **265** bl Jon Arnold/Telegraph Colour Library, tr TW *after* Arnold, 1991; **266** t PW & b TW *after* Arnold, 1991; **267** HG; **268** G.B. Belzoni, *Six New Plates*, 1822; **269** Jeremy Stafford-Deitsch; **270** PW; **271** Matthew W.Stirling/NGS; **272** Antonio Attini/AWS; **273l** Robert Frerck/RHPL, r Irmgard Groth Kimball; **274** bl,t,br TW; **275b** Robert Estall, t *after* Moseley; **276–7** Tony Morrison, South American Pictures; **278–9** PW; **279t** Foteca Unione, b Editions La Cigogne; **280** Roger Wilson; **281–5** Dr David Phillipson; **286 & 287** l TW *after* Tarzi, 1977; **287** Robert E. Fisher; **288** Edgar Knobloch; **290** Elizabeth Pendleton; **290–1** Masterfile/ Telegraph Colour Library; **291** Elizabeth Pendleton; **292** tl Annick Petersen, tr Peter Bellwood; b Elizabeth Pendleton.

Sources of quotations:

21 V. Denon, *Travels in Upper and Lower Egypt*, 1803; **27** Josephus, Antiquities, X,11; **30** E. Gibbon, *The History of the Decline and Fall of the Roman Empire, c.* 1776; **33** Strabo, *Geography*, VIII,3,30; **37** W. Birnie, *The Blame of Kirk-buriall*, 1606; **42** Pliny, *Natural History*, XXXIV,41; **45** Strabo, *Geography*, XVII,1; **51** E. Lhwyd, Letter to Henry Rowlands, 1700; **54** A.J.B. Wace, *Mycenae*, 1949; **56** G. Steindorff, *Baedeker, Egypt*, 1902; **61** D.H. Lawrence, *Etruscan Places*, 1932; **68** A.H. Layard, *Early Adventures in Persia, Susiana and Babylonia*, 1887; **74** Nihongi, *Chronicles of Japan from the Earliest Times to* AD 697, 1972; **76** J.L. Stephens, *Incidents of Travel in Central America, Chiapas, and Yucatan*, 1842; **81** H. Mouhot, *Travels in the Central Parts of Indochina*, 1861; **89** A. Mayr, *The Prehistoric Remains of Malta*, 1908; **92** W. Harrison, *Description of Britaine*, XXIV; **97** Herodotus, *Histories*, 1.181-2; **100, 105** D. Roberts, *Diary*,1838; **111**, Plutarch, *Life of Pericles*; **132** C. Atwater, 'Descriptions of Antiquities…', *Trans. American Antiquarian Society* 1, 1820; **136** A. Foucher, 1909; **140** H. Brackenridge, *A View of Louisiana…*, 1814; **159, 185** A.H. Layard, *Nineveh and Babylon*, 1853; **163** Lord Curzon, *Persia and the Persian Question*, 1892; **167** Martial, *The Book of Spectacles*, I; **172** Augustan Histories, Life of Hadrian, 26.5; **177** Augustan Histories, Life of Antoninus Caracalla, 9, 4–5; **190** P. Garlake, *Great Zimbabwe Described and Explained*, 1985; **197** Pausanias, *Description of Greece*, II,xvi, 5–6; **201** H.B.F. Lynch, *Armenia, Travels and Studies*, 1901; **207** Thomas Hardy, 'A Tryst at an Ancient Earthwork', 1885; **210** Diodorus XIV,18.3–7; **217** S.W. Wolcott, *Researches in Palestine*, 1843; **227** J. Marshall, *Mohenjo-Daro and the Indus Civilization*, 1931; **234** Pliny the Elder, *Natural History*, 36,123; **239** Procopius, *The Gothic Wars*, XIV, 6–11; **242** Josephus, *The Jewish War*, I; **246** D. Schwartz, in Noble, D.G., *New Light on Chaco Canyon*, 1984; **258** Pliny the Elder, *Natural History*, **271** I. Bernal, *The Olmec World*, 1969; **275** E. Hadingham, *Lines to the Mountain Gods, Nazca and the Mysteries of Peru*, 1987; **278** Pliny the Elder, *Natural History*, 3,20; **281** Y. Kobishchanov, *Axum*, 1979; **289** Capt. J. Cook, *A Voyage towards the South Pole…*, 1777.

Index